Utah

Tom and Gayen Wharton
Photography by Tom Till

COMPASS AMERICAN GUIDES

Utah

Copyright © 1993 Fodor's Travel Publications, Inc.
Maps Copyright © 1991 Moon Publications, Inc.

Second Edition
Library of Congress Cataloging in Publication Data
Wharton, Tom, 1950
    Utah / Tom and Gayen Wharton : photography by Tom Till. —2nd ed.
    p.   cm.
    Includes bibliographical references and index.
    ISBN 1-878867-31-8 : $16.95
    1. Utah—Description and travel—1981—Guide-books.
I. Wharton, Gayen. II. Till, Tom III. Title.
F824.3.W48 1993
917.9204'33—dc20   91-40404
                                  CIP

Series Editor: Kit Duane   Contributing Editors: Barry Parr, Deke Castleman
Assistant Editors: Taran March, Peter Zimmerman   Designers: David Hurst, Chris Burt   Map Design: Bob Race
Production house: Twin Age Limited, Hong Kong

Printed in Hong Kong

First published in 1991 by Compass American Guides, Inc., 6051 Margarido Drive, Oakland, CA 94618, USA

ACKNOWLEDGMENTS

WE WOULD LIKE TO THANK editor Barry Parr for patiently reviewing and re-reviewing our manuscript. Not only was Barry an editor, but a friend. Tom Till's fine photographs reveal the diversity of Utah's landscapes. We also appreciate the efforts of contributing photographers Steve Griffin and Tim Kelly. Mural on pages 184-185 used with permission from the Peabody Museum at Yale University. We also wish to thank the following individuals: Bob Donohoe, our expert reader, for invaluable advice; Gary Topping, Manuscripts Curator of the Utah State Historical Society; the society's Photograph and Map Librarian, Susan Whetstone, who helped us track down the historical photos used in the book; and Dr. William Lee Stokes, our geology professor at the University of Utah, who graciously edited our text for accuracy. Mark Goodwin of U.C. Berkeley contributed much on the subject of dinosaurs. The Utah Wilderness Association's Dick Carter, Alta's Alf Engen, Lagoon's Peter and David Freed, the Pack Creek Ranch's Ken Sleight, Gordon Topham of Fremont Indian State Park, Monsignor Jerome Stoeffel, Larry Davis at Anasazi State Park, and modern-day mountain man Timothy Toker Many Hats all made themselves available for interviews.

Rick Reese of the Utah Geographic Series, Ward Roylance, and Mel Davis and John Veranth of Wasatch Publishers were generous in granting permission to quote from their books. Joe Rutherford of the Utah Travel Council, and the staff of the Salt Lake County Convention and Visitors Bureau were also extremely helpful. Dawn House and Ralph Wheeler helped edit the chapter on the Mormon Church for accuracy.

Other institutions providing invaluable help include: Utah Division of Wildlife Resources, Utah Division of Parks and Recreation, National Park Service, U.S. Forest Service, Bureau of Land Management, Utah Symphony, Utah Opera Company, Ririe-Woodbury Dance Company, Ballet West, Pioneer Memorial Theatre, Salt Lake Acting Company, Repertory Dance Theater, University of Utah, Brigham Young University, Utah State University, Weber State College, and Southern Utah State College. Tom's long-time employer, *The Salt Lake Tribune*, has given him a chance to explore Utah for the past 20 years. For this, he is extremely grateful.

Finally, we would like to thank our children—Emma, Jacob, Rawl, and Bryer—for putting up with their parents' book-writing effort, which took precious time away from family activities.

To our parents, Max and Althea Bennett and Jack and Vi Wharton,
who encouraged us to write, and instilled in us their love of travel.

C O N T E N T S

Literary Extracts

Topical Essays

Maps

Delicate Arch in Arches National Park.

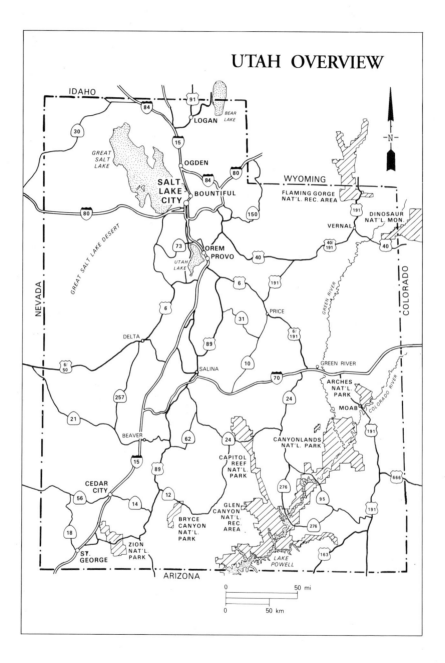

UTAH OVERVIEW

INTRODUCTION
A PIONEERING PLACE

ON THE EAST BENCH OF SALT LAKE CITY, A WEATHERED STATUE GAZES silently at the valley below. A brown haze from automobiles and industrial stacks obscures the view slightly to the west, but the blue waters of the Great Salt Lake and the mighty peaks of the Oquirrh Mountains are still visible, as they were on July 24th, 1847, when Brigham Young first looked out from this spot, ending a perilous 1,500-mile journey by declaring, "This is the right place." Could even a wise and visionary man like Young have imagined what Salt Lake City—and, for that matter, all of Utah—would become?

Those who have made Utah their home, from the ancient Indians who built magnificent cliff dwellings in the southern canyons to contemporary scientists who flirt with the infinite possibilities of nuclear fusion, have possessed the courageous spirit of true pioneers.

This land brings out a conservative, independent streak in people. *Industry* is Utah's official motto, and the beehive its state symbol. Utahns take their work seriously.

Utah's earliest residents may not have known much about their homeland's geography and geology when they arrived, but they were quick studies. Largely by trial and error, the Native Americans, mountain men, explorers, and first settlers learned how to make a living from the land.

In the mid-nineteenth century, newcomers from across the plains brought a distinctive, energetic spirit, which the independent mountain men, the Catholic explorer-priests, and even the Indians who preceded them might have respected. These Mormon pioneers sought the freedom to worship God in their own way, and dreamed of turning Utah into a modern-day Zion through hard work and community effort. The soldiers, miners, railroad workers, and other non-Mormon "gentiles" who came later may not have possessed the same religious beliefs, but certainly they were caught up in the pioneering spirit.

This book, to a great degree, is about all sorts of pioneers. It is based on the premise that residents and visitors cannot fully appreciate Utah's magnificent natural and cultural heritage without first understanding the spirit of the people who turned what many regarded as a wasteland into a thriving state.

Many know the story of Utah's most famous pioneer, Brigham Young, a man who knew the value of planning for the future. Young built Salt Lake City from almost nothing, laying it out in wide, square, well-organized blocks. He sent out Mormon settlers to remote corners of the unsettled West, armed with little more than faith, a willingness to work hard, and a rare courage to face the unknown. He is, by most accounts, the archetypal Utah pioneer.

But Utah's pioneering spirit did not die with Brigham Young. Witness the Greek musician, Maurice Abravanel, who came to Utah with the desire of building a world-renowned symphony, and did not retire until his vision became reality. Or consider the team of researchers and doctors at the University of Utah who, for the first time, built an artificial heart and successfully implanted it in a living human being. And remember people like Utah Jazz owner Larry Miller, who spent much of his own money to open the glittering Delta Center in the early nineties, revitalizing the western part of Salt Lake City.

Evidence of this pioneering spirit can be seen everywhere in the Beehive State. Walk down the clean, wide streets of Salt Lake City, where dozens of new buildings rose in the 1980s, and where business executives and government leaders plot the course of the state into the twenty-first century. Listen to a symphony, or attend a play, opera, ballet, or modern dance company performance, and savor the enthusiasm of a community willing to support all kinds of artistic endeavors.

Then escape to the wild lands which lie in all directions from the Wasatch Front. Get a sense for the courage of explorer John Wesley Powell by taking a white-water raft trip through Cataract Canyon. Visit the site where the first transcontinental railroad was completed in 1869, to glean some feeling for the exciting day when West and East were joined for the first time. With a pack on your back, hike through one of Utah's five national parks to experience first-hand the incredibly rugged geography that the early explorers, settlers, and prospectors had to face and conquer. As you wander through the High Uintas Wilderness Area, or follow the old Pony Express Trail across the western desert, or bounce up and down in the seat of an old Jeep through an obscure southern Utah canyon, imagine yourself as a mountain man, daring Pony Express rider, or grizzled prospector. The state's wild places still allow visitors to get a sense of what our forefathers faced in this desolate but wonderful land.

Lower Calf Creek Falls near the Escalante River.

STORIES IN STONE

THERE ARE MANY WAYS TO CONTEMPLATE THE GEOLOGICAL FORCES which have shaped Utah. Hike to the top of an alpine peak overlooking the Great Salt Lake Valley and look down on the sprawling metropolitan area. Drive across the desolate Bonneville Salt Flats, where mirages of floating mountains and disappearing lakes shimmer across the glistening, salt-encrusted surface. Listen to the roar of the rapids on a raft trip through Cataract Canyon and watch the colors and shapes of steep sandstone ledges change dramatically along the way. Then fly back over the same country and look out over the convoluted canyons, stately fins, windblown arches, and rock bridges formed by erosion. Wander down a remote, narrow canyon in Zion National Park. Examine the texture of the sandstone closely; feel the warm, red rock with your hands. Ascend an almost vertical cliff. Lie on a hard, smooth rock surface, and study the countless hues.

Nowhere in the world, perhaps, have the elements of earth, wind, and water come together with such drama. Underground forces have heaved and pushed, thrusting massive plateaus and mountain ranges up more than a mile above sea level. Erosion has cut and gouged plateaus into spectacular pinnacles and canyons.

In most places, water, soil, or vegetation cover the rock layers that tell the earth's geological history. Things are different in Utah, which geologist William Lee Stokes calls "The Bedrock State." Only three percent of Utah's land is agricultural—an area which could fit into the Great Salt Lake. The remaining 97 percent is bare rock or unproductive soil.

Much of Utah has a high desert climate. Little rain falls, and vegetation is sparse. As a result, rivers and streams cut directly into layers of rock, exposing them for study. Utah is one of the few states where all 13 periods of the geologic time scale are represented in the rock record. Sedimentary layers of rock from every era have yielded thousands of fossils. Even the famed Grand Canyon in Arizona exposes only seven periods of time.

A visitor to Utah can discover great varieties of every basic rock type. Rockhounds can pick up sedimentary, metamorphic, and igneous specimens. Rich and diverse mineral deposits are scattered throughout the state.

One need not be a geologist to appreciate the qualities that make Utah unique. The arrangement of its physical features has dictated the state's human settlement and economic development throughout history, and still shapes its future.

Utah is divided into four major geological regions, all extending beyond the state boundaries: the Colorado Plateau, the Basin and Range, the Middle Rocky Mountains, and the Basin and Range/Colorado Plateau Transition provinces. Each province provides its own unique recreational opportunities and monumental vistas.

■ THE COLORADO PLATEAU

The Colorado Plateau covers a large portion of southeastern Utah. It also extends into adjacent areas drained by the Colorado River in Colorado, New Mexico, and Arizona. This sparsely vegetated landscape of plateaus, mesas, deep canyons, sloping foothills, imposing vertical cliffs, and barren badlands contains some of the world's most unusual scenery. "Here," writes Stokes the geologist, "is a kingdom of rocks, an arena where the elemental forces of time and weather meet the raw stuff of the earth with nothing to soften or hide the scars of battle."

According to some geologists, the Colorado Plateau has existed as a distinct entity for at least 500 million years. One hundred and fifty million years ago, the area was beachfront property—the west coast of North America. Thick layers of sand deposits on the shoreline, which advanced and retreated repeatedly over a period of 40 million years, created a vast, Sahara-like desert. Whenever ocean or streams spread over these dunes, thinner, softer layers of marine sediments were laid down. Over the centuries, these layers of sediment were sandwiched between layers of sand. In time, all the layers hardened into rock.

About 10 million years ago, the entire western half of North America was elevated a mile or so above sea level. Most geologists feel this movement was caused by the pressures of continental drift. This increase in elevation resulted in new weather patterns, and, most important, increased precipitation. With little vegetation to soak it up, rain falling on the young plateau flowed into rivulets and gullies, picking up sand and scouring the rock with increased erosive power. The softer marine sediments eroded the fastest, leaving the harder sand sediments as blocks of sandstone. Following the path of least resistance, these new stream courses—the Colorado and its tributaries—in time carved southern Utah into a fascinating maze of canyons and gorges. Most of the impressive sandstone cliffs seen by visi-

The classic geological formation of Comb Ridge in extreme southeastern Utah.

tors to Arches, Zion, Capitol Reef, and Canyonlands national parks are solidified sand dunes.

Erosion has also created the extraordinary number of fins, arches, natural bridges, and "reefs" that can be found in the Colorado Plateau. Water cuts, breaks, and wears down sandstone layers both when moving and standing still. Moving water cuts away the soft layers of rock from between harder layers. When a layer of harder rock is left standing by itself, it's called a fin. A good example is the Fiery Furnace in Arches National Park. Natural bridges are formed when water works its way completely through portions of a rock fin or narrow rock wall.

Flowing water is not the only agent of erosion. Water standing in pools and potholes wears down the rock more slowly by dissolving the binding minerals in the sandstone, loosening separate grains, which are then blown away by the wind. In winter, water freezing in the cracks between rocks further breaks apart sandstone layers, enlarging the gaps and freeing huge slabs from canyon walls. When a fin has been left standing alone through years of ice-cracking and exposure to wind, an opening can appear and slowly widen into an arch. A sandstone spire is created when a thin wall collapses, leaving behind only a single monolithic remnant.

Several highland areas of the Colorado Plateau are the remnants of geological uplifts. These appear as gigantic blisters in the sandstone, with rock strata tilted almost perpendicular to the horizon. Over time, erosion carves crack-like canyons in the upturned sandstone. These near-vertical ridges are often referred to as "reefs" because they resemble underwater coral reefs, and present similar barriers to travel. The San Rafael Swell and Comb Ridge are prime examples of such eroded "reefs."

Rock strata millions of years in the making are exposed at the confluence of the Green and Colorado rivers.

The mountain ranges found within the Colorado Plateau are also unusual. Geologists describe them as volcanoes which did not quite erupt. The La Sal, Abajo, and Henry mountains, as well as Navajo Mountain near Lake Powell, were formed by molten rock pushing up through overlying strata to (or close to) the surface. Erosion and glacial action removed the upper layers of rock, revealing their igneous inner cores. Of these ranges, only Navajo Mountain still retains its outer shell of sedimentary rock.

Four of Utah's five national parks are found on the Colorado Plateau. Visiting them will help you understand the forces that form this unique and beautiful part of the world. Geological guides are sold at the park visitor centers, or you can read interpretive signs along the roads.

■ THE GREAT BASIN

Think of the Great Basin as a large, imperfect bowl full of ridges and valleys. It's called a basin not only for its topography but for its effect on drainage. The water in the Great Basin has no escape to the sea. Rainfall is too sparse to fill the basin.

During the last ice age, which ended 10,000 years ago, many lakes and rivers filled the basin. Utah's Lake Bonneville was the largest. This massive, freshwater inland sea dominated the landscape for at least 250,000 years. It covered the northwest corner of Utah with shallow bays extending into Idaho and Nevada. At one time, it measured 1,050 feet (318 m) deep, 145 miles (232 km) wide, and 346 miles (577 km) long.

The pounding waves carved out terraces or benches, many of which are still preserved along the eastern edge of the Great Basin. These terraces are especially prominent around the mountains encircling Salt Lake City. Utah's state Capitol stands on one of them.

Travelers to Utah can see the remnants of Lake Bonneville by visiting the Great Salt Lake, largest saltwater lake in the Western Hemisphere, and Utah Lake, the state's largest freshwater lake, which drains into the Great Salt Lake by way of the Jordan River.

Another remnant of Lake Bonneville can be found at the Little Sahara Recreation Area (often called Jericho). Utah's largest sand-dune field is located on the east-central edge of the Great Basin.

The salinity of the Great Salt Lake results from its position on the floor of the Great Basin, where it receives all the salts and dissolved minerals that would normally be carried by rivers to the sea. When water evaporates, the salts and minerals remain in their solid form. There are 15 natural salts (in addition to the ordinary table-salt variety) in and around the Great Salt Lake. The most important of these are magnesium and potassium, both extracted from the lake by large commercial operations.

The Great Salt Lake has several islands, some of which become peninsulas at low-water levels. Antelope Island, the largest, is the site of a mostly undeveloped state park, and home to a wild buffalo herd.

Sixty-five million years ago, the area that was to become the Great Basin was a vast highland, slowly expanding outward like the surface of a loaf of bread when it rises. After expanding to its limit, it collapsed. Like the rubble of a collapsed building, the remains of this highland take the shape of narrow, eroded mountain ranges interspersed with sediment-filled valleys.

While this highland was collapsing, volcanic intrusions of magma were simultaneously being forced to the surface. Volcanic products pushing up through the earth often yield valuable mineral ore deposits such as gold, silver, and copper. The world's largest open-pit mine, Bingham Copper Mine in the Oquirrh Range, has produced in excess of $15 million of ore, mostly copper, but also gold, lead, and zinc.

Earthquakes of all magnitudes have shaken the lands bordering the Great Basin. Geologists believe that a major quake could hit the area within the next 100 years.

■ THE MIDDLE ROCKY MOUNTAIN PROVINCE

North-central Utah is dominated by the Wasatch Range. The high Uinta Mountains, a rarity among ranges in the United States in that they run from east to west, dominate the skyline of northeastern Utah. Both lie within the Utah portion of the Middle Rocky Mountain Province.

The Wasatch Mountains rise to the east of the Great Basin along the boundaries of Utah's major cities—Provo, Logan, Ogden, and Salt Lake City. They belong to a longer chain of mountains called the Wasatch Line. The Wasatch Line is one of the most important geological features of North America because of the great differences in the geology and landforms on its east and west sides. To the east lies the Uinta Basin (not a true basin, as its rivers flow eventually into the sea), and the canyons and tablelands of the Colorado Plateau. To the west lies the Great Basin and the remnants of Lake Bonneville.

The Wasatch Mountains have an unusual assemblage of sedimentary, igneous, and metamorphic rocks. Each canyon along the Wasatch Front exposes a different era of rock. The rich sediment deposits of these canyon streams account for almost all of Utah's fertile soil.

A heavy concentration of hot springs, usually associated with earthquake faults, is found along the Wasatch Line. Not surprisingly, several of the longest normal faults in North America also have been mapped here. (A normal fault is one in which a block of strata drops in relation to another.) The Wasatch Fault, which runs along the east bench of Salt Lake City, is Utah's longest. The concentration of earthquakes along the Wasatch Line is so great that it has been named "the Intermountain Seismic Belt." The largest recorded earthquake in this area, with an estimated magnitude of 6.4 on the Richter Scale, occurred around the turn of the century. Smaller quakes regularly make the needle jump at the University of Utah's seismographic station, but are seldom noticed by the public. A large earthquake

The granite of the Wasatch Range comes both polished and rough.

would cause serious damage in Utah. Salt Lake City, built on an old lake bed (similar to Mexico City), would jiggle like gelatin in the event of a major tremor.

The Central Wasatch Range, like other ranges in the Rocky Mountains, has a core of igneous or metamorphic rock. The area around Alta and Park City has yielded millions of dollars worth of precious metals.

To the east of the Wasatch Line rises the Uinta Range. These mountains were pushed up in a east-west direction, perpendicular to every other major range in the Rockies, and indeed, the continental United States. These mountains have no record of igneous activity, and consequently no important ore deposits.

The two mountain ranges intersect near Park City. The geology of this "crossroads" region is extremely complex.

■ BASIN AND RANGE/COLORADO PLATEAU TRANSITION PROVINCE

An exact boundary between the Great Basin and the Colorado Plateau is difficult to draw. The Transition Province has features common to both. Here are eight plateaus ranging in elevation from 8,000 to 11,000 feet (2,425-3,330 m). These

Utah's Capitol Reef National Park.

run southerly from near the center of the state, with drainage about equally divided between the Great Basin and the Colorado River.

The Tushar Mountains, remnants of extinct volcanoes, were formed 20 to 31 million years ago. Numerous mineral deposits are found there, including those that give the Big Rock Candy Mountain, near Marysville, its distinctive coloration.

The high plateaus of Iron, Garfield, Wayne, Piute, and Sevier counties are part of the Transition Province. Brian Head, the site of the popular Brian Head Ski Resort south of Parowan, is a dominant protrusion on top of such a plateau. Nearby Bryce Canyon National Park and Cedar Breaks National Monument each embrace colorful, limestone-capped subsections of this same region.

The Tonoquints volcanic section, which includes the Escalante Desert portion of the Great Basin, is another interesting geological area. Iron Mountain and Iron County received their names from the ore deposits found here. Travelers interested in the early history of mining should visit Iron Mission State Park in Cedar City.

■ PREHISTORIC LIFE

Utah's rocks hold fossils from every geological age. Dinosaurs once roamed this area, and visitors can follow the tracks of these ancient beasts.

A boater at Lake Powell strolling on the shoreline may discover dinosaur tracks. At Dinosaur National Monument, paleontologists work in an active quarry. Thousands of dinosaur bones were taken from the Cleveland-Lloyd Quarry in Emery County. Utah has been called "a King Tut's tomb of fossils."

Why is Utah so full of dinosaur and other fossils? The Morrison Formation—a geologic designation for a series of strata deposited at the height of the dinosaur age—is found throughout eastern Utah. A combination of erosion and dry climate has exposed it to an extent unusual for any formation. Dinosaur National Monument, in northeastern Utah, and the Cleveland-Lloyd Dinosaur Quarry, near the town of Cleveland in central Utah, are miles apart, but both are in the Morrison Formation, and both have yielded some of the finest fossilized dinosaur skeletons found anywhere. These are the most obvious places to view actual remains. But there are sites all over Utah where amateur rockhounds and budding geologists can examine the remains of ancient worlds.

The Dinosaur Gardens at the Utah Field House of Natural History in Vernal.

For detailed information on Utah's fossil treasures and an overview of prehistoric history, visitors can stop by the museums in Vernal or Price, or the Utah Museum of Natural History in Salt Lake City.

The best place to actually see paleontologists extract and reassemble dinosaur bones is the quarry at Dinosaur National Monument. An ancient riverbed where the prehistoric animals were buried has been encased in a large working laboratory at the monument's visitor center. For the most part, the bones of plant-eating dinosaurs are found at the monument. *Stegosaurus* is common, as are several types of sauropods, the largest animals ever to roam on land, and the tiny *Nanosaurus,* a creature no larger than a chicken.

Andrew Carnegie, the famous capitalist and philanthropist, stirred dinosaur fever throughout the world with specimens from Utah. He constructed a huge museum for the people of Pittsburgh, Pennsylvania, but could find nothing grand enough to fill it.

"Someone slapped a picture of a *Brontosaurus* from the monument on his desk," recounts Dr. William Stokes, the geologist, "and his eyes lit up. He said, 'Get me one!' Here was something finally big enough to fill up his big halls. He had a huge cast made for a 60-foot (18-m) diplodocus. Carnegie had duplicates sent all over the world to the kings, potentates, and emperors." The model outside the museum in Vernal is the last one made from this mold.

Dr. William Stokes, a leading geologist at the University of Utah. A colleague named the Stokesosaurus *after him.*

The Cleveland-Lloyd quarry is a more remote and rustic site. Relatively greater numbers of carnivorous dinosaur fossils are found there. The area was once a bog where large plant-eating dinosaurs became trapped and eventually entombed. The meat-eating *Allosaurus* is the most common species found here. *Stokesosaurus,* a sauropod, was discovered here and named for Stokes.

Dinosaur National Monument and the Cleveland-Lloyd quarry are managed by different government agencies for somewhat different purposes. The bones at the monument are uncovered but left in place. The Cleveland site, managed by the Bureau of Land Management, is an active quarry from which bones are removed for research and study. Anyone with a proper permit may dig for bones at the Cleveland quarry. In addition to these two locations, fossilized trilobites are common in the western desert regions of the Great Basin. Miners in Price, located in the heart of dinosaur country, have uncovered many dinosaur footprints in the coal deposits.

Petrified wood can also be found throughout the Colorado Plateau. Visitors to Escalante State Park can hike along a trail among the petrified logs of an ancient coniferous forest.

Certain areas in northeastern Utah are rich in fossils.

UTAH'S FIRST INHABITANTS

THE AMERICAN SOUTHWEST, AND UTAH IN PARTICULAR, contains some of the country's most spectacular traces of Native American civilization. Many of these ruins, artifacts, and rock pictures were left by the vanished Anasazi and Fremont cultures, while others were the work of the more recently arrived Shoshone, Ute, Navajo, and Paiute peoples. The human history of Utah, however, begins much earlier.

Paleo-Indians (as archaeologists call the first colonizers of America) were hunting and gathering throughout the area now known as Utah as early as 11,000 B.C. Their stone-tipped spears, used to fell large fauna of the Ice Age, have been discovered in caves along the long-vanished shoreline of Lake Bonneville. Meat from animals like the mammoth and giant bison were probably cached in the frozen ground to sustain the Paleo-Indians, who also depended on seeds, nuts, and small rodents for food.

When Ice Age glaciers started to recede around 6000 B.C., wind patterns changed. By A.D. 1, great inland deserts were forming in the Southwest. Many of the Ice Age mammals became extinct. The people who once depended on very large mammals to sustain them had to change their way of life, spending more time collecting wild seeds and nuts, and trapping game such as elk, deer, mountain sheep, antelope, rabbits, and rodents.

Around A.D. 500, corn and other crops were introduced into the Southwest from Mexico. With a more dependable food source, the Indians could stay in one place and produce enough corn, beans, and squash to store for the winter and times of drought. They made clay pottery and intricate baskets for harvesting and storing the crops. This new agricultural life differed so much from the old hunting and gathering cultures that archaeologists distinguish its practitioners with new names: the Fremont and the Anasazi. The Anasazi, in general, flourished on the Colorado Plateau south of the Colorado River, while the Fremont people lived north of the Colorado and east of the Virgin rivers in the Great Basin and Uinta Basin.

Sunlight streams into a kiva, *a ceremonial structure used among pueblo-dwelling tribes.*

■ THE ANASAZI

The first Anasazi people, known to archaeologists as the Basketmakers, lived in pithouses, saucer-shaped dwellings half above ground and half underground, walled and roofed with a combination of logs and mud mortar. They apparently had frequent contact with other peoples, and their dramatic cultural advancement from A.D. 700 to 1300, designated as the Pueblo Period by archaeologists, shows them to have been extremely adaptable and dynamic. Around A.D. 700, the bow and arrow made its appearance, replacing the less efficient spear and *atlatl* (wooden spear-thrower). Cotton weaving was introduced, and dogs and turkeys were domesticated.

Circa A.D. 900, the Anasazi began to build multi-story stone structures grouped around courtyards. Beneath the courtyards were underground chambers called *kiva*. The roofs were mud on top of a wooden framework, level with the surrounding plaza. A hole in the center of the roof served as entrance and smoke hole. Each kiva had a place for a fire, ventilation to keep the fire going, and a small indentation in the floor called a *sipapu*. Because modern Hopi use the same kind of room for their ceremonies, archaeologists theorize that the use and purpose of the Anasazi kiva was similar. To the Hopi, the sipapu symbolizes the opening through which mankind entered the world. The kiva was a place for the men to come and weave and pass on their culture. Women were not allowed.

During the latter part of the Pueblo Period, dwellings were constructed in the protected alcoves of sandstone canyons. Built on cliffs high above the valley floor, most were reached by ladders or handholds and footholds chipped in the rock. Some were nestled back into large open caves in the rock walls of the canyons. Thousands of remnants of this civilization can be found throughout the Colorado Plateau in what the Utah Travel Council calls the Grand Circle. Among the sites on the Grand Circle described later in this book are Edge of the Cedars State Historic Park, Butler Wash, Grand Gulch Primitive Area, Natural Bridges and Hovenweep national monuments, Anasazi State Park, Canyonlands National Park, and Newspaper Rock.

■ THE FREMONT INDIANS

Much less is known about the Fremont Indians, who inhabited the region north of the Anasazi, along the edge of the Great Basin and the Colorado Plateau. Such an extreme range of climate and geography prompted individual bands to adapt in different ways. Some lived as nomadic hunters and plant collectors. Others established villages and lived as farmers. Consequently, they have fewer communal characteristics to identify them as a common people. Among these are a particular style of basketry and leather moccasins (as opposed to the sandals of yucca fibers worn by the Anasazi). Their pictographs, petroglyphs, and clay figurines generally have distinctive hair "boles" and necklaces. Also unique was the Fremont recipe for making pottery by mixing granular rock or sand with the wet clay.

Five distinct Fremont groups have been identified by archaeologists, each determined by geographical location and differences in styles of pottery, figurines, and projectile points: the Parowan Gap, Uintah, Sevier Fremont, San Rafael, and Great Salt Lake.

There are fewer known Fremont village sites than Anasazi sites. One reason for this is that the pit houses of the Fremont deteriorated faster than the stone and mortar of the Anasazi. The pit houses are hard for the layman to differentiate from the desert floor, but the granaries and rock graphics stand out clearly.

An excellent place to learn about these early settlers is Fremont Indian State Park, where Five Finger Ridge Village was uncovered when the interstate was built built through Clear Creek Canyon, about 15 miles (24 km) southwest of Richfield. The state of Utah collected the artifacts together in a museum showing how the Fremont hunted for game and wild plant foods, and farmed in the canyon bottoms. Visitors can examine full-sized replicas of a pit house and granary and see the Fremont rock graphics along the Show Me Rock Art and Discovery trails.

Fremont Indian State Park superintendent Gordon Topham often invites Indians who live in the area to give demonstrations of their traditional way of life. The park frequently sponsors special events at which guests are invited to learn an Indian dance, chip stone into an arrowhead, or make a pot in the ancient Fremont way.

Fremont Indian petroglyphs may also be viewed at Parowan Gap, 12 miles (19 km) north of Parowan in Iron County, and in Nine-Mile Canyon, northwest of Price.

■ FINDING INDIAN SITES

There are thousands of sites containing Anasazi and Fremont remains throughout Utah. Go to a state or federal park, such as Anasazi State Park, Fremont Indian State Park, or Hovenweep National Monument, to research the prehistoric inhabitants of the area. You might take one of the tours available in towns like Blanding, Bluff, or Moab.

Next, set off on your own to smaller areas in these parks or to several BLM sites throughout Utah.

Our family has turned Indian ruin hunting into a hobby. Before the children could walk, they were carried through the doorways of the magnificent pueblos of Mesa Verde in Colorado and Chaco Canyon in New Mexico. They grew up listening to lectures from mom at the museums, and often fancied themselves as the half-naked Anasazi children they saw in displays. After educating ourselves, we decided it was time to go exploring on our own. One Easter, we walked into a BLM ranger station in Monticello, looking for a backpacking trail we could take to see Indian ruins. We don't like to say where we went because, like many, we cherish our own secret places. After a few hours on the trail, we were lost. We acknowledge the fact that we are horrible map-readers, so we always keep track of landmarks, should we have to backtrack, as we did that evening. By the time we were

Hunting scenes on a prehistoric fresco in Nine-Mile Canyon.

This ancient reptile appears to have been drawn yesterday.

hiking on another trail, the sun was low in the sky. We set up our tents for the night within a mile of our car. We heard coyotes in the distance and slept under a blanket of stars. The next morning was like Christmas, Easter, and birthdays all wrapped together. Before setting off down the trail, the youngest looked back and said, "What's that?" He saw the unmistakable walls of a cliff dwelling tucked into an alcove. For the next half hour, our exclamations of delight and discovery echoed off the walls of the canyon. Here were pieces of pottery—white, red, black, some smooth, some crimped. The patterns on them were reminiscent of jigsaw puzzles. One gray piece had an unmistakeable fingerprint in black, as if it were a photograph negative. We saw fingerprints, too, in the clay mortar between the stones of the walls. A fingerprint is so personal and so immediate. What would the owner say if he saw us here? A small corn cob lay back in the sand of one of the rooms. Here were so many things we had seen behind the glass of museum displays. Here was a kind of dwelling we had seen before but never on our own and never with so many pieces of pottery scattered wherever we looked. That night we set up camp far down the trail from the Anasazi ruins—but still we found pottery. Our dreams were filled with visions of brown-skinned women sitting in front of their neatly plastered homes, grinding corn and painting geometric designs on their smooth white pots.

(following pages) Anasazi ruins at Island-in-the-Sky, Canyonlands National Park.

Sit in the stillness of the canyon. Try to hear the echoes of the Anasazi as they go about their daily chores. Women chatter as they grind corn, children chase domesticated turkeys. Young adults carefully beat the tops of rice grass, letting the seeds fall into their ornate baskets. While you try to recreate the centuries-old scene, please remember the words of modern Hopi, Navajo, Ute, Paiute, Shoshone, all who trace their ancestry to canyons such as this. You are in someone's home, resting in someone's cemetery. Treat it with respect. Ruin walls are fragile; the mortar holding them together crumbles easily. Please do not walk or lean on them. Please leave all artifacts in place. The beauty of these places is that pieces of the past can be seen. If any one artifact is taken or destroyed, the quality of the experience for hundreds of visitors to come is diminished. Touching rock graphics deposits skin oils which hasten deterioration of the pigments and rock surfaces. Besides, all prehistoric remains are protected by law by the United States government. Fines of up to $20,000 and or imprisonment may be imposed on anyone removing or destroying these cultural resources on public lands. Rewards are offered for information leading to the arrest and conviction of anyone disturbing a site.

■ THE FATE OF THE ANCIENT ONES

Many ask the question, what became of the Anasazi and Fremont? Several theories have been proposed but no solid evidence has been produced to support one theory over the other. By studying tree rings, scientists have documented that a severe 20-year drought hit the Southwest where the Anasazi and Fremont lived. Cutting timber for fuel and building material and clearing land for agriculture may have started a cycle of erosion, ending with a loss of fields due to gullying. With a diminished capacity to grow and store enough food, social disruptions undoubtably took place. While no evidence of violence has been found in the cliff dwellings, their relative inaccessibility makes them seem like fortresses. The abandonment of the ancestral lands was gradual. Perhaps a few people at a time migrated south to more hospitable lands until no one was left. It is believed the Anasazi migrated to the northern Rio Grande tributaries and the upper Little Colorado River drainage on the Hopi Mesa and Zuni Plateau, where active settlements were already prospering. By 1300, the pueblos were sprawling. New rooms could be easily added.

Anasazi pots from the vicinity of Cedars State Park.

Their construction was less formal than the classic cliff dwellings. Indians living in pueblos probably traded corn and pottery for the Plains Indians' meat and hides.

While anthropologists and archaeologists dig into Anasazi and Fremont village sites trying to solve the mystery of what happened to their old occupants, many modern Indians feel the answers can be found somewhere else. May Perry, a Shoshone, says, "If you want to find out what happened to the Fremont Indians, just ask us." Perry explains that in a recent trip through the Utah Natural History Museum the curators showed her several round stone balls. She said, "My people use these for juggling! We always have." May found many items on display at the museum that closely resembled her own household utensils. The styles of grinding stones, jewelry-making tools, and moccasins are all very similar.

Will Numkena, a Hopi, says, "The Hopi feel a strong kinship with those you call Fremont and Anasazi." The Hopi recognize many petroglyphs and pictographs as representations of their *kachinas*, or offspring of the Creator. Many of the symbols found on the rocks are an integral part of their daily lives.

Perhaps with a changing climate and pressure from migrating tribes, the Fremont were assimilated into the erstwhile separate groups, like the Shoshone. Research into the Fremont Indian culture is still inconclusive.

■ THE LATER TRIBES

Although it is not scientifically proven that the contemporary Indians of Utah and the Southwest are direct descendants of the Fremont and Anasazi, it is a fact that the Ute, Shoshone, Paiute, Goshute, and Navajo people inhabited Utah long before the non-Indian explorers and settlers came along.

During a panel discussion in which representatives from the Ute, Paiute, Shoshone, Navajo, and Hopi tribes talked about their kinship with the Fremont, every speaker expressed the desire to see all visitors respect the Anasazi and Fremont cultures, and particularly their burial sites. Travis Parashonts, a Paiute, said, "Archaeologists see it as a science—Indians see it as a spiritual or emotional thing. There is a reason for everything. Our forefathers were put away with special things. When they are dug up, an imbalance is made." Clifford Duncan, a Ute from the Uintah Basin, agrees. He says, "The Indian people have roots here in this country. When people bother the remains of the ancients, it is us they are bothering. Those who

(top) Poncho House ruins at Chinle Wash. (bottom) Anasazi ruins in Road Canyon. The Anasazi vanished 600 years ago as mysteriously as they had appeared centuries before.

tell others to leave the dwellings and rock markings alone are speaking for the Indian. They are landmarks and sacred areas. They remind the world that The People once lived there."

Modern Indians feel their ancestral heritage, geography, and religion are common bonds between all the different tribes. They see the religious symbols of the Anasazi and Fremont as proof that the modern Indian religion grew out of the old. Will Numkena says that when he is among the symbols on the canyon walls, he is among spirits of his family.

The story of Utah's Indians, their domination and frequent betrayal at the hands of non-Indian settlers and politicians, parallels that of other tribes throughout the United States. The first Spanish explorers in the Southwest encouraged Utes to prey on Paiutes and Goshutes and bring them as slaves for trade. The settlers were generally accepted by the Indians in the beginning until the number of non-Indians increased along with their demand for more land.

Historically, Utah's Indians were hunters and gatherers, moving from place to place within a particular boundary. Small bands camped near water in cooler areas in the summer and moved to warmer areas in the winter. There were many different bands belonging to each Indian tribe. The bands would come together occasionally for seasonal celebrations. Each band had its own leader, but there was no one head of the Shoshone, Hopi, Navajo or Ute. The concept of "chief" seemed to develop after the arrival of non-Indians, who were accustomed to negotiating with a spokesman for every nation. This lack of an overall leader led to many misunderstandings. A treaty signed between one group of Utes and the pioneers did not, in the Ute scheme of things, bind all Utes to its promises. At Fort Panguitch in the early days of the Walker War, a man was killed by an Indian arrow. When another group of Indians later came to the fort, they were not asked their purpose, but were murdered as enemies.

The Utes and Shoshone picked up the idea of using teepees for housing from the Plains Indians. Horses obtained from the Spanish changed the way of life of the Utes by enabling them to chase and hunt larger game, like buffalo and antelope, and to trade more easily.

The Paiute and Goshute used conical pole lodgings covered with grass or brush. The article of clothing used universally by the Indians was the rabbitskin blanket, made of long strips of skin with the fur on. A wide variety of baskets were produced by coiled and twined techniques. A pitch-covered bottle with a globular

These Northern Shoshone were photographed around the turn of the century.

body and constricted neck was used for carrying liquids on long treks into the desert in search of wild seeds.

The first Spanish to visit the Indians in Utah were Dominguez and Escalante. They found the Laguna Utes living along the shores of Utah Lake and described them in this way: "Their dwellings are some sheds or little wattle huts of osier (willows) out of which they have interestingly crafted baskets and other instruments of ordinary use. They are very poor as regards dress. The most becoming one they wear is a deerskin jacket and long leggings of the same. For cold seasons they wear blankets made of jackrabbit and coney rabbit furs. They employ the Yuta language but with noticeable variances in pronunciation, and even in some words. They possess good features, and most of them are fully bearded. All the sections of this sierra along the southeast, south-southwest, and west are inhabited by a great number of peoples of the same nations, language, and easy-going character as these Laguna, with whom a very populous and extensive province could be formed."

The Paiute were also farmers, growing corn, beans, and squash in the river bottoms. Every autumn the Paiute and other Indians of Utah went to gather pine nuts from the piñon pine forests. This practice was adopted by the pioneer settlers.

Something else the pioneer settlers adopted was the Indians' water supply. In a dry climate like Utah's, whoever had access to the water was able to dominate all others. In many cases, Indians would go off to a seasonal hunting or gathering area and return to find their traditional water source fenced off or in some way

Chief Kanosh

(opposite) Spires in Monument Valley at Navajo Tribal Park.

appropriated. Varied ways were used to encourage the Indians to leave. Pioneers around Huntsville in northern Utah were digging a ditch to the South Fork of the Ogden River when a band of Indians told the settlers to leave the valley or they would pollute the water. Captain Hunt told the Indians that at their first suspicious act he would burn all the water in the canyons. When they looked incredulous, he grabbed a dipperful of colorless liquid, probably alcohol, and burned it. The Indians backed down. Sometimes the Indians were left parcels of land, not always the prime parcels, and encouraged to take up the same lifestyle as their new non-Indian neighbors. Brigham Young preached that it was far cheaper to feed and clothe the Indians than to fight them. He encouraged the Mormon pioneers to hand out food, tobacco, and clothing whenever the need arose. One of the first settlers of Kanosh remembered occasionally passing out food and blankets to members of Chief Kanosh's band when the Indians occasionally showed up at her door. She also remembered employing an Indian woman to do the family's wash.

As one band of Indians was forced from its traditional land, it entered the lands of another band. This caused conflict between groups, but they often joined against the common invader. It is surprising that the Indian conflicts in Utah did not last longer than they did. It has been suggested that this is because the Indians were not warlike to begin with. According to the 1941 edition of *Utah, A Guide to the State*, "The Walker War of 1853-54 was precipitated by the occupation of Indian lands by white people, and would probably have been more serious except for the restraining influence of the Ute war chief, Sowiette. Shoshone resistance to white settlement was crushed when six hundred Indians were surrounded and killed by Federal soldiers in January, 1863. The Black Hawk War of 1865-68 was waged over the same question of white preemption of hunting grounds, and had the same sort of ending. In 1879, the Indian agent, N.C. Meeker, and others were killed at the White River Agency in western Colorado by Ute Indians who objected to maltreatment and to having soldiers on the reservation. The outbreak was quickly subdued, mainly because of the peaceful attitude of Chief Ouray, and the Utes were afterward moved to reservations. There were Navajo raids into southwestern Utah in the 1860s and 1870s, and trouble with Paiutes and Utes in the San Juan area in the 1880s and 1890s. Between 1861, when the Uinta Basin was set aside for Indian use by President Lincoln, and 1929, when the Kanosh reservation was established, all of the Indians within the state were settled on reservations."

Goulding's Trading Post circa 1950.

The "last battle" between Indians and non-Indians in the remaining frontier of the United States took place in 1923 outside of Blanding, Utah. Chief Posey and his band had eluded capture by a large posse by making a 15-foot (5-m) jump in west Comb Wash. Posey was wounded and died of blood poisoning. His band gave itself up two days later. The event brought the tribe's plight to the nation's attention and they were later given the White Mesa Indian Reservation, 12 miles (19 km) south of Bluff.

The inevitable ending to the clash between the Indian and non-Indian cultures was a virtual elimination of the Indians' way of life. The Indians were forced to stay on reservations and become ranchers and farmers. Those who chose not to live on the reservations where the conditions were never very good had to fit into a society that did not accept the Indians' culture. Most Indians adopted non-Indian clothes and homes. Perhaps worst of all was the attitude that the Indians had to abandon their religious beliefs and social customs. Children were sent away to school to learn "civilized" ways. The federal government ran a large boarding school in Brigham City. The Mormon Church sponsored an Indian Placement Program where Indian children were placed in Mormon homes to be raised and educated.

■ MEETING CONTEMPORARY INDIANS

As the consciousness of many Americans was raised in the 1960s in respect to the Indians' plight, Utah began to change with the rest of the country. The Intermountain Indian School was closed, and schools were built on the reservations where students could live at home and learn many of the traditional ways both from their families and schools. The challenge still remains, however, of how the Indian can live in the modern world and retain his cultural roots.

Besides visiting the Anasazi and Fremont ruins in the state, visitors to Utah should get to know its modern Indians, many of whom do not live on reservations.

The White Mesa Institute in Blanding, sponsored by the College of Eastern Utah, offers educational programs for youth and adults on Southwest archaeology, modern Indian tribes, pioneer history, wildlife, and geology. The Museum of Natural History in Salt Lake City and the Canyonlands Field Institute in Moab offer similar programs.

In Cedar City in June, the local Indian community sponsors the Paiute Restoration Gathering, with a parade, dances, traditional games, native food, and a beauty pageant. Many Indians from southern Utah attend Southern Utah State University in Cedar City.

The Annual Southern Utah Folklife Festival is held in Springdale, outside of Zion National Park, every September. Southern Utah's Paiutes are included in this festival.

In Bluff, Indians from the Navajo reservation across the San Juan River occasionally have dance performances, horse races, rodeos, and other get-togethers.

Utes from Fort Duchesne, on the Uintah and Ouray Indian Reservation, hold a "Ute Indian Powwow" every summer, with tribes from all over the West in attendance. Rodeo action, craft displays, and food booths entertain the crowds. Other Indian powwows, dances and rodeos are held throughout the year. Information on dates and times is available at Bottle Hollow Resort on US Route 40 near Roosevelt. The Uintah and Ouray Indian Reservation covers nearly one million acres scattered across the East Tavaputs Plateau. Non-members are asked to keep to the main roads on the reservation and purchase permits for most activities, such as camping, hunting, boating, or fishing. Bottle Hollow Reservoir and campground are on the reservation, as is the Bottle Hollow Resort.

Monument Valley, in the southeast corner of Utah, has been described as the "Eighth Wonder of the World," an enduring symbol of the West. Monument Valley is located on the Navajo Indian Reservation, which sprawls over vast areas of Utah, Arizona, and New Mexico. Like their neighbors, the Hopi, the Navajo have been able to retain much of their ancestral lands and therefore maintain more of their old ways of life. Round mud and log hogans, the Navajo winter homes, are scattered throughout the reservation. Fine examples of Indian jewelry and blankets can be seen and purchased from stores like Hatch Trading Post, on the way to Hovenweep National Monument, and Montezuma Creek Trading Post, just east of Bluff. Once in awhile a few individuals will set up a stand by the side of the road to sell their wares. Expect to pay high prices for the jewelry and blankets. These articles take a long time to produce and are priced as works of art.

In the Mystery Valley section of Monument Valley Tribal Park are several hundred Anasazi dwellings, most of them small and unnamed. Guides are needed to locate them. The caretakers of this land, the Navajo, though unrelated to the Anasazi, live in a similar fashion to that of their predecessors. They are isolated and clannish, depending on the land and little else to survive.

The Indians of Utah have a rich heritage. Their history is told in the markings on the rocks and in their dwelling places. It is told through the legends and traditions of those who came after—the Hopi, Ute, Paiute, Goshute, Shoshone, and Navajo. In a state that claims so many diverse natural wonders, the added dimension of a proud native people is a bonus. As those who travel Utah come to love the beauty of its canyons, mesas, mountains, and deserts, they must learn to appreciate the beliefs of the first Americans. The idea that mankind must live in harmony with the earth and protect it from harm is gaining more and more acceptance. It would be sad to see the end of the wide open spaces and the ancient caretakers of the land.

THE EARLY EXPLORERS

UTAH IS A VAST TERRITORY JUST WAITING FOR ADVENTURERS. Freeways may crisscross the land, the nearest town might loom just around the corner, and an airplane can fly across the entire state in less than an hour. But great expanses of alpine forest still remain wild and natural. Red-rock canyons, forbidding-looking deserts, high pristine mountains, and gleaming white salt flats stretch far into the horizon.

Take a day—or better yet, several—to explore a wild part of Utah. Find a place without roads, reservoirs, or restaurants. Imagine that you are an early adventurer seeing this country for the first time. Conjure up visions of mysterious Indian tribes camped nearby. Dream that grizzly bears and wolves roam the forests.

Perhaps then can you imagine what Utah's early explorers—Escalante, Dominguez, Bridger, Smith, and Powell—experienced as they ventured into this fascinating land.

■ THE SPANISH EXPLORERS

Soon after Cortez conquered Mexico, Coronado pushed northward in search of the legendary Seven Cities of Cibola. The conquistador came searching for cities made of gold, but found only adobe pueblos belonging to the Hopi Indians. Catholic missionaries came to the land—now including parts of New Mexico, California, and Arizona—and established outposts at Santa Fe and all along the Pacific coast. Their purpose was to convert the Native Americans and reap whatever bounty they could from the vast new land. The Indians were also encouraged to capture and sell slaves.

To ensure the success of the precarious California missions, the Spanish needed a trade route from Santa Fe to the Pacific. Hopis and Apaches, tribes that stubbornly resisted foreign incursions into their territories, inhabited the country in between. The Spanish desperately sought a northern route around them.

Father Silvestre Velez de Escalante came to Santa Fe. He talked to the visiting Ute (whom he called *Yuta*) Indians from what is now Utah. He sensed from the information they gave him that he could find a way to California, perhaps by water, by heading north.

THE DOMINGUEZ-ESCALANTE JOURNAL, 1776

Sept. 25 near Utah Lake, on first learning of the Great Salt Lake from the Indians. . . The other lake with which this one comes in contact covers many leagues, so we were informed, and its waters are harmful and extremely salty, for the Timpanois assured us that anyone who wet some part of the body with them immediately felt a lot of itching in the part moistened.

Oct. 11: Many times before leaving La Villa de Santa Fe we had reminded each and every one of our companions that in this journey we had no other destination than the one which God would grant us; nor did this tempt us to any worldly purpose whatsoever; and that whosoever among them tried either to trade with the infidels or to follow out his private notions by not keeping before him the sole aim of this undertaking, which has been and is God's greater glory and the spreading of the faith, had better not go in our company. On the way we time and again admonished (some) to rectify their intentions, because otherwise we would suffer hardships and misfortunes and would not achieve all that we were aiming for—as they saw in part come true under circumstances which, unless they close their eyes to the Light, they could never attribute to accident. With all this they plagued us more each day, and we were very much disheartened by seeing how in the business of heaven the one of earth was being sought first and foremost. . . .

Oct. 14 in the vicinity of present-day Toquerville, Utah . . . Here it is already very temperate country for, in spite of our having experienced plenty of heat yesterday, last night, and today, the river poplars were so green and leafy, the flowers and blooms which the land produces so flamboyant and without damage whatsoever, that they indicated there had been no freezing or frosting around here. We also saw growths of mesquite, which does not flourish in very cold lands. . . .

Escalante enters Utah Valley, as portrayed by Eddington. (Utah State Historical Society)

Escalante and Father Francisco Atanasio Dominguez, the expedition's leader, set out in 1776, a month after members of the Continental Congress signed the Declaration of Independence. His superiors charged the expedition with scouting out any new Indian settlements favorable for missionary work. With a party of six explorers and a map-maker, they became probably the first Europeans to enter the uncharted regions that would later become Utah. Several Indians joined in the expedition as guides along the way.

Dominguez and Escalante did not succeed. The explorers found no northern route to California, and the Indians did not convert. The priests died in obscurity. Yet, the expedition did open Utah to further exploration. The expedition's map-maker, Don Bernardo Miera y Pacheco, charted Utah's first maps. Modern travelers who read Escalante's journal and visit the rugged country of the Colorado Plateau, the Uintas, and the Wasatch Front can only marvel at the exploits of these brave men.

How different might Utah have been if the fathers had succeeded! The Utes (or *Lagunas*, as the Spanish fathers called them) on the shores of Utah Lake grew to like the missionaries so much that they begged them to return. Dominguez and Escalante promised to send missionaries but their superiors in Mexico chose not to. Almost a hundred years passed before another church, the Latter-day Saints, arrived in their land. Utah was never colonized by the Spanish even though the early explorers described it as "the most pleasing, beautiful, and fertile site in all New Spain." Colonization was left to the Mormons. If Dominguez and Escalante had succeeded, Utahns might speak Spanish as their native language and Provo would be home for Catholic priests instead of Mormon bishops.

Monsignor Jerome Stoffel, a retired Catholic pastor in Salt Lake City, appreciates the efforts of the explorers more than most. Using maps and descriptions from old journals, he researched and followed Escalante and Dominguez's route on a 1976 trek sponsored by the Utah Bicentennial Commission.

Though the expedition's original journal has never been found, Monsignor Stoffel used copies made by subsequent explorers, written in eighteenth-century Spanish, each slightly different from the others. No map of the route is absolutely dependable.

Like a detective working to solve a mystery, Monsignor Stoffel and his fellow historians used the journal to search for the original trail and campsites. His eyes twinkle as he relates a discovery he made in comparing the journal entries and his

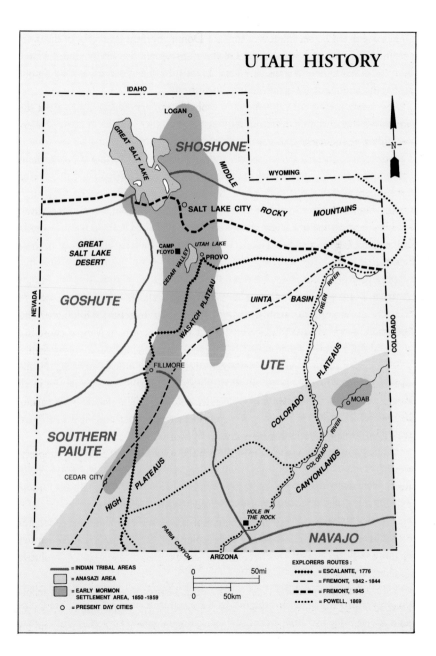

UTAH HISTORY

-N-

IDAHO

LOGAN

GREAT SALT LAKE

SHOSHONE

MIDDLE

WYOMING

SALT LAKE CITY   ROCKY   MOUNTAINS

GREAT
SALT LAKE
DESERT

CAMP
FLOYD   UTAH LAKE
CEDAR VALLEY   PROVO

NEVADA

GOSHUTE

WASATCH PLATEAU

UINTA   BASIN

GREEN RIVER

COLORADO

UTE

FILLMORE

COLORADO   PLATEAUS

MOAB

SOUTHERN
PAIUTE

COLORADO   RIVER

CEDAR CITY

HIGH   PLATEAUS

CANYONLANDS

HOLE IN
THE ROCK

PARIA CANYON

NAVAJO

ARIZONA

= INDIAN TRIBAL AREAS

= ANASAZI AREA

= EARLY MORMON
SETTLEMENT AREA, 1850-1859

O = PRESENT DAY CITIES

0   50mi

0   50km

EXPLORERS ROUTES :

♦♦♦♦♦♦ = ESCALANTE, 1776

- - - = FREMONT, 1842 - 1844

■ ■ ■ = FREMONT, 1845

•••••• = POWELL, 1869

knowledge of the landscape at that time. "Escalante became suspicious of his Indian guides. Upon reaching a ridge, Escalante discovered a route obviously easier than the one his guide was using. 'Why,' he must have wondered, 'do they not go in that direction? Are we being led into an ambush?'

"We know there were Comanches in that part of the country," Monsignor explains. "Comanches were feared by Europeans and other Indians. It came to us as we looked at the route that Escalante's guide was probably trying to save them. The explorers possessed horses, mules, and supplies that the Comanches would do anything to get. We appreciated the wisdom of the guides, apparently more than did Escalante!"

Arriving at what is now Utah Lake, called *Timpanogos* (the Stone One) by the Indians, they learned of a larger lake to the north that the Utes said was filled with bitter water (the Great Salt Lake). There were also tantalizing tales of a river, Tizon, that flowed from the salty lake to the Pacific Ocean. With neither time nor supplies to explore this route, however, the explorers instead headed south toward Santa Fe, hoping to find Indians who would trade with them for food. The myth of a river connecting the Great Salt Lake to the Pacific Ocean persisted until the mountain man Jedediah Smith explored the lake.

It is ironic that the physical barriers to travel that exasperated Dominguez and Escalante now are popular tourist destinations. Split Mountain, where the priests crossed the Green River, guards a campground in Dinosaur National Monument. When Monsignor Stoffel tried to determine the exact point at which the fathers crossed the river, he was baffled. The river had changed too much in the past 200 years to cross at the exact location.

Escalante described a canyon near present-day Palmyra campground on the Diamond Fork River of Spanish Fork Canyon, southeast of Provo, as a place where "there were many dangerous defiles and slides, with no other trail than the one we went opening all along, and over the sierra's corrugated ruggedness which all over here made us change direction and wind about excessively at every step." Visitors to the canyon today travel on pavement to view the same rugged mountains that so vexed the Spanish fathers.

Hikers in Paria Canyon near the Utah-Arizona border carry maps and water and enjoy the spectacular red-rock scenery. In 1776, the tall, vertical walls of Paria Canyon stifled the Spanish explorers in their search for a way to ford the Colorado River. They had been warned by local Indians not to continue south to the

Colorado because of the impassable sandstone terrain. They distrusted this advice. For ten days they struggled to find their way through trackless mesas, across massive gorges, suffering from hunger and thirst. Horses were killed to feed the starving party. Finally they reached the only point where, for 50 miles (80 km) upstream and 150 miles (240 km) downstream, a horse could reach the water. The river was wide and deep here. "We found nothing but insuperable obstacles for getting to the ford without retracing much terrain," wrote Escalante. The fathers called their camp in Paria Canyon *Salispuedes* ("Get Out if You Can"). The Crossing of the Fathers, as it is now called, where the explorers forded the Colorado is now submerged under Lake Powell. Escalante described the climb out of the canyon as having "extremely difficult stretches and most dangerous ledges." They made the arduous climb and camped that night above the present-day swimming beach at Wahweap, on Lake Powell.

■ MOUNTAIN MEN

Fashionable citizens no longer wear tall hats manufactured from beaver pelts. Mountain men, who forged a path through the wilderness in search of beaver, otter, and other furry creatures, are no longer needed to supply the wants of twentieth-century fashion. Gore-Tex jackets, hiking boots with Vibram soles and backpacks constructed of nylon have long replaced buckskins and moccasins. But the spirit of men like Jedediah Smith, Jim Bridger, Miles Goodyear, and Peter Skene Ogden lives on in the hearts of people like Timothy Toker Many Hats, a modern-day trapper born 150 years too late.

"I guess we never died off," says Many Hats, who frequently lives in a teepee, still traps, and does his best to keep the tradition of the mountain man alive. "I don't believe in reincarnation, but I've seen a few guys who must have come back."

Fort Buenaventura State Park in Ogden, where Many Hats works part-time, regularly joins with other state parks and black-powder muzzle-loading organizations to sponsor mountain-man rendezvous throughout Utah. At rendezvous, visitors walk from one teepee to the next, watching men or women in buckskins or furs work on Indian beadwork or stir up Dutch-oven meals. There are skilled gunsmiths, tanners, leatherworkers, and hat makers. The cracking black-powder muskets echo in the distance while Indian drums and chanting beckon visitors toward a dancing circle. And mountain men and women like Timothy Toker Many Hats begin to feel like the trappers and traders of the old American West.

"Actually, the whole fur trading era was a fad," says T.T. Many Hats. "The men who got involved in it at the beginning got very rich. They would pay $17.50 for an English long rifle. They would then go to an Indian, who would say, 'Yes, I would like a thunderstick.' Then they would say to the Indian, 'Oh, very expensive. You must bring in beaver pelts and pile them this high. . .' So, these Indians were paying almost $2,000 in furs for a rifle that only cost $17.50. But, for the Indians, it was worth it."

The old fur-trading business provided employment to loners, colorful characters, and adventurers. Some lived and trapped together in small groups. Others were independent types who saw other humans only at rendezvous to exchange goods and news. Many had Indian wives and families. All mountain men soon learned to live with the land or perish. Often, the Indians taught the trappers how to survive in the mountains. Indian crafts are still taught at the rendezvous.

T.T. Many Hats is one of the few modern mountain men who can say he got his start in the old way. He was born in Canada. His mother was French. His father was a hunter, trapper, gold prospector, and an American citizen. A Blackfoot Indian guardian helped to raise him, teaching him about the Blackfoot religion in the process.

The mountain-man rendezvouz has its roots in the early days of fur trapping in the West. John Jacob Astor, who established a fur company at the mouth of the Columbia River in Oregon, sent the first non-Indian trappers to northern Utah in 1811. Twelve years later, General William H. Ashley led a party sent by the British-owned Hudson's Bay Company to Cache Valley, near present-day Logan. Jim Bridger, a member of that party, is believed to be the first non-Indian to see the Great Salt Lake.

General Ashley quickly realized the country did not lend itself to established methods of trapping, which used rivers to transport goods and furs. He ambitiously organized a system of pack trains and an annual rendezvous at designated spots. The rendevouz became the most important link with the outside world for many trappers, a chance to stock up on civilized goods, and the premier social event of their long, lonely year.

General Ashley took buffalo hide boats down the Green River through Flaming Gorge searching for a western passage to the Pacific. Instead, he found the

JIM BRIDGER, 1804-81

Jim had a marked linguistic gift and, wandering over the West as he did for so long, had picked up Spanish and frontier French, besides nearly a dozen Indian tongues, including those of the Snake, Bannock, Crow, Flathead, Nez Perce, Ute, and Pend Oreille, with a smattering of others. He was so adept in the use of the sign language that he habitually accompanied his remarks with slight unconscious corroborative gestures. He was a crack shot and an expert trapper—none better—while his courage and good judgement were acknowledged by all who knew him.

Jim also excelled at trailing. He could read and recognize signs made by any critter on four legs or on two, readily determining the sex, age, gait, and often the purpose of any animal whose trail he picked up. He could at once identify the tribe of any Indian whose moccasin tracks crossed his trail, and was so familiar with his own horse and those of his companions that he could usually recognize the tracks of any horse in the *caballada*. He could estimate accurately by the warmth of the ashes of a dead campfire how long it had been since those who had built it had departed. If a track were in sand, he could tell by the amount of sand that had crumbled into it how long before it had been made. In grass he could tell whether or not the tracks had been made before or after dewfall, before or after a shower. Even at night, by dismounting and feeling the ground with his hands, he could usually make out the trail with his hands.

—Stanley Vestal, *Jim Bridger, Mountain Man*, 1946

Trappers spend an evening around the fire. (Special Collections, Utah State University)

Colorado Plateau and a maze of red rock canyons. "The river," he wrote, "is bounded by lofty mountains heaped together in the greatest disorder, exhibiting a surface as barren as can be imagined." Giving up his journey, he purchased horses from the Ute Indians for the return trip, and circled around the Uinta Mountains on his way to a rendezvous at Henry's Fork.

Ashley soon announced that he had seen enough of the mountains, sold his fur-trading interests, and departed to greener pastures. But the tradition of the rendezvous lived on, and still lives on. Most of the men and women who attend rendezvous today do so as a brief escape from the modern world, to barter, trade, share ideas, and exchange stories. They come to dance and rejoin their family, other mountain men and women. The meetings are seldom as uproarious as in times past; after all, there are more opportunities these days to party.

It is at night, when most of the tourists have gone, that the feeling of the past returns like the flames of the campfire. Tales are told of the first mountain men, and legends grow larger. Many of their deeds died along with the trappers and their families. "There were so many people that were in the mountain man era who didn't write down what they did," explains T.T. Many Hats. "Some went out and trapped for a few years. Some went out and just got killed."

Many left their names on Utah's map. The city of Ogden honors the memory of Peter Skene Ogden. Provo bears the name of Etienne Provot. The trapper custom of hiding or "caching" their furs until rendezvous time gave Cache County its name.

Other trappers left their marks without their names. Miles Goodyear erected the first fort in the Wasatch Mountains. A replica of it can be seen at Fort Buenaventura in Ogden. In 1837, Philip Thompson and David Craig constructed Fort Davy Crockett in Brown's Hole, south of where the Flaming Gorge Dam was later built. It was renamed Fort Misery by the trappers who frequented it, who called it "the meanest fort in the West."

■ JEDEDIAH SMITH

Perhaps the most remarkable of all the mountain men was Jedediah Smith.

"He was a very enthusiastic man," says T.T. Many Hats. "He'd be very excited and enthusiastic about his ideas and he'd convince a large group of men to go with

An old miner's cabin near Ophir.

him. Then they'd all meet with disaster. He was just beautiful for living through disasters."

These disasters, chronicled in a very literate and colorful journal kept by Smith and later discovered and published, turned Jedediah into a legend. The mountain man possessed a reputation for being different. Unlike most men of his day, he disdained the use of tobacco, did not drink liquor, never swore, and stayed away from loose women. If he had a flaw, it was his recklessness with both his life and the lives of others.

Smith opened South Pass to the great route of Western migration. He traveled the length of Utah from north to south before any other non-Indian. He used the maps and journals of Spanish explorers to blaze the trail between California and the rest of America. Crossing the Great Basin, he proved once and for all that the legendary Buenaventura River linking the Great Salt Lake to the ocean did not exist. He was the first non-Indian to cross the Sierra Nevada and follow the California and Oregon coasts to the Columbia River.

Smith returned in 1826 from an expedition to California, where he had been imprisoned by the Spanish, battled snow in the Sierras, and became separated from his men.

Jedediah and his companions, Silas Gobel and Robert Evans, left most of the group in California and set out in May for Utah. On June 20, they entered Utah just north of present-day Great Basin National Park in Nevada. After turning north through the Snake Valley, the bogs of Salt Marsh Lake trapped them. One of their six horses became hopelessly mired in the mud. They killed it and saved the meat.

Smith described the Great Salt Lake Desert as "a country completely barren and destitute of game. We frequently traveled without water, sometimes for two days over sandy deserts where there was no sign of vegetation. When we found water in some of the rocky hills, we generally found some Indians who appeared the most miserable of the human race, having nothing to subsist on (nor any clothing) except grass-seed, grasshopper, etc. With our best exertion, we pushed forward walking as we had been for a long time over the soft sand. That kind of traveling is very tiresome to men in good health who can eat when they choose and drink as often as they desire. To us, worn down with hunger and fatigue and burning with thirst increased by the blazing sands, it was almost insupportable."

During the day, the men buried themselves in the sand to escape the heat. At night, they pushed on through what is now the Dugway Proving Grounds (a government bombing range and nerve-gas testing area because of its isolation and desolation). The men ate the horses and mules as the animals died along the way.

On June 25, Robert Evans could go no further. Smith left him under a small juniper tree and headed for the distant mountains in search of water. He found it three miles away at the foot of the Stansbury Mountains, on the edge of Skull Valley. The men plunged into the water and drank their fill. Jedediah took five quarts back to Evans, who was barely alive. Evans drank every drop and asked for more. The three rested for a day and moved on.

Two days later, they saw the Great Salt Lake.

"Those who may chance to read this at a distance from the scene may perhaps be surprised that the sight of this lake surrounded by the wilderness of more than 2,000 miles diameter excited in me these feelings known to a traveler who after long and perilous journeying comes again in view of his home," wrote Smith. "But so it was with me for I had traveled so much in the vicinity of the Salt Lake that it had become my home in the wilderness."

In two days' time, Smith, Gobel, and Evans reached the rendezvous on the south shore of Bear Lake, a rendezvous that is still held annually. Because they had been thought to be dead, their presence caused a commotion. Ashley fired a cannon, the first wheeled vehicle to cross South Pass, to salute the returning heroes.

Unfortunately, a few years later, Smith's luck ran out. He was killed by Comanches on the Santa Fe Trail.

■ JOHN WESLEY POWELL

"On the right, the rocks are broken and ragged, and the water fills the channel from cliff to cliff," wrote John Wesley Powell, the first man to explore the Green and Colorado rivers in 1869. Every new river runner who floats through Cataract, Westwater, Desolation, and other Utah canyons sees the same wild river and feels the same excitement. "Now the river turns abruptly around a point to the right and the waters plunge swiftly down among great rocks. . . . I stand up on the deck of my boat to seek a way among the wave-beaten rocks. All untried as we are with such waters, the moments are filled with intense anxiety. Soon our boats reach the swift current; and a stroke or two, now on this side, now on that, and we thread the narrow passage with exhilarating velocity, mounting the high waves, whose foaming crests dash over us, and plunging into the troughs, until we reach the quiet water below. Then comes a feeling of great relief. Our first rapid is run."

Boatmen may take dozens of trips down the same stretch of river in a summer, but each time is different because the rivers are ever-changing. Sometimes they are low, with new boulders looming above the rapids. In high-water years, the rivers become raging torrents, whipping the rafts downriver with frightening speed. The Flaming Gorge and Glen Canyon dams have altered the Colorado and Green rivers of Powell's day, but these waterways inevitably surge and swell in wet years and wither in dry ones.

Thousands of adventurers try the Green and Colorado each year. In the evening, at the water's edge in the remote wilderness, the reflections of Powell written long ago, softly echo from the canyon walls.

"As the twilight deepens," he wrote, "the rocks grow dark and somber; the threatening roar of the water is loud and constant and I lie awake with the thought of the morrow and the canyons to come, interrupted now and then by characteristics of the scenery that attract my attention."

In the morning, as the rafts full of people dart past rocks and brown water, their thoughts are similar to Powell's: "Today we have an exciting ride. The river rolls down the canyon at a wonderful rate and, with no rocks in the way, we make almost railroad speed. Here and there the water rushes into a narrow gorge; the rocks on the side roll it into the center in great waves, and the boats go leaping and bounding over these like things of life, reminding me of the scenes witnessed in Middle Park—herds of startled deer bounding through forest beset with fallen timber."

It is all but impossible to run a Utah river and not hear of the exploits of John Wesley Powell at some time during the trip. Guides often read from the early explorer's journal around the campfire and tell of the one-armed man who ran the river sitting in an armchair, lashed onto the bow deck of a flatboat.

Powell named most of the rapids and many of the physical features of the canyons shaped by the Colorado and Green rivers. Names like Disaster Falls, 'Bin Hurt, Brown Betty, and 10 Cent most likely recall the experiences of the first men down the river. Most river runners know and appreciate the Major's knowledge of the rivers, but few realize the impact that Powell had in bringing the West into the twentieth century.

John Wesley Powell conversing with an Indian who was probably one of his guides.
(Utah State Historical Society)

Though Powell advanced to the rank of lieutenant colonel in the Civil War, it was the title of major that stuck with him. He lost his right forearm in the Battle of Shiloh. After the North won the war, he secured a college professorship of geology and natural history from Illinois State Normal University without benefit of a college degree. He was, in essence, a self-taught man.

After two years of field work, he became convinced that he could explore the canyons of the Colorado and its tributary, the Green, even though it would be impossible to replenish supplies for more than 500 miles (800 km) of the river's length. He used his own money, secured private contributions, solicited money from several colleges and friends, and secured free railroad passes for his men and supplies. The Smithsonian Institute loaned scientific instruments to the expedition. The brave men of his crew received no pay and little glory for their work.

The journey into the last great unknown and unmapped country of the continental United States began at Green River Station, Wyoming, and passed through places like Flaming Gorge, Echo Park, Desolation Canyon, and Cataract Canyon.

By the time Powell left the Colorado, at the mouth of Utah's Virgin River, he was making plans for a second trip. On this adventure, he stopped along the way to study the Indians living in the territory surrounding the Colorado River. He also took notes on the area's geology.

The chief topographer of Powell's expedition, A.H. Thompson, discovered and named the last major river added to the United States map while on the expedition. He called it "Escalante" in honor of the Spanish fathers who explored the region in 1776.

Together with photographer John

James Baker (1818-1898) was the quintessential mountain man. He drank and gambled, trapped with Jim Bridger, and married an Indian princess named Flying Dawn. (Utah State Historical Society)

Hillers, in 1871, Powell studied the Ute and Paiute Indian tribes at a time when their way of life was beginning to disappear. He was appointed special commissioner to the Indians in Utah and eastern Nevada in 1873 to help establish the tribes on reservations. He told his superiors that the Indians, numbering only 5,500 in the territory, were on the verge of extinction. His suggestions for reservation sites were adopted, but unfortunately, his vision of a reservation as a school of industry, where instructors taught trades, skills, and English to help the Indians prosper in the modern world, was not. America was not ready to accept responsibility for Indian welfare. The Indians were simply herded onto the reservations and largely ignored. Powell later joined the Smithsonian Institute, where he continued his work with the Indians as director of the Bureau of Ethnology.

ROCKY MOUNTAIN TALE

As is generally known, the Great Salt Lake, though fed by the Bear, Jordan, and possibly other rivers, has no outlet, and it was a common belief that the great lake had a subterranean outlet, otherwise the vast quantity of water poured into it by the two considerable rivers would cause it to overflow its banks. Down in southern Colorado there was, at the time I am writing of, and it may yet be there, a good sized lake that had neither inlet nor outlet, so far as surface indications showed, and it was the general belief that the lake was kept supplied by a subterranean inlet.

According to one, a certain man ventured out on the Utah lake in a small boat. The boat was caught in a whirlpool and, then some distance from the shore, sucked beneath the surface. Clinging to the sides of the boat, with desperation born of despair, the man found himself plunging almost straight downward, with water roaring over and all around him. Suddenly the boat, riding on an even keel, shot forward through a wonderful tunnel-like cavern, the roof and walls covered with vari-colored stalactites, presenting a scene surpassing description. Just how long he floated in the underground channel the man could not tell, but an end came to his trip eventually when he found his boat shooting upward, with its occupant holding on for dear life. As perhaps the reader has guessed, the boat and its owner reached the surface of the Colorado lake, but little the worse for the underground voyage, and the great mystery of the outlet and inlet of the two lakes had been solved.

—Edited by Levette Davidson and Forrester Blake,
Rocky Mountain Tales, 1892

Powell's travels and studies of Indian philosophy taught him that mankind needs to keep in balance with the land. His geological training helped him realize that the Colorado Plateau and River, and its tributaries, are part of an equilibrium of precipitation, evaporation, and erosion. He preached that civilization must fit within the system or run out of water.

His travels led to suggestions on ways the lands of the West should be managed. Systems that worked in the water-rich East did not apply to the arid West, where the right to own water had to go along with the deed to the land. Engineers needed to create reservoirs so that precious water could be managed for recreation, agriculture, and flood prevention. He called for the preservation of forests, land-use studies, and the setting aside of public land for the use of all citizens.

JOHN WESLEY POWELL, *DIARY OF COLORADO RIVER EXPLORATIONS, 1869*

Describing Grandview Point in what is now Canyonlands National Park

What a world of grandeur is spread before us! Below is the canyon through which the Colorado runs. We can trace its route for miles, and at points catch glimpses of the river. From the northwest comes the Green in a narrow winding gorge. From the northeast comes the Grand, through a canyon that seems bottomless from where we stand. Away to the west are lines of cliff and ledges of rock—not such ledges as the reader may have seen where the quarryman splits his blocks, but ledges from which the gods might quarry mountains that, rolled out on the plain below, would stand a lofty range; and not such cliffs as the reader may have seen where the swallow builds its nest, but cliffs where the soaring eagle is lost to view ere he reaches the summit. . . . Wherever we look there is but a wilderness of rocks—deep gorges where the rivers are lost below cliffs and towers and pinnacles, and ten thousand strangely carved forms in every direction, and beyond them mountains blending with the clouds.

Now we return to camp. While eating supper we very naturally speak of better fare, as musty bread and spoiled bacon are not palatable. Soon I see Hawkins down by the boat, taking up the sextant—rather a strange proceeding for him—and I question him concerning it. He replies that he is trying to find the latitude and longitude of the nearest pie.

When Powell became the second director of the United States Geologic Survey, in 1881, he went to work establishing both an irrigation survey for the West and a department of science to help the government make intelligent decisions about its future handling of the environment and the Indians. Many of his ideas failed to be implemented until after his death in 1902. His part in the development of environmental conservation came to fruition with the withdrawal of public lands for the public good, the harnessing of the Colorado River, a bureau of forestry, and a federal department or agency for the encouragement of science.

To get a feel for John Wesley Powell's exploits visit the **John Wesley Powell River Running Museum** in Green River. A multi-media show also examines the history of river running in the state. Exhibits include the Utah River Runners Hall of Fame and several of the earliest boats used by rafters. For an even more first-hand look, try taking a spring "ghost boat" trip down the Yampa or Green rivers with Holiday River Expeditions of Salt Lake. Some of the rafts used are replicas of the originals. Plus, river historians offer guided walks and campfire discussions on Powell and other adventurers.

As a river runner floats down the mighty Colorado into the canyons and over rapids named by John Wesley Powell, he lives the legacy of the man whose bravery and vision helped preserve this part of the country for all Americans.

THE MORMON PIONEERS

TO UNDERSTAND THE MANY NUANCES OF UTAH'S CULTURE without knowing anything about the Mormon pioneers would be like visiting Italy and overlooking the Catholic tradition.

Travelers in Utah cannot fail to sense the presence and heritage of the Mormon Church. Its influence is evident in the gleaming white temples found in cities like Manti and St. George. It is preserved at historical sites and museums. It is woven into the fabric of the state's politics, cultural activities, and laws. Many names on the state's road map—Brigham City, Moroni, Nephi, Lehi, and Heber City—reflect Utah's Mormon origins. The Mormons play, and will continue to play, a tremendous and often misunderstood role. This is their story.

■ THE FOUNDING OF THE MORMON CHURCH

Persecution either destroys or unifies a people. Seventeen years of persecution gave the Mormons the strength and religious faith to leave the civilized world east of the Missouri River and cross the Great Plains and Rocky Mountains in order to practice their faith. Under adverse conditions they took a dry and inhospitable wilderness avoided by the rest of the immigrants and made it "blossom like a rose."

The history of the Mormon Church begins with Joseph Smith. As a young man in the early 1800s, Smith questioned the many Christian religions competing for converts in the eastern United States. Mormons believe that when Smith prayed for an answer as to which church to join, God and Jesus told him that they had chosen him to institute the true religion. Later, an angel named Moroni appeared and showed Smith where he could uncover some gold plates containing the history of Ephriam and Manasseh, two of the ten tribes of Israel that had fled Jerusalem before it was destroyed by the Babylonians.

The plates told of their escape to the Western Hemisphere, where they established a new civilization. Eventually they divided into two warring camps, the Nephites and the Lamanites. The plates recorded the ultimate victory of the Lamanites, from whom the Mormons believe American Indians are descended. Moroni was himself one of the characters in this history, being the last surviving member of the Nephites and the one who buried the gold plates.

THE BOOK OF MORMON

Does the Bible Contain All of God's Word?

2 Nephi 29:6-9: Thou fool, that shall say: A Bible, we have got a Bible, and we need no more Bible. Have ye obtained a Bible save it were the Jews?

Know ye not that there are more nations than one? Know ye not that I, the Lord your God, have created all men, and that I remember those who are upon the isles of the sea; and that I rule in the heavens above and in the earth beneath; and I bring forth my word unto the children of men, yea, even upon all the nations of the earth?

Wherefore murmur ye, because that ye shall receive more of my word? Know ye not that the testimony of two nations is a witness unto you that I am God, that I remember one nation like unto another? Wherefore, I speak the same words unto one nation like unto another. And when the two nations shall run together the testimony of the two nations shall run together also.

And I do this that I may prove unto many that I am the same yesterday, today, and forever; and that I speak forth my words according to mine own pleasure. And because that I have spoken one word ye need not suppose that I cannot speak another; for my work is not yet finished; neither shall it be until the end of man, neither from that time henceforth and forever.

The Plates

Mosiah 8:9-11: And for a testimony that the things that they had said are true they have brought twenty-four plates which are filled with engravings, and they are of pure gold.

And behold, also, they have brought breastplates, which are large, and they are of brass and of copper, and are perfectly sound.

And again, they have brought swords, the hilts thereof have perished, and the blades thereof were cankered with rust; and there is no one in the land that is able to interpret the language or the engravings that are on the plates. Therefore I said unto thee: Canst thou translate?

—The Book of Mormon

Besides showing Joseph Smith the location of the gold plates, Moroni also gave him some stone spectacles with which to translate the plates from an ancient language into English. When he was finished with his translation, the angel Moroni took the plates back. Smith later produced witnesses who claimed to have seen the gold plates.

In the spring of 1830, Joseph Smith published the *Book of Mormon* and founded the Church of Jesus Christ of Latter-day Saints (LDS) in Fayette, New York. Members of the LDS faith hold the Book of Mormon to be divinely inspired. They called themselves Latter-day Saints in reference to a prophecy by Paul in the New Testament that the true believers in the last days of the world would be called saints. Smith was believed to be bringing about these last, or *latter*, days by restoring the Gospel to the world. Contemporary visitors to Salt Lake City find the angel Moroni depicted in gold atop the Mormon Temple, blowing his horn to announce the restoration of the Gospel of Jesus Christ.

The popular term of *Mormon*, incidentally, comes from the name of a Nephite general who wrote the Book of Mormon contained on the gold plates.

■ PERSECUTION

Persecution of the Mormons began almost immediately. Members of the new church called themselves the "chosen of God." They were active missionaries and quietly practiced polygamy. Their zeal and fervor were not appreciated by other citizen or religious leaders. It wasn't long before Smith and his followers were forced to move from New York to Kirkland, Ohio, and Independence, Missouri.

Tensions between Mormons and non-Mormons were inflamed further by the depression of 1837, when many banks all over the United States collapsed, sending their depositors into a panic, and heightening suspicions against newcomers, or those who appeared to be different. Joseph Smith owned several banks, which undoubtedly inflamed the resentment. In short, the Mormans were again expelled from their new homes.

After leaving Ohio and Missouri, the Mormons founded the city of Nauvoo, Illinois, which became home for 20,000 inhabitants, making it the second largest city in that state. Smith and the city council were permitted by the state to raise a militia, levy taxes, and make laws, thus provoking concern in the surrounding non-Mormon communities. The first municipal university in the United States was built in Nauvoo. The city's prosperity, however, brought jealousy. The Mormons soon irritated both political parties in Illinois by voting for neither one.

The Illinois Legislature considered repeal of Nauvoo's charter. Again and again, mobs descended on outlying Mormon farms, killing and mutilating Mormons, and burning their houses and crops. Joseph Smith decided it was time to move again and sent scouts to look for a suitable place. Meanwhile, on May 17, 1844, he declared his candidacy for president of the United States. His stated intention was to spread "the dominion of the Kingdom of God" throughout the country. If this didn't work, he was prepared to head west.

Smith's political ambitions were cut short when he and his brother were arrested in connection with the unlawful smashing of a printing press by members of the Mormon city council, who believed the press was being used to print anti-church libel. Joseph and his brother Hyrum were taken to await trial in a jail in Carthage, the county seat 15 miles (24 km) to the east. On the night of June 27th, 1844, a mob stormed the jail and killed Joseph and his brother.

A rare portrait of Joseph Smith standing over his brother, Hyrum, from the late 1830s. No photograph of Smith is known to exist. (From History of the Mormons, 1852*)*

■ EXODUS TO UTAH

Brigham Young became the second leader of the LDS Church. He had grown up near Joseph Smith's New York home, and was baptized into the church in 1832. At the time of Smith's death, Young was president of the ruling body of the church, the Council of the Twelve. Since that time, the leader of the Council of the Twelve has assumed church presidency upon the death of an existing president.

Descriptions of Brigham Young vary with writers' views of Mormonism. Some describe him in glowing terms, others with suspicion and contempt. At the time of the exodus to Iowa, he was a thick-chested man of middle age. In *Giants of the Old West*, Frederick R. Bechdolt wrote that the first impression one received from him was of heavy strength: "There was no fineness in his lines. Throughout, there was a certain homely indomitability. His face was large and fair; the blue eyes keen. A brown beard ringed his strong jaw; his upper lip was shaven, revealing the coarse, firm mouth. He would have passed for a well-to-do farmer or a British drover. He was, by trade, a carpenter. By destiny he had become leader of a people."

After Smith's death, the Mormons continued to have problems with their non-Mormon neighbors. Looting, arson, and riot repeatedly tore through the town and surrounding countryside. Fearing for their safety, Young sent scouts to search for sites for possible resettlement. Maps of explorers and mountain men were studied.

Late in 1845, the state of Illinois repealed Nauvoo's city charter and the violence increased. Young sent an advance party to the plains of Iowa, which arrived in February of 1846. The exodus of the Mormons from Nauvoo took several months.

In Council Bluffs, Iowa, the Mormons were asked by U.S. Army Captain James Allen to supply 500 men to help the United States in the Mexican War. Church leaders had a right to be bitter about the lack of support the United States government had given them in the past. Instead, this was seen as an opportunity to prove their patriotism and earn some needed cash. The Mormon Battalion departed in July for a 2,000-mile march (3,200-km) to California. They saw no military action but were in the San Francisco area when gold was discovered. It is said San Francisco's first lawsuit was between the LDS church and battalion leader Sam Brannan, who stayed in California to become the state's first millionaire. The LDS Church wanted its share of it. Sam kept the money.

Winter quarters for the remaining church members were established near the site of present-day Omaha, Nebraska. Many Mormons died during the severe winter of 1846. Young decided that there could be no lasting peace until his people found a place where they could live unmolested by the outside world. He felt that if the Church could remain isolated for at least 10 years, it would become strong and able to survive. Young used maps made by explorers of the West, like John C. Frémont, to find a place where the Mormons might be left undisturbed. When Sam Brannan urged him to go on to California, Young said, "Brannan, if there is a place on earth that nobody else wants, that's the place I am hunting for."

Brigham Young found such a place. Two early Mormon pioneers, George Washington Brimhall and Gilbert Belnap, described the Great Salt Lake Valley as "a vast desert whose dry and parched soil seemed to bid defiance to the husbandryman." On July 24, 1847, Young led an advance party of 143 men, three women, and two children to the mouth of Emigration Canyon overlooking the Great Salt Lake Valley. The Mormon leader, sick with mountain fever, raised himself from his wagon bed and announced that they had found what they were looking for. That same afternoon, the pioneers began diverting streams for irrigation, plowing and planting, even before starting construction of their homes. Thus began the transformation of Utah.

A renovated pioneer wagon, reminiscent of the ones used by the first Mormon immigrants.

The Mormons named the territory they settled the State of Deseret. The word Deseret comes from the *Book of Mormon* and means "honeybee." Thus, the bee and hive have become symbols of the state, signifying industry and community. Both are depicted on the Utah state flag. The emphasis by Young on these qualities made the new territory prosper.

■ ESTABLISHING ZION

Brigham Young proved to be a master planner with a vision for what the future Mormon "Zion" should look like. Mormon history records that he was instrumental in attracting 100,000 people to Utah, founding more than 200 cities, towns and villages, and establishing many schools and factories. To this day, the state has benefited from his far-sighted planning.

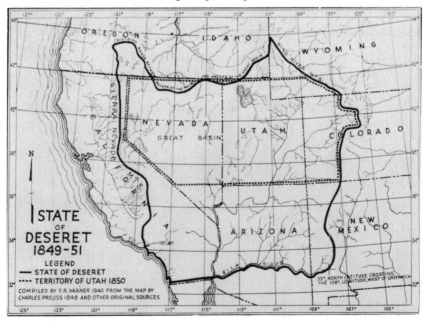

Brigham Young's original boundaries for the State of Deseret. (Utah State Historical Society)

(opposite) These witnesses testified to the existence of the Book of Mormon when Joseph Smith first began to translate it from the "reformed Egyptian." (LDS Archives)

The settlers faced innumerable hardships. In the spring of 1848, a late frost hurt much of the beans, corn, and wheat. Then came a cloud of crickets, "by the thousands of tons." The pioneers fruitlessly tried to beat them off the crops, but were rescued finally by hungry sea gulls who flew in to gobble up the crickets. This "miracle of the gulls" is a cherished part of Mormon folklore, and the seagull is the state bird. The state flower, the sego lily, also helped the pioneers survive their first year. Its nourishing, edible bulb was eaten when there was little else.

Church leaders initially divided up the land among all married males. Each received one city lot and one country lot, and was required either to work the land or lose the right to own it. The early settlers lived in Salt Lake City both for protection and companionship.

The early Mormons held property in common. They were also required to give 10 percent of their income for the good of the Church, a practice called tithing that dates to Biblical times. An extensive welfare system was established, whereby large storehouses were built to house excess crops that were passed out to members in accordance to their needs. The arrangement proved so successful that it still exists in much the same form today.

Swasey Cabin near San Rafael Swell is typical of the sod-roof structures of the early pioneers.

Polygamy remained one of the main tenets of the Latter-day Saints' faith. Church members believed that the only way to achieve the highest reward in heaven was to have more than one wife. In some cases, women entered into purely contractual marriages, providing themselves and their children with a means of financial support.

All Mormon men were (and are) expected to serve as missionaries for a period of time, usually two years. Deseret was to be the gathering place for all Latter-day Saints. A Perpetual Emigration Fund Company was established in 1849, with voluntary donations given to help converts travel to the Salt Lake Valley. Those taking advantage of these funds were expected to pay back the amount they had borrowed as soon as possible so that others could come. In the early years, missionaries to Scandinavia and Europe sent tens of thousands of immigrants to Utah. When organized funding became insufficient to help the flood of converts, Brigham Young came up with a unique solution.

"We cannot purchase wagons and teams as in years past," he told the faithful. "I am consequently thrown back on my old plan and that is to make handcarts and let the emigrants foot it. They can come just as quick, if not quicker, and much cheaper—can start earlier and escape the prevailing sickness which annually lays so many of our brethren in the dust."

Three thousand immigrants pulled handcarts across the United States to join the Latter-day Saints in Utah. There were surprisingly few fatalities. Only the two largest parties, the Willie and Martin companies, suffered disaster. They had left the East too late in the year and then were hit with unusually early winter storms. Brigham Young sent rescuers to the companies stuck on the Wyoming plains. Mormon leader George D. Grant was one of the first Mormons to reach the stranded handcart company. According to William Smart in *Old Utah Trails*, Grant found "between five and six hundred men, women and children, worn down by drawing handcarts through snow and mud; fainting by the wayside; falling, chilled by the cold, their feet bleeding and some of them bare to the snow and frost. The sight is almost too much for the stoutest of us."

As the crippled company was brought into the Great Salt Lake Valley, Brigham Young cut short the church meeting and sent the Saints to ready their homes for the new immigrants. "Prayer is good," he told the faithful, "but when baked potatoes and pudding and milk are needed, prayer will not supply their place."

As the Mormon population grew, so did its "capital" between the Wasatch

Salt Lake City founder and upholder of the Mormon faith, Brigham Young. (Utah State Historical Society)

Mountains and the Great Salt Lake. Civil engineering projects initiated by Young and the Mormon pioneers still impress modern visitors to Salt Lake City. The broad, tree-lined streets are laid out in a grid-like pattern, and clear water runs down the gutters today—just as it did a hundred years ago. All street numbers start from the corner of South Temple and Main Street, and radiate out from the temple, making it easier to find one's way around in Salt Lake City than in other large cities lacking such urban planning.

Brigham Young built Temple Square in the heart of Salt Lake City. The temple itself, which took 40 years to build, was constructed of granite quarried in Little Cottonwood Canyon, some 20 miles (32 km) away. Because sacraments like marriage had to be performed in the temple to make them eternal, Mormons were for many years obliged to make pilgrimages to the Salt Lake City temple until other temples could be built.

Another major feature of Temple Square is the famed Mormon Tabernacle, designed by bridge-builders William Folsom and Henry Grow. An egg-shaped dome set above a series of stone buttresses, the Tabernacle is a remarkable building, especially when one considers the primitive conditions under which it was constructed. Because nails were scarce, wooden pins and rawhide were used in construction. The Tabernacle is now home to the world-famous Mormon Tabernacle Choir.

Young's city home was located just east of Temple Square, where it still stands today. It is called the Beehive House because of the sculpted beehive on its roof. Here, Young entertained visitors and passing dignitaries. One of Brigham's 27 wives lived with her children in the Beehive House; more of his families lived next door in the Lion House. Another family lived on the outskirts of the city in his farm home. A store was part of the Beehive House, where all of his wives and children had accounts.

With more than four million visitors a year, Temple Square today is Utah's most popular tourist attraction.

■ END OF ISOLATION

The Great Salt Lake Valley's isolation had been advantageous for the church leaders of the young State of Deseret, but isolation could not last forever. In fact, Salt Lake City was becoming an important stop-over on the trail linking the East and West coasts.

The outside world first intruded in 1849 when throngs of miners en route to the gold fields of California stopped in the valley to buy supplies for their journey. Mark Twain passed through during the Comstock silver boom of the 1860s. He recorded in *Roughing It* the sentiments shared by many immigrants during this early period: "The high prices charged for trifles were eloquent of high freights and bewildering distances of freightages. In the east, in those days, the smallest moneyed denomination was a penny and it represented the smallest purchasable quantity of any commodity. But, in Salt Lake there did not seem to be any money in circulation smaller than a quarter, or any smaller quantity purchasable of any commodity than twenty-five cents' worth."

In 1850, the legislature of the State of Deseret sent a delegate to Congress to petition for statehood. Instead, Congress passed a proposal by Henry Clay to admit California as a state, and New Mexico and Utah as territories. Utah Territory embraced the present states of Nevada and Utah, and its capital was Fillmore. The Mormon name of "Deseret" was repulsive to Congress because of its religious connotations. Congress instead named it after the Ute Indians, but the Mormons persisted in calling it the "State of Deseret."

Tensions during this period of American history were rampant. There were rumblings that the South was about to secede from the Union. Compounding this crisis was the Mormons insistence on governing themselves in a manner much different from the rest of the United States.

Utah Territory was unusual in that Mormon religious leaders also wielded political power. The Mormons resented the federal government's attempts to install its own representatives in the territory. And polygamy was deemed an assault on morality. The Republican National Convention platform of 1856 labeled polygamy and slavery "the twin relics of barbarism." Authorities in Washington were eager to focus public attention on something other than the constant strife over slavery. Given the political climate of the time, it was perhaps a surprise only to the Mormons when President Buchanan revoked Brigham Young's governorship and sent an army detachment commanded by Colonel Albert Sydney Johnston—a man who would later distinguish himself as a commander for the South in the Civil War—to the Great Salt Lake Valley to put down any insurrection which might arise.

This persecution was familiar to the Mormons who, although intent on staying in Utah, were nonetheless prepared to flee the Great Salt Lake Valley and to fight

The Mormon Temple and nearby Tabernacle are the holiest places of the Church of the Latter-day Saints.

BRIGHAM YOUNG AND SIR RICHARD BURTON ON POLYGAMY

In the full eloquence of his later years Brigham once told his congregation: "Ladies who come into my office very frequently say, 'I wonder if it would hurt his feelings if I were to ask him how many wives he has?' Let me say to all creation that I would as lief they should ask me that question as any other; but I would rather see them anxious to learn about the Gospel. Having wives is a secondary consideration; it is within the pale of duty, and, consequently, it is all right. But to preach the Gospel, save the children of men, build up the kingdom of God, produce righteousness in the midst of the people; govern and control ourselves and our families and all we have influence over; make us of one heart and one mind. . . is our business, no matter how many wives a man has got, that makes no difference here or there. I want to say, and I wish to publish it, that I would as soon be asked how many wives a man has got, that makes no difference here or there. I would as soon be asked how many wives I have got as any other question, just as soon; but I would rather see something else in their minds, instead of all the time thinking, 'How many wives have you;' or 'I wonder whom he slept with last night.' I can tell those who are curious on this point. I slept with all that slept, and we slept on one universal bed—the bosom of our mother earth, and we slept together. 'Did you have anybody in bed with you?' 'Yes.' 'Who was it?' It was my wife, it was not your wife, nor your daughter nor sister, unless she was my wife and that too legally. I can say that to all creation, and every honest man can say the same; but it is not all who are professed Christians who can say it."

❖ ❖ ❖

Refused admittance to the Church, [in 1860 Captain Richard] Burton defended his sincerity. He had, he said, traveled from the Old World to the New simply to become part of a people "sensible enough to permit polygamy." Persuasive though his visitor's argument was, Brigham would not relent. Instead he firmly changed the subject. Had his visitor, in his African explorations, covered the same ground as Dr. David Livingston, the Scottish missionary? Burton replied that he had traveled ten degrees north of Zambezi and the Victoria Falls. One of the Apostles present, Albert Carrington, rose to locate Burton's route on a wall map but moved his finger too near the equator. Brigham called to Carrington, "A little lower down." Carrington obeyed, dropping his finger lower on the map. This was accurate and Burton was impressed. "There are many educated men in England," he wrote, "who could not have corrected the mistake as well." With this the interview was terminated, and Burton left without the license to practice polygamy, which he had hoped to acquire.

Burton remained almost a month in Salt Lake City and continued to study polygamy as an outsider. He had arrived favorably disposed toward the doctrine. What he saw at firsthand did not disappoint him. "To the unprejudiced traveller," he wrote, "it appears that polygamy is the rule where population is required, and where the great social evil has not had time to develop itself. In Paris or London the institution would, like slavery, die a natural death; in Arabia and in the wilds of the Rocky Mountains it maintains a strong hold upon the affections of mankind. . . . The other motive for polygamy in Utah is economy. Servants are rare and costly; it is cheaper and more comfortable to marry them."

This idealized portrait of a pioneer family contrasts sharply with the harsh conditions faced by original settlers. (Utah State Historical Society)

Of course, admitted Burton, the Mormons had, with plural marriage, reduced romance and love "into a calm and unimpassioned domestic attachment." The monogamous company of two encouraged tenderness; the polygamous company of three made it rather a crowd. Still, perhaps this was not too bad. "Womanhood is not petted and spoiled as in the Eastern States; the inevitable cyclical revolution, indeed, has rather placed her below par, where, however, I believe her to be happier than when set upon an uncomfortable and unnatural eminence."

Before leaving Utah for California, Panama, and England, Burton came to this conclusion: "The Mormon household has been described by its enemies as a hell of hatred, envy, and malice— a den of murder and suicide. The same has been said of the Moslem harem. Both, I believe, suffer from the assertions of prejudice or ignorance. The temper of the new is so far superior to that of the old country, that, incredible as the statement may appear, rival wives do dwell together in amity; and do quote the proverb 'the more the merrier.' . . . They know that nine tenths of the miseries of the poor in large cities arise from early and imprudent marriages, and they would rather be the fiftieth 'sealing' of Dives than the toilsome single wife of Lazarus."

❖ ❖ ❖

HORACE GREELEY ON BRIGHAM YOUNG

At two o'clock in the afternoon of July 13, 1859, Horace Greeley sat down across from Brigham Young. . . . Greeley began to pose his questions, and Brigham replied with pleasing frankness. "He spoke readily," Greeley told his readers, "not always with grammatical accuracy, but with no appearance of hesitation or reserve, and with no apparent desire to conceal anything, nor did he repel any of my questions as impertinent. He was very plainly dressed in thin summer clothing, and with no air of sanctimony or fanaticism. In appearance, he is a portly, frank, good-natured, rather thick-set man of fifty-five, seeming to enjoy life, and to be in no particular hurry to get to heaven."

—Irving Wallace, *The Twenty-Seventh Wife,* 1961

the United States government. The populace was willing to burn the city if the army threatened occupation. When interviewed by Captain Van Vliet for a response to President Buchanan on September 8, 1857, Brigham Young replied boldly: "We shall do the best we can; and I will tell you, as the Lord lives, we shall come off conquerors. . . . We have three years' provisions on hand, which we will cache, and then take to the mountains and bid defiance to all the powers of the government."

The Mormons' early attempts at guerrilla warfare were impressive. They first burned all the available forage between South Pass and Fort Bridger, Wyoming, cutting off the advance army supply trains and burning them. Swinging behind the main column of the Utah Expedition, they burned several more supply trains. Fewer than 50 shots were fired, and no one was killed, but the troops were forced to spend the winter near Fort Bridger, 300 miles (480 km) short of their objective.

While the Mormons were under siege and with U.S. troops marching on Utah, the infamous Mountain Meadow Massacre occurred. In the fall of 1857, a wagon train of 140 immigrants from Arkansas and Missouri (a state where Mormons had been severely persecuted) passed through Salt Lake City. The wagon train was rich with livestock and had picked up a few defecting Mormons. Rumors flew that the Arkansans had poisoned springs and even poisoned beef which they had given the Indians. Some said that members of the wagon train had boasted about plans to attack the Mormons. For these reasons, the wagon train was marked for attack. A group of men under President Issac Haight and Bishop John D. Lee disguised themselves as Indians and convinced several hundred Paiute Indians to join them in attacking the immigrants. When the direct attack failed and the Indians would not finish the job, the Mormons took off their disguises and offered a flag of truce and a chance for the men, women, and children to put down their arms and walk away from the wagons. The frightened immigrants complied. The men under Haight and Lee then fell upon the unarmed party and within five minutes the entire group, except for a number of children believed too young to talk, was massacred. All participants swore themselves to secrecy but the story leaked out and evidence was discovered by a wagon train which happened upon the site. Haight was excommunicated. It wasn't until 1874, however, that John D. Lee was caught, convicted and taken to Mountain Meadow, where he was shot. (Lee's Ferry on the Colorado River was operated by Lee during his period of hiding.)

While Johnston's army was camped for the winter near Fort Bridger, the political mood in Washington changed. Captain Van Vliet had reached Washington with Brigham Young's message. A scandal concerning army contracts was exposed. Because millions of dollars were being spent with questionable results, the press started calling the whole affair "Buchanan's Blunder." Through an intermediary, Colonel Thomas L. Kane, Brigham Young agreed to admit the army into the territory as long as it neither molested the people nor settled there permanently. Johnston assured the Mormons they would not be disturbed. He marched his men through Salt Lake Valley and on to the west side of Utah Lake in Cedar Valley, where he established Camp Floyd near the present-day hamlet of Fairfield.

The camp followers of Johnston's army soon transplanted themselves to Great Salt Lake City, bringing with them tendencies toward alcohol, theft, and violence. The capital's main thoroughfare became known as Whiskey Street. Yet, at the same time, farmers could now sell surplus foodstuffs and livestock to the army at high prices, and cheap manufactured good were available in Utah for the first time.

Although Johnston's army left at the outbreak of the Civil War in 1861, government pressure on the Mormons did not end. In 1862, the Mormons drew up their third constitution for a "State of Deseret," and elected Brigham Young as governor. The federal government viewed this as an act of rebellion and passed a new law aimed at preventing polygamy. They sent Colonel Patrick Edward Connor to Utah with 300 volunteers from California and Nevada. He vowed to "subdue the

TWO ACCOUNTS OF A DISPUTE BETWEEN JIM BRIDGER AND MORMONS, 1853

Bridger's description of usurpation of his fort as described by his friend Captain William L. Marcy:

At length. . . his prosperity excited the cupidity of the Mormons, and they intimated to him that his presence in such close proximity to their settlements was not agreeable, and advised him to pull up stakes and leave forthwith; and upon his questioning the legality or justice of this arbitrary summons, they came to his place with an army of 'avenging angels' and forced him to make his escape to the woods in order to save his life. He remained secreted for several days, and through the assistance of his Indian wife was enabled to elude the search of the Danites and make his way to Fort Laramie, leaving all his cattle and other property in possession of the Mormons.

Bridger's letter to his Senator, G.B. Butler, gives the story in his own words:

I was robbed and threatened with death by the Mormons, by the direction of Brigham Young, of all my merchandise, livestock, in fact everything I possessed, amounting to more than $100,000 worth, the buildings in the fort partially destroyed by fire, and I barely escaped with my life.

obstreperous Mormons though all Hell yawned." Connor marched his men into the Great Salt Lake Valley, building Fort Douglas on a bench overlooking the city. Many of the original sandstone buildings at Fort Douglas remain today, as well as a small museum tracing the history both of Fort Douglas and the U.S. Army in the Beehive State.

The Mormons may have caused Connor and his men no trouble, but the influence of the army certainly troubled the Latter-day Saints. Connor set out to undermine the totalitarianism of the Mormon Church. He encouraged his men to prospect for minerals, a practice frowned upon by the Church. He organized the first mining district in the Territory in 1863 and wrote its mining code. He never personally benefited from his efforts, yet he earned the title "the father of Utah mining." Silver was found in nearby Park City; copper in the Oquirrh Mountains west of Salt Lake. Mining thrived, so more "outsiders" poured into Utah, diluting the once homogeneous culture.

The Pony Express, and especially the transcontinental telegraph and railroad systems, signalled the end of Utah's isolation. Church leaders who had worked hard to ingrain in their society the idea of cooperation and communal life now worried that gentile (non-Mormon) traders would come to economically enslave the Mormons, who were expected to maintain their spiritual goals before achieving financial reward. On the other hand, the improvements in communication and transport allowed church leaders better contact with members scattered throughout their large territory.

■ GROWTH OF ZION

The new railroad facilitated the expansion of Utah's mining industry. Boomtowns sprang up along the Wasatch and Oquirrh mountains. The coal-rich areas of Carbon and Emery counties was exploited. Cattle and sheep ranching prospered. But Mormons were exhorted to trade with Mormon merchants rather than with gentiles.

Brigham Young envisioned his new society as completely self-sufficient socially, religiously, and economically. He frowned upon the export of his people's money, goods, and crops in payment for merchandise. Pioneer lore details experiments undertaken to fulfill the Church president's wishes. Mulberry trees, for example,

ON THE MORMON FRONTIER—THE DIARY OF HOSEA STOUT, 1844-61

(as it appears in the original)

Tuesday 28th 1851 January. This morning quite a company went out with the Band to meet the governor B. Young & others who were gone to Weber County Davis & the settlements North to preach visit & Organize the County of Davis.

The went to congratulate him on the news of his appointment of Gov. by the President of the U.S. They returned about and were recieved here by the firing of artillery and the shouts of a large concourse of citizens and a display of fire works at Messrs Kinkead & Levingston's Store. The whole scene was joyful peaceable and quiet. The Gov when he was escorted home delivered a short address to the people assembled.

I spent the day at home and around the Council house Weather fine clear & warm

Monday July 5th 1852. This morning the citizens of this city were awakened by the roar of artillery at break of day followed by a Serenade by two Bands of music to hail the birth day of our national liberty and at half past seven I went to the Tabernacle to meet the Committee of arraingements preparitory to forming the Gov escort after which according to a previous invitation from his excellency the Gov I repaired to his house at half past 8 o'clock to join his suit to be escorted to the Tabernacle where the ceremonis of our celebration would commence

When the escort arrived The 31 veterans, then the "Mormon Battalion" The escorted pay and Gov forming betwen them while the Minute company of Horse were in the rear the escort proceeded with proper cerimonies to the Tabernacle under the continual roar of cannon. After which the meeting was opened by prayer and the order of the celebration commenced which consisted of alternate speaches, songs, airs, toasts & c.

I read the Declaration of Independence, immediately after the opening prayer.

Had a short adjournment for dinner. The day past off well and all seemed to enjoy themselves well. About four the assembly dispersed. Had some legal business for Thomas Moor to attend to about dark. So well was Mr Lely satisfied with the compromising manifested that he gave me 5 dollars in the presence of Br Moor although I was Moor's attorney vs him

Thursday 15 June 1854. Mr Elisha Ryan with some seven Shoshone Indians arrived here, There is several lodges of shoshonee's been encamped here sevral days. In the after noon we had a regular talk with Ryan, as chief, and his braves He aid he was sent by the Head Chief to learn what our intentions were. Whether we intened to take their land & if so whether peaceably or not. What was the feelings of the General Government & also Governor Young and the mormons, towards them. That they did not want their timber cut or have houses built on their land nor have settlements established. That if we did not and were friendly all was well for they desired to live in peace with all men but at the same time they would not allow any infringement on their lands.

That they had given Green River to him the said Ryan and those mountaineers who had married shoshonee wives. They complained bitterly about the general government neglecting them in never making a treaty with them and not sending men to trade for their skins and furs &c Ryan said he had been robbed of his last bottom dollar (refering to the suit against him last year) That he considered this land his own and no one had a right to keep a ferry here but himself and those who had married shoshonee wives. He said he [had] nothing against the mormons as a people but had againts those individuals who robbed him last year, and many such things spake he.

—*On the Mormon Frontier: The Diary of Hosea Stout, 1844-1861*
(Hosea Stout was a lawyer and an officer in the Nauvoo Legion)

The furniture in this pioneer cabin was laboriously hauled West by covered wagon. (Utah State Historical Society)

were imported along with silkworms to produce silk for ladies' fine garments. Perhaps the best-known experiment was the establishment of a cotton mission in sunny St. George. Cotton and silk were produced there, but abandoned with the advent of the railroad.

Drawing on examples of existing cooperative tanneries and mills, the Mormons formed Zion's Cooperative Mercantile Institution (ZCMI) in 1868. This department store still operates in Salt Lake City today.

Mormon leaders believed that only by extensive settlement could Deseret remain in Church hands. There was to be no room for outsiders in the promised land of Zion. Mormon pioneers spread to all corners of the territory and into lands now part of Nevada, Idaho, Arizona, Wyoming, Colorado, New Mexico, and California.

As new immigrants arrived, they were organized into groups and assigned land for development into self-sufficient communities. Many were dispatched to settle remote parts of Deseret, guided by experienced settlers, who were often called upon to leave the farms that they had established earlier. These moves often tested the faith of Church members who had spent long, hard hours working to make their land prosper, only to be asked to leave and begin someplace else. Much of Utah is dry and must be irrigated in order to cultivate. Only faith in their leaders and the Mormon belief that good works on earth promised salvation induced these pioneers to start over again.

Settler Parley P. Pratt described the feelings of many: "My family and myself, in common with many of the camp, suffered much for food. I had ploughed and subdued land to the amount of near 40 acres and had cultivated the same in grain and vegetables. In this labor every woman and child in my family. . . had joined to help me. . . . Myself and some of them were compelled to go with bare feet for several months, reserving our Indian moccasins for extra occasions. We toiled hard and lived on a few greens and on thistle and other roots. We had sometimes a little flour and some cheese, and sometimes we were able to procure from neighbors a little sour skimmed milk or buttermilk." But he would write his brother in England, "All is quiet—stillness. No elections, no police reports, no murders, no wars, in our little world. . . . It is the dream of the poets actually fulfilled."

Even occasional threats from sometimes hostile Indians seemed minor compared with threats the Mormons had received from their old neighbors in Illinois.

One of the most inspirational stories about the pioneers' faith and perseverance in the settlement of Utah was the Hole-In-The-Rock expedition. Two hundred and fifty men, women, and children took 82 wagons and hundreds of head of livestock to colonize the most remote corner of the state. The most difficult part of the journey was the descent down a narrow, 2,000-foot (600-m) cliff, where they crossed the Colorado River. The pioneers had to cut their path through solid rock, from ledge to ledge, a disheartening, week-long task. "While they were doing it, Mons Larson and his 23-year-old wife, Olivia, reached the top of the mesa in a blizzard," wrote William B. Smart in *Old Utah Trails*. "On the climb up, Olivia had carried a two-and-one-half-year-old under one arm and a one-and-one-half-year-old child under the other, just as she had carried them down the Hole. The children's feet had been frost-bitten in the bitter cold, and the parents spent most of the night doctoring them. The next day, February 21, lying in the wagon seat while her husband struggled to pitch a tent against the raging blizzard, Olivia delivered her third child, a healthy boy."

A passage had to be cut through solid rock so that the wagons of the Hole-in-the-Rock expedition could proceed. (Utah State Historical Society)

Today, boaters on Lake Powell can look up at the route the pioneers took down the Hole-In-The-Rock. Four-wheel-drive enthusiasts can peer down into the crevice after driving to the spot from Escalante over Bureau of Land Management property. Dance Hall Rock, where the brave company relaxed and danced before their difficult journey, can be seen along the way.

Pioneer cabin stove.

■ ENTRANCE TO THE UNION

By 1868, Congress had taken sizeable chunks of land away from the Territory of Utah, paring it to its present shape.

When Ulysses S. Grant became president in 1869, the issue of polygamy was eliciting increasing criticism of the Mormons. In 1882, Congress passed the Edmunds Bill, allowing the federal government to fine and imprison polygamists. Many polygamists hid their plural wives and children when federal marshals came to town. Mormons were not allowed to vote or hold office in the territory. By the end of 1885, hundreds of Mormons were pouring into the Mexican state of Chihuahua to escape persecution. The Mexican government had outlawed polygamy also but did not actively prosecute. Anti-Mormons formed the Liberal Party. Its voice for many years was the *Salt Lake Tribune*. The Mormon Church owned, and continues to own and operate, *The Deseret News*. The competition between the two worlds of thought in Utah still exists.

In 1877, with controversy whirling around him, Brigham Young died in the Lion House. Many wondered if Mormonism would die with him. The succeeding church president, John Taylor, died in hiding in 1887. That same year, the Edmunds-Tucker Act dealt another severe blow to the Mormons by disincorporating the LDS Church, confiscating all of its property, abolishing female suffrage and the Perpetual Emigration Fund, mandating a federally appointed government for Utah, and requiring an oath that they were not polygamists before they could vote, hold elective office, or serve on juries.

In September of 1890, the new Church president, Wilford Woodruff, published a manifesto in *The Deseret News* describing some revelations in which the Lord had directed him to ask his followers to cease practicing polygamy. "The Lord showed me by vision and revelation exactly what would take place if we did not stop this practice," he wrote. "If we had not stopped throughout the land of Zion, confusion would have come upon the whole Church, and we should have been compelled to stop the practice. Now, the question is, whether it should be stopped in this manner, or in the way the Lord has manifested to us, and leave our Prophets and Apostles and fathers free men, and the temples in the hands of the people, so that the dead may be redeemed. . . . The Lord has decreed the establishment of Zion. He has decreed that the Devil should not thwart it. If you can understand that, that is the key to it."

This significant change made life easier for the Mormons. After publicly abandoning the practice of polygamy, they were allowed to vote and hold public office. They formed the People's Party. In a gesture of reconciliation in 1889, the Mormon People's Party offered four places on their Salt Lake City ticket to prominent gentiles. As a result of the infusion of gentiles into politics, the Territorial Legislature established public schools in 1890, further separating church and state. A year later, to offer proof of their desire to keep religious leaders from governing, the LDS leaders asked members to join the Democratic and Republican parties instead. The Church, however, continues to wield power in Utah's politics to this day.

A seventh constitutional convention met in Salt Lake City in 1895 in hope of getting Utah Territory admitted to the Union. Those attending gave women the right to vote and officially outlawed polygamy, though polygamous marriages already in existence were allowed to continue. On January 4, 1896, President Cleveland proclaimed Utah the 45th state in the Union.

■ THE MORMONS TODAY

At one time, being Utahn meant being Mormon. This is no longer the case; the isolationism of the past is gone. The Mormon Church's influence is everywhere in Utah, but other creeds are found, as well. Mormons are in the majority in most rural communities and many suburban neighborhoods. The religious population of the urban areas is much more diverse (though still 50 percent Mormon).

State politics is influenced by the conservative opinions of the Church. Most Mormons tend to vote Republican, though there have been and are many Democratic officials, including governors and congressmen. Most candidates are sensitive to Mormon thought and avoid being labeled as "liberal."

The Mormon church owns KSL Radio and Television, as well as the state's third largest newspaper, *The Deseret News*. Mormon viewpoints are expressed therein, along with differing opinions. The Church also owns radio and television stations in other parts of the country. Deseret Book is an LDS-owned bookstore where Mormon as well as non-Mormon publications are sold.

The Mormon Church maintains many landholdings in Utah and around the world. In downtown Salt Lake City, more than two full city blocks, including Temple Square, are owned by the Church, since it was the first landowner. The

Utah became a state on January 4, 1896, after decades of conflict with the federal government over polygamy. (Heritage Prints, photo courtesy of Rell Francis)

A Glimpse of The Church of Jesus Christ of Latter-Day Saints

BACKGROUND

If given the word "Mormon" during free association, most Americans would probably respond, "polygamy." This is unfortunate because the Mormon faith, with over five million adherents worldwide, offers a rich body of original religious thought and springs from one of the most fascinating histories that America has to offer. In fact, polygamy (which has been banned by the church since 1890), played a very minor role in the overall development of the church since its conception by the Prophet Joseph Smith.

In *Mormonism*, Jan Shipp indicates that Joseph Smith's "First Vision" at the age of fourteen is considered to be the first episode in Mormon history. The young Joseph Smith, confused about which church he ought to join, prayed that the truth would be revealed to him. One spring morning in 1820, he entered a grove of trees near Palmyra, New York. A state of despair which had fallen upon him was lifted at the onset of the vision. Joseph Fielding Smith's *Essentials in Church History* presents us with the Prophet's own words describing the event:

"'It no sooner appeared than I found myself delivered from the enemy which held me bound. When the light rested upon me I saw two personages, whose brightness and glory defy all description, standing above me in the air. One of them spake unto me, calling me by name, and said, pointing to the other—'This is my beloved Son, hear him!'

"My object in going to inquire of the Lord was to know which of all the sects was right, that I might know which to join. No sooner, therefore, did I get possession of myself, so as to be able to speak, than I asked the personages who stood before me in the light, which of all the sects was right—and which I should join. I was answered that I must join none of them, for they were all wrong; and the personage who addressed me said that all their creeds were an abomination in his sight; that those professors were all corrupt; that they draw near to me with their lips, but their hearts are far from me; they teach for doctrines the commandments of men, having a form of godliness but they deny the power thereof. He again forbade me to join with any of them. . ."

According to Shipp, Joseph Smith had a second vision the night of September 22, 1823:

"This time it was a vision of an angel who identified himself as Moroni, 'a messenger sent from the presence of God to tell of records written on gold plates which, along with two special stones called the Urim and Thummim, were buried in a hill not far from the Smith family farm. From Moroni the young man learned that the possession and use of these stones were what constituted 'seers' in ancient or former times, and that God had prepared them for the purpose of translating the book that was engraved in Reformed Egyptian characters on the gold plates."

Smith made four annual visits to the site where the plates were buried (where he would also converse with the angel Moroni) but was not able to obtain the plates until September 22, 1827.

The Mormons believe that through Joseph Smith, the true church was restored. He is considered to be the authentic successor of the priesthood which began with Adam but for centuries had been interrupted by the establishment of the Roman Empire. Certain priestly powers (the "Aaronic priesthood") were restored when John the Baptist layed hands on Smith; further priestly powers (the "Melchizedek priesthood") were restored by the laying on of hands by the Apostles Peter, James, and John. Joseph Smith's later visitations by the Apostles Peter, James, John, and the angel Moroni, supplied details pertaining to the lost history of the Americas. In *The Mormon Corporate Empire*, John Heinerman and Anson Shupe provide a summary of this history,

"In about 600 B.C. a band of inspired Hebrews had left Jerusalem shortly before the Babylonian army overran the city. These Hebrew refugees sailed west across the Atlantic and founded a mighty civilization in both the North and South American continents, where Jesus Christ manifested himself several times again to supplement His Middle Eastern visitations. Moroni, the last prophet of one warring Jewish faction called the Nephites and son of Mormon, the Nephites final historian, led Joseph Smith to ancient gold plates on which the account of these events was written. Fourteen centuries earlier, Moroni had hidden the plates beneath a large rock on a hillside near Smith's house after the Lamanites (who became the root stock from which American Indians sprang) wiped out the Nephites. The Lamanites' advanced civilization then deteriorated into barbarism. Smith was appointed to translate the golden texts, creating from them a third biblical testament, the *Book of Mormon*, which would establish the legitimacy of the new Zion in North America and complete the books of the Bible."

In 1830, after a few years of arduous work by Smith, the translator, and his appointed scribe, Oliver Cowdery, *The Book of Mormon* was published.

The name "Mormon" comes from the name of a Prophet in *The Book of Mormon* —a second witness to Jesus Christ. The King James Version of *The Bible*, *The Doctrine and Covenants*, and *The Pearl of Great Price*, are fundamental to the faith, as well.

The growing band of Mormons suffered continuous persecution in New York. In search of a place where the new Zion might be based, Smith led the group to Kirtland, Ohio and then on to various counties in Missouri. They finally settled in Nauvoo (Commerce), Illinois. Heinerman and Shupe note that at each stop, "they were pursued by angry mobs, denounced by the local newspapers and clergy, and spied on by suspicious politicians." It was not long after Joseph Smith and his brother, Hyrum, were murdered in a jail in Carthage, Illinois (they were being held for suppressing the *Nauvoo Expositor*—an anti-Mormon paper), that the Mormons, faced with renewed persecution, fled to Iowa. There, four temporary settlements were established. Shipp writes that "The Pioneer Company" left the settlement at Winter Quarters, Iowa "to search for a permanent settlement site." On July 22-24, the pioneers reached the Great Salt Lake Valley and, four days later, a site was selected for the Temple.

MORMON CUSTOMS

The first thing that strikes the inquirer about the Mormon faith is its adherents' deep, abiding commitment to family—the second is their emphasis on order. David O. McKay, President of The Church of Latter-Day Saints in the late sixties, once stated that, "There is no success that can compensate for failure in your own home."

The Mormon love of family and adherence to what is recognized by them to be the natural order of things is reflected in such church customs as baptisms and sealings.

There are two baptisms for the remission of sins: one for those who are repenting and another for the deceased. Children are not baptized until the age of eight. The Mormons believe that children come into the world innocent—each child is thought of as being a child of God—and are not able to choose clearly between good and evil, right and wrong, until around this age. The baptisms of the living take place in a baptismal font in the chapel.

The baptisms of the dead take place in the Temple's font. A Mormon is encouraged to trace his or her genealogy as far back as possible and to submit the name of non-member relatives to headquarters in Salt Lake City. They are then baptized vicariously; Mormons claim that all individuals are free moral agents. They hold that even the spirit of the dead has the choice to accept or not to accept the teachings of the church. (The spirits of all persons come from the spirit world and at death return until the time of the Resurrection.) Good human agency, for them, is a matter of presenting humans with the correct principles and letting them govern themselves.

Sealings are defined, in Bruce R. McConkie's *Mormon Doctrine* as, "ordinances performed in the Temple whereby husbands and wives are sealed together in the marriage union for time and eternity, and whereby children are sealed eternally to parents. . ." McConkie informs the reader that sealings for the dead are available on a proxy basis, too.

There are approximately 47 Temples and over 26,000 chapels worldwide. Services are held in the chapel on Sunday but ordinances such as baptisms for the dead and sealings are performed at the Temple.

Another striking feature of Mormonism is that the Temple is not open to everyone. Admission to the Temple requires what is called a "Temple recommend," that is, a certificate issued by the church. Some of the qualifications which must be met in order to enter the Temple are as follows: Upholding the Testimony of Jesus Christ, sustaining general authorities of the church, paying full tithe, honesty in all business dealings, being morally clean (this includes being free of sexual sin), and abstaining from drugs, alcohol, coffee, tea, and tobacco. One must also wear his or her "Temple garment," that is, special underclothing worn daily by all who are worthy to wear them. Temple garments are symbolic of the promise to Father in Heaven.

A prominent feature of the Mormon religion is its extensive missionary program. Typically, Mormon men are sent (anywhere in the world) on a two-year mission when they reach nineteen years of age. Women who are not married at the age of twenty-one are eligible for an eighteen-month mission. Each missionary is guided by an older church member of the same sex. The places the missionaries are sent are not decided at random but are, rather, individually chosen by the church authorities in Salt Lake City. During the mission, missionaries must obey a set of strict rules pertaining to moral purity. They are not permitted to swim, date, attend parties, and the like, or they will be sent home—something akin to receiving a dishonorable discharge from the military. Conversely, the completion of one's mission is regarded as a great honor.

What of holidays? The Mormons celebrate most traditional holidays. Christmas is celebrated on December 25th, although the Mormons do not believe that Jesus Christ was born on that day. Traditional holiday lore is downplayed in favor of the original religious essence of the holidays, however, the appearance of Santa Claus and the Easter Bunny is generally tolerated for the sake of the young children. Pioneer Day—a day replete with huge festivities—takes place annually on July 24th, in honor of the settlers entering Salt Lake City.

—Holly Cratty

city has benefited from this in many ways. For instance, the land where Salt Lake County's convention center, The Salt Palace, sits, is loaned to the city for $1 a year. (These and other Church businesses do not have non-profit status, and are handled separately from the religious affairs of the Church.)

The heart of the Church is Temple Square. In 1989, some four million people visited Temple Square to see the headquarters of the LDS Church. Authorities estimate that two-thirds of this number are not Church members.

The Church of the Latter-day Saints, likewise, is no longer confined to Utah. As of 1987, 34,750 Mormon missionaries resided in 113 different countries, while the number of foreign converts runs into the hundreds of thousands. The Church has an ambitious program of building new temples throughout the world, so Mormons no longer have to come to Salt Lake City for sacraments.

Today, mainly young men between the ages of 18 and 20 are expected to spend two years as missionaries. Young women have been allowed to become missionaries, too, and their numbers are growing. Married couples are volunteering more and more to do mission work. Women and married couples may serve from one to one-and-a-half years.

Mormon boys are expected to start saving for their missions early, as it is primarily the family's responsibility to finance the mission. Money spent supporting a missionary is not tax deductible. The missionaries are given intense language training if necessary, and sent out in pairs. Several sets of missionaries may work in the same area. They must adhere to strict moral guidelines while in the field. Dating, and even holding hands, is not allowed. Many a Mormon woman, however, will wait for her missionary and keep in touch by mail and telephone while his two-year commitment is fulfilled.

Visitors to Utah often notice the abundance of children in the state. The Church's teaching that children are blessings and that family life is essential has helped give the state the youngest population in the nation.

The Church teaches that alcoholic beverages, caffeine, and tobacco are harmful to the body, and discourages their use by Mormons. This has resulted in a state population statistically healthier than the rest of the country, as well as some unusual liquor laws. The state has slowly been working on changing these laws, however, to attract more tourists.

Though punishable by law and excommunication, the practice of polygamy still exists in a few isolated places. It is not actively prosecuted in Utah. Several fundamentalist groups have broken from the established Church over the polygamy issue, and also over the idea of communal property.

With its emphasis on family life and clean living, the Mormon Church has enabled a prosperous and vital state to evolve. As it holds on to these values into the future, Utah will remain a great and beautiful place to live.

WATER IN AN ARID LAND

No group of people in the West since the coming of the whites has been more aware of the importance of water, more cohesive and diligent in searching, capturing, and distributing it, or more suitably adapted to preserving and perpetuating a water-dependent culture in an arid land than the Mormons, those members of the Church of Jesus Christ of Latter-day Saints who make up the vast bulk of Utah's population. Like the Indians, the Mormons have their own distinctive relationship to the waters of the Colorado River system. The Mormons have shared in it greatly,

the Indians minimally. Unlike the disparate, transient whites that make up most of the West's population, these two groups (not really minorities since they dominate and rule their own lands to a great extent) possess separate identities and unique institutions that have survived despite constant encroachments from the outside world. To wander through their separate nations is to feel like a stranger in one's own land.

The Mormons wasted no time in establishing their own special relationship to water that was later to be emulated throughout the West. . . .

Sunset over Utah Lake, Utah Lake State Park.

From the start it was the Mormons conquering the desert, ceaselessly seeking prosperity and progress in an inhospitable locale—what was to become the second driest state. There was no private ownership of water. The church controlled its distribution and made the decisions on where and how to capture it. The family was the basic social unit, and farming, not mining, was the preferred occupation. With the coming of the energy shortages in the early 1970s, all these basic Mormon tenets would be challenged during the mad scramble for Utah's mineral wealth. But until then, in the small Mormon towns scattered like frontier outposts throughout the Colorado River basin in the remote eastern and southern portions of Utah, it would still be an almost completely closed, agrarian society, one which viewed the goings-on in the metropolitan area of Salt Lake City as being somewhat akin to those of ancient Babylon. . . .

❖ ❖ ❖

Farming had been the traditionally approved Mormon occupation in Utah; search for and production of minerals was historically discouraged. Water followed socio-religious preferences, with 90 percent of it diverted to agriculture. But in the last ten to fifteen years, mineral production—particularly if it was energy-related—has gained an accepted, even preferred, status in the Beehive State. Employment was a principal reason. No longer did agriculture supply jobs in sufficient numbers, so water was to be directed more and more toward municipal and industrial use. Agriculture would remain stable, but energy uses of water would expand, or so it was hoped. A 1967 policy statement of the Utah Board of Water Resources, reiterated in 1975, was revealing: "The Board considers the use of water for the irrigation of new lands to be relatively less advantageous to the State under conditions now existing than some possible alternative uses." Energy, for instance. The state's large reserves of coal, oil, oil shale, tar sands, and uranium were located in the Colorado River basin, precisely in those remote regions where the population was dropping most alarmingly and that basic Mormon unit, the family, was disintegrating. The problem was to get the water there, back to its basin of origin, since most of it was already committed to urban areas west of the divide. . . .

❖ ❖ ❖

That there was any controversy in the 1970s, or even a difference of opinion on something so basic as the use of water, was a rarity in monolithic Utah and a testimony to how tight things were getting. Again, the Indians were central to the differences, but there were other elements— environmentalists, Uinta Valley residents, agricultural and energy interests.

—Philip L. Fradkin, *A River No More,* 1981

MODERN PIONEERS

ALF ENGEN: SKI PIONEER

A native of Norway, Alf Engen first ventured into Utah in 1930 to compete for the world ski-jumping title. While there, he and his brother Sverre were invited to examine Ecker Hill in Parleys Canyon as a potential ski-jumping site. "It didn't look like much," recalls Engen, "but we could see that it had possibilities." Ecker Hill became a reality, and thus began one of Alf Engen's many careers: that of evaluating sites for potential ski resorts.

A fierce competitor who would become an eight-time national ski-jumping champion, Engen competed both at Ecker Hill and at Becker Hill (which is near the site of present-day Snowbasin in Ogden Canyon).

Much of this time, Engen also worked as a technical advisor for the U.S. Forest Service and the Civilian Conservation Corps, and it was with the ccc that Engen was sent to investigate Alta in Little Cottonwood Canyon as a possible site for a ski resort. Once a prosperous silver mining area, Alta was by that time pretty much in decline, and the only way to get there at all was to take in an old mining train.

Elgen didn't feel like taking the railroad, so he strapped on his Nordic skis, and crossed the pass of Big Cottonwood Canyon from Brighton into Alta and then skied Little Cottonwood Canyon.

"The chamber of commerce had already talked to Alta Mayor George Watson about a ski area," recalls Engen, "and Watson basically told the Forest Service that if they wanted to build a ski area there, he would give them the land he had. Pretty soon we had a CCC crew in there filling all the mine holes. When we didn't have enough rocks and dirt to plug the holes, we laid heavy logs over the entrances. Then we built the rope tow there in 1937."

Alta's first lift—the second to be built in the United States after the one at Sun Valley, Idaho—was constructed near the present-day Collins lift for the 1938-39 ski season.

"The lift was a single chair, and its design was based on the idea of a mining tram. It had a double cable, and instead of mining buckets, some seats. The cost of a lift ticket was 75 cents a day.

"I think about when I first saw Alta and what it is today," muses Engen looking about himself thoughtfully. "Can you imagine all the changes?"

Avalanche control, a problem even today in Little Cottonwood Canyon, was a dangerous undertaking in Alta's early days. Engen's brother Sverre served as one of the first avalanche rangers.

"You had to have a sixth sense for avalanches," recalls Engen, who now watches U.S. Forest Service technicians shoot down the snow slides with mortar guns after a big snowfall. "We didn't have anything then. Sverre would go up on the mountain after a snowfall, tamp on them, and let them go. It was quite dangerous."

Though he competed until he was 55, Engen turned to teaching to make a living. During World War II, he instructed Army officers and enlisted men in skiing techniques. Later he helped with the rehabilitation of veterans at the Bushnell Hospital in Brigham City, Utah, and at the Navy Convalescent Hospital at Sun Valley, Idaho. In 1948, he coached the U.S. Olympic ski team, and then returned to Alta to head the resort's ski school and to teach thousands of youngsters the joy of skiing.

"I'd like to be remembered as a heckuva good teacher in my day," says Engen. "I loved it because I loved people, and my favorite people are the little ones. They call me grandpa and are friends for life. The little ones I taught in 1948, now bring their grandchildren for me to teach."

Each ski season, Engen learns something new about his beloved sport. And he has a bit of advice for those who come to enjoy Alta's famous powder. "You never want to lose your enthusiasm," he says. "You want to keep it. If you start sitting in front of a television all day, you're dead. I tell both young and old men to get up and walk. I think being 80 is great. It's no problem for me. I don't try to be 79 either. I know something most of you guys don't know. I know how it is to ski when you're 80."

In 1989 at 80 years of age, Engen was named Alta's director of skiing. As the grand old man of the Utah mountains, he has lived to see skiing develop from a curiosity into a major Utah industry. Eight double chairlifts now carry Alta skiers up 39 packed runs, and nearby Snowbird, with its concrete condominiums, a high-tech tram, and seven chairlifts draws powder hounds from all over the world.

DICK CARTER: WILDERNESS PIONEER

Dick Carter looks, talks, and acts like an environmental radical. His eyes gleam with passion. His long hair and beard give him the appearance of a 1960s-era protestor out of sync with an increasingly materialistic modern world.

The description, "Utah's best-known environmentalist," fits the Utah State University forestry graduate well. In 1979, as an idealistic ex-wilderness ranger, Carter founded the Utah Wilderness Association. This was during the early stages of both the Bureau of Land Management and U.S. Forest Service wilderness review programs, and Carter believed Utah needed a statewide nonprofit environmental organization, funded through committed membership, to build a foundation for wilderness preservation and to assure a local voice in natural resource allocation.

The fledgling, poorly funded association immediately found itself attacked from all sides. National environmental organizations accused the group of being too willing to compromise. Utah politicians, among the most conservative and pro-development legislators in the United States, looked at Carter and his compatriots as "tree-huggers" out to kill the state's economy, and wilderness foes hanged him in effigy in more than one Utah town.

Carter's philosophy differs from that of many of his contemporaries. He believes in approaching wilderness issues by building a consensus among diverse interests. "I would like to be an environmentalist who resolves problems," he says. "The easiest thing in the world is to create controversy. But how do we actually go about getting bighorn sheep into the High Uintas Wilderness Area without destroying the sheep industry? How do we protect BLM wilderness and bring people who are terrified of government intervention into the discussion, so they see they have nothing to fear? We won't have a wilderness system unless people support it. We can't just say wilderness is good and those who disagree are bad, because that's not going to solve any problems."

The Utah Wilderness Association holds seminars, workshops, lectures, field trips, and hikes. It publishes a newsletter six times a year, has initiated a national wilderness poetry competition, sponsors an annual wilderness rendezvous, and brings nationally known authors and speakers to talk to Utahns about important environmental issues. Carter and his staff also work with school groups.

"It is exceedingly important to make sure that young people see the value of wilderness," he says. "I want to take kids out of those malls they like to hang around in and let them hang around in the wilderness instead."

Carter's organization has worked hard to give Wasatch Front children a chance to do just that. With the passage of the Utah Wilderness Act of 1984, wilderness areas like Mount Nebo, F, and Mount Timpanogos were established.

For Carter a key part of the bill was the 460,000 acres of wilderness set aside in his beloved High Uintas Mountains—a place he has hiked, fished, and explored since he was a junior high student. It epitomizes, for him, everything untamed and beautiful. He calls it "the flagship of Utah's wild lands."

"The Uintas, to me, are the quintessential wilderness," he says with typical passion. "You can go up there to Henry's Fork and sit at the top of the North Slope and know that 15 miles to the north is wilderness, 25 miles to the south is wilderness, and 25 miles on both sides are wilderness. That's what wilderness is all about. Anywhere you have that much undeveloped land, you can come to know the value of isolation and solitude."

As Carter gazes out from the top of Red Knob Peak or Kings Peak, he experiences the same sense of mystery he knew as a boy. "I can look down now on a green sea of timber that is entirely protected," he says with satisfaction. "One hundred years ago, it was filled with grizzly bears, and 150 years ago, it was filled with wolves. Sometimes I pretend they are still there. I dream that there is a very lonely, gnarly old grizzly bear still wandering around looking for 'a soul mate, and that some day, we will be wise enough and capable enough to put critters like that back into the Uintas."

As he sits on the mountain top, Carter no doubt imagines wilderness fights to come—battles over the future of property managed by the Bureau of Land Management and involving some of Utah's most spectacular Great Basin and Colorado Plateau backcountry. He hopes to take part in deciding how much should be preserved.

"Most people really believe wilderness is good," he says. "Nobody complains about the concept of leaving land alone, leaving it for wildlife, protecting it for watershed, and preserving it for future generations.

"I consistently find people—both kids and adults—who have run across a sign saying they're in a wilderness area when they're hiking and then call us to ask about it. They don't know anything about what we've done. They just ask where they can find other wilderness areas.

"The world won't ever be again what it was a hundred years ago. A kid born today is never going to see that past wilderness. And, in 100 years, we're going to have less." But, if Dick Carter and the Utah Wilderness Association have their say, enough Beehive State areas will be set aside so that future generations can experience the solitude and the dreams that only come from wild places.

LAGOON: A PIONEERING AMUSEMENT PARK

Peter Freed wanders through the well-manicured grounds of his Lagoon amusement park in awe of what he and his family have created. A new $7 million water slide park sits on the site of what was once a mere swimming pool. Nearby, people laugh and shriek as they are whirled upside down on the park's new metal roller coaster. High above the park, riders on the tramway peer down to the midway below, and the Lagoon band belts out a spunky tune in a place where entertainers as diverse as Duke Ellington and the Rolling Stones have performed.

Lagoon Park at the turn of the century. (Utah State Historical Society)

Lagoon, located about halfway between Ogden and Salt Lake City just off I-80, is the nation's second oldest operating amusement park. Only Pennsylvania's Dorny Park—which is three years older—predates the opening of the Utah park in 1886.

Lagoon was founded by railroad magnate Simon Bamberger, who would later serve as Utah's fourth governor. Bamberger owned the railroad line connecting Salt Lake City and Ogden, and built the park in order to encourage people to ride his train. "Lakeside," as the park was originally called, was constructed four miles west of present-day Lagoon, on the shores of the Great Salt Lake, but met its demise when the lake receded. Eventually, the park was moved to a spot near a pair of ponds and some artesian wells, and renamed "Lagoon."

For many years the park was a tremendous success, but it was closed during World War II and by 1945 was derelict. "There were waist-high weeds all over the place," recalls Peter Freed, who with his brothers Robert and Dave took over the amusement park from the Bambergers in 1945. "It looked like a ghost town. You had to use a lot of imagination to envision it as an amusement park again."

A few remnants of the original Lagoon can still be seen. The oldest building, the Lake Park picnic terrace, dates back to the "Lakeside" resort. A turn of the century carousel, one of fewer than 200 of its kind in the United States, is still in operation. The park's first roller coaster, built in 1921, has retained its original design, although it has been rebuilt many times, and Freed believes it to be one of the oldest operating wooden coasters of its kind in the country.

When Lagoon was first conceived, it was, like most amusement parks of its time, relatively simple. "The big things in those days," recalls Freed, "were dancing and bathing. We put in the swimming pool, and it was the first one in the area. When we started buying rides, we started out slowly because we didn't have any money. There was nothing like we have now."

In 1953, a fire started near the roller coaster and destroyed most of the west midway. The Freeds rebuilt with a vengeance, and soon Lagoon was one of the largest amusement parks of its kind between the Mississippi River and the West Coast.

In the 1960s, legendary rock performers like the Doors, the Beach Boys, the Rolling Stones, and Janis Joplin performed at Lagoon's Patio Gardens. The Beach Boys even composed a song—"Salt Lake City"—which mentioned the park. But, with the advent of the drug culture, the Freeds decided to turn Patio Gardens into a spook alley and roller skating rink, because they were afraid that rock-concert patrons wouldn't mix well with wholesome families enjoying the rides. As an alternate

The dancing pavilion at Lagoon.

entertainment, they built an opera house where they staged theater performances and musicals.

In 1974, the Freeds purchased the "Pioneer Village" collection of buildings and Utah artifacts then near the east bench of Salt Lake City and brought it all to Lagoon. Their interest in preserving and presenting Utah's pioneer history to the public is understandable. Their maternal grandfather was Brigham Young's older brother.

Visitors to Pioneer Village get a sense of what it was like to be an early Utah settler. On view, in one of the best gun museums in the United States, are several of gun inventor John Browning's early prototypes, as well as his tools and workbench. Rare Civil War and Mormon Battalion flags hang near the safe of Mormon leader Porter Rockwell. Kids can be "locked" into an old rock jailhouse, ride a horse-drawn carriage through the streets of the little village, and imagine what school was like inside the old Wanship schoolhouse. Brigham Young's china, a tiny organ which survived the Mormon trek across the plains to Utah, the state's first soda fountain, a drug store, and a rock chapel moved piece by piece from Coalville, are on display. There's also the old Charleston post office, a train station moved from Kaysville, and the carriages of some of Utah's most prominent early citizens. The more modern thrills of a log flume ride—a modern-day equivalent of the water chute built at Lagoon at the turn of the century—and Old West shootouts on Main Street, add to the attraction of Pioneer Village.

Now, with the construction of the water slide park, Lagoon seems to have come full circle to its origins as a place to swim. The park draws over one million visitors annually, and on a busy summer day, it is not unusual to see 15,000 people enjoying the rides, playing games, listening to music, and viewing the gardens, exhibits, and fountains.

"My late brother Robert loved the amusement park industry," recalls Peter, "and made it his life. If he came back today, though, he wouldn't recognize it. The big change now is that the rides are so much more sophisticated. You really can't buy any kind of a ride at all for under $1 million. Some cost as much as $14 million."

Then, Utah's soft-spoken amusement park pioneer smiles, almost shyly. "The greatest thing about the business is that our product is fun."

PIONEERS ON THE SALT

Utah's Bonneville Salt Flats are for the most part devoid of life. Only the hardy in search of strange, surrealistic desert experiences venture beyond the interstate and into this land of white salt and mirages.

To most people, the salt flats are a wasteland, a place to spend a few minutes gazing at stark whiteness and sparkling salt crystals from a freeway rest stop before wandering on into the air-conditioned casinos seven miles to the west in Wendover, Nevada. To those who run mineral industries around the salt flats, this area is a gold mine. Within it, there are fifteen different salts, potassium, and manganese, all of which are gathered from evaporation ponds. But another select group of people look at the Bonneville Salt Flats and see in their mind's eye sleek racing cars, because for them these salt flats are a world-famous racing strip.

It was Sir Malcolm Campbell of Great Britain who first put Bonneville Speedway on the map. The year was 1935, and his speed as he raced across the salt was 301.13 miles per hour. Other racing pioneers soon followed. Craig Breedlove became the first to break the 400 and 500 mile-per-hour speed barriers, and then on Nov. 15, 1965, his "Spirit of America" racing machine sped across the salt at a record 600.601 miles per hour. Gary Gabelich utilized another rocket-powered wheeled vehicle on Oct. 23, 1970, traveling 622.407 miles per hour and becoming the fastest man on land.

Lesser-known racing enthusiasts have pioneered innovations in speed on this track each year. Today it is one of the few remaining bastions of amateur motor racing.

Sanctioning organizations like the Southern California Timing Association and the Utah Salt Flats Racing Association arrange events each summer that allow amateur racers to establish land speed records. Spectators who make the drive on I-80, 120 miles west of Salt Lake City near the Nevada-Utah state line, are welcome to talk to the race car drivers and watch them as they attempt to set records.

"People from all walks of life and all financial backgrounds come here with one common goal, and that goal is to go fast," says Southern California Timing Association official Andrea Williams, who has spent a week in August on the salt ever since she was a youngster. "We have over 200 classes based on body style, engine type, and type of fuel used. There is room here for anybody with imagination, skill, and creativity. This is one of the few motor sports in which ordinary people can afford to compete."

Al Teague, a California construction worker, dreams of breaking Bob Summers's 1965 piston-driven speed record of 409.227 miles per hour. "Ego is involved here," says Teague. "This is a challenge and something to do in life. The average guy can't go to Indy and race in the 500. The cost of drag racing is out of sight. Here, we can do something." Not surprisingly, Teague, and many other enthusiasts, do not view the rocket cars driven by Breedlove and Gabelich as true automobiles.

Rick Vesco, owner of a northern Utah motorcycle dealership, constructed a twin-engine streamliner for his brother Don to drive in an attempt to smash Summers's record. "The engines that run our vehicle are a lot like your grandmother's V-8," says Vesco, pointing to a sleek 30-foot long automobile with rear wheels 12 inches apart. "I do all my own fabrication and construction. Friends volunteer labor. Our hobby is building cars."

The Vesco team invested $350,000 for its record attempt. Others hoping to qualify for a land speed run spend far less. A spectator at the races will see in the competition cars off the factory showroom, motorcycles powered by solar cells, mopeds, 1950 Nash Ramblers, and Lakesters resembling the famed Mormon Meteor that Abe Jenkins used to set records in the early 1950s. Many participants are old-timers, having followed their fathers to the salt when the tradition of Speed Week started in 1949.

"It's a family reunion every year," says Vesco. "These people are like your brothers, only you see them just once a year. My father began racing here in the 1920s. We learned from his experience. I have no formal engineering experience, but normally our cars go faster than the engineers' cars. And that's kind of fun."

Vesco looks out toward the salt with one concern. Changes in the landscape, related to man's highway building and mining activities, are causing the salt to deteriorate. The U.S. Bureau of Land Management, owner and manager of much of the Bonneville Speedway, has taken salt samples for 28 years. Studies show that the thickness of the salt on the Bonneville Speedway is shrinking at a rate of about one percent a year, including a 30-percent reduction of salt volume during the past 28 years.

"Given this long-term trend, it is apparent that the Salt Flats, as we know them, are in trouble," says BLM official Deane Zeller. "Clearly, some hard questions need to be addressed."

KEN SLEIGHT: PIONEERING RIVER-RUNNER

Ken Sleight struggled to keep the raft upright through the roaring foam of Skull Rapid in the Colorado River's Westwater Canyon. His passengers screamed in fright and delight. A wave of water engulfed the rubber boat, but somehow, some way, the guide and his passengers survived their run through the swirling rapids.

Relieved, the passengers slapped the river runner on the back and complimented him on the way he handled the boat. Sleight smiled but didn't let on that anything much almost happened.

"Shoot," he jokingly admitted years later, "I didn't have anything to do with getting us through there safely. I just got us out alive. I did a lousy job, but everybody thought it was really great stuff."

Ken Sleight belongs to an elite group of veteran Utah guides who pioneered river-running and backcountry touring in southern Utah during the early 1950s. Like many of these guides, he's spent his life living on the edge, greeting each day with the desire to learn something new and to introduce visitors to self-discovery and adventure, too.

"The biggest thrill in the world is to be able to lead a group of people up a canyon and let them discover something for themselves rather than to say, 'Okay, now we're going to see Rainbow Bridge right around the corner.' You see guide after guide after guide telling people to prepare themselves to see something. I think this is wrong. People who come on trips don't want to be classified as tourists or onlookers. I like them to feel like they're going to discover the river just like John Wesley Powell did.

"When I was a kid, my favorite pastime was going to the library and reading about all those people who were the first to discover something. When I went out and nobody else was in a place, I felt a thrill of discovery. People think a discovery is something that only happens once, but things are discovered anew in each and everyone's experience. I'm a watcher. And I love to watch people turn into the canyons for the first time. It blows their mind."

Sleight started running rivers commercially in 1951, and he's seen most of those in southern Utah. He took his boats through Glen Canyon before a dam created Lake Powell. He's run the Grand Canyon, Cataract and Westwater canyons on the Colorado, and most of the canyons on the Green River. As a horsepacker and hiker, the veteran guide helped explore famed Utah backcountry like Grand Gulch, Dark

Canyon, Coyote Gulch, and the Maze. Though he enjoys giving his customers the feeling of adventure, like on the Westwater Canyon trip, he can't recall ever being in a life-threatening situation on one of his trips.

He is a man with definite opinions about what makes a good trip and what doesn't. He thinks, for example, that many modern-day river excursions are too short. "It takes time to bring a group together," he says. "The first day, when you meet the people, they're trying to analyze you, and you're doing the same to them. It usually takes three days for everyone to feel comfortable. The third day is the charm. Personally, trips six to 10 days long are my favorites."

Sleight loves taking excursions through canyons he's never explored before. "The more you've seen, the more you realize what you haven't seen," he says. "When I was a kid running the rivers, I thought I'd see them all, but there are so damn many, one guy in a lifetime couldn't see them all. That's the beauty of the canyons."

Sleight, whom many believe to be the prototype for the character of Seldom Seen Smith in Edward Abbey's novel *The Monkey Wrench Gang*, is, with one very big exception, the prototype of a typical conservative southern Utah businessman. He owns a small business, operating out of the Pack Creek Ranch 14 miles south of Moab at the base of the La Sal Mountains. He possesses a healthy distrust of government and its regulations. Like the prospectors, cattle ranchers, and farmers who struggle to make a living in this desolate country, Sleight is by nature independent.

He differs greatly, though, from many of his fellow southern Utah citizens in his concern for the preservation of wilderness in the canyonlands country where he lives and works. Many Utah residents want more development. Sleight fights to preserve the country he loves.

For example, he professes a profound hatred of Lake Powell, the huge man-made reservoir which inundated some of his favorite canyons and brought more motorized recreation to southern Utah. When it was built, he left the Moab area for a few years and ventured to Alaska. But the lure of his beloved red rock canyons drew him home again.

"The canyons are terrific," he says. "I guess that's why I'm so adamant that, if I'm going to stay here, I'm going to make damn sure they don't overdevelop them. If there was canyon country all over the world, I'd just move on. But it's so limited, really. It's just one section of the entire earth. There's no place else to go. You have to make your stand. You have to keep it the way it ought to be and that's as wilderness."

So, Sleight does a bit of fighting politically. But, most of all, he helps people discover the joy of his beloved rivers and canyons on their own, knowing in his heart that the land will help them make up their mind about how much of it should be preserved.

WILLIAM STOKES: PIONEERING GEOLOGIST

His hair is pure white, and a lifetime spent outside in bright sun and dust barely shows in his pale face. A snowy moustache highlights a wry grin. He's a man with a vision who speaks with boyish enthusiasm. Dr. William Lee Stokes still gets excited about rocks and dinosaurs and tomorrow.

Most kids are born collectors and dinosaur-lovers. But they are not all lucky enough to spend their childhoods, as Stokes did, roaming the badlands of Emery County, picking up moss agate, jasper, petrified wood, and fossils. Coming home again, sometimes with his family's lost cattle in tow, Stokes would look at what he'd found and ask those eternal childhood questions, why and how?

Not surprisingly, Stokes eventually studied geology, first at Brigham Young University and then at Princeton University. When he learned that Princeton wanted a dinosaur skeleton for its geology hall but was concerned about the price of dinosaur skeletons, he volunteered to find a less expensive one. He knew where to go—back home in the Morrison Formation. Digging in the soft clay-like rock was fairly easy, and it wasn't long before he found an *Allosaurus*. Soon, Stokes was unearthing one dinosaur after another at the Cleveland-Lloyd Quarry (named after a financial benefactor). His goal was to provide fossils for anyone who wanted them, and it evidently pleases him that millions of people now can see dinosaur skeletons from the quarry on display all over the world.

Eight fossils, including the *Stokesosaurus*, have been named for him. "You never name a fossil after yourself," he says, "That's too egotistical!"

Stokes has a gift for sharing his wealth of geological information about Utah and the world, in part because his sense of wonder is infectious. For thirty-two years he has taught geology as a professor and dean of the geology department of the University of Utah, and he has authored classic texts on the subject.

Guidebooks became a popular means of transmitting information about an area in the 1950s, and Stokes is a pioneer in this medium as well. "A tourist can spend loads of time and money to get to a place, go into a gift shop and find a book on the birds and bees, the flowers and the trees, but find nothing there on the scenery which he came to see. So I wrote a series of tourist-oriented books. I want everybody, even a little six-year-old, to get an understanding of dinosaurs and geology. It is the worst failing of science, and geology in particular, that it isn't explained so the average tourist can understand it." Most parks in the state carry Stokes's invaluable guides. (A list is found in the "Recommended Reading" section of this book.)

During World War II, Dr. Stokes worked for the United States Geological Survey, mapping and evaluating vanadium, which is used as a hardening agent for steel. At the time, the Geological Survey spoke of the uranium found in conjunction with vanadium as a "byproduct." Stokes now recalls ironically, "When they dropped the atom bomb, why, then we knew what that was all about."

A mixture of delight and curiosity shines in Stokes's eyes when he talks about the future. "Where does geology go from here? We've got to go deeper and deeper into the earth. That's where the mystery is. The deepest wells are around 24,000 feet (7,315 m) deep. Just think of all those mountains and plateaus that are pushing up through the earth—there must be some terrific energy down there. The earth's crust is moving. It's dynamic. Once the whole Colorado Plateau was down at sea level, and here it is now at 6,000 to 10,000 feet (1,828-3,048 m). Something lifted it up. Unlocking this mystery is the unknown frontier. We've gone to the moon, but we know practically nothing about the earth's interior, and from this interior we may eventually get inexhaustible energy. It's hot! It's molten! Why can't we bring all that energy up?"

Stokes sees Utah's numerous geothermal areas, as excellent natural laboratories for the study of energy from the earth's interior.

Calling himself a "third generation pioneer," Stokes has also used data gathered by explorers like John C. Frémont and early U.S. Geologic surveyors, to put together the first detailed geologic map of the state. It is more comprehensive than any other Western state map, and has led to the discovery of many natural resources. Similarly, Stokes was first to assemble a complete set of guides and indexes to fossils for the Western interior, enabling geologists to classify certain earth layers by the fossils they contain.

Dr. Stokes's endless questioning and his search for answers to the eternal questions have led him from geology to religion. He actively seeks to merge science with religion. "It is a fault of modern society that it compartmentalizes the two," he says. "There needs to be better communication between them."

GORDON TOPHAM: INTERPRETER

As a boy, Gordon Topham picked up the arrowheads and pottery in the southern Utah desert where he grew up.

He didn't know that what he brought home in his pockets were antiquities or that collecting them was illegal.

Many years later, Gordon Topham, as state park superintendent, opened Fremont Indian State Park on I-70 southwest of Richfield. He is an authority on the kinds of arrowheads and pottery pieces that he used to collect, and he works to educate others about the need to protect the ancient Indian civilizations they represent.

"Perhaps it is my penance for inadvertently breaking the law so many times," he says. "I feel it is important to educate people about our cultural resources so they will be eager to protect them."

The names Fremont and Anasazi are given to groups of prehistoric Indians that inhabited the southwestern United States and then mysteriously disappeared. Little is known about the Fremont, who were contemporaries of the Anasazi but who inhabited a different region west of the Colorado River and north of the Virgin River in Utah. Topham's work is shedding some light on this little-known people.

"Every couple of weeks, something new pops up," Topham says. "A while ago we were digging a trench and uncovered some cobs of corn we carbon-dated back to 175 B.C., a time before corn was thought to be cultivated in this part of the world!"

The artifacts found in prehistoric Indian habitation sites are like pieces in a giant puzzle, explains Topham. They give clues to such questions as: Where did the Fremont come from? What were their lives like? Why did they disappear? Topham challenges visitors to Fremont Indian State Park to join archaeologists in asking questions about the Fremont and finding answers.

What use was that twisted piece of cord found in an ancient storage room put to? Why did the Fremont live in pit houses on level ground while their contemporaries to the southwest, the Anasazi, lived in cliff dwellings? Why was it that the Fremont left more rock art than their Anasazi neighbors?

"Right now I have so many things to do here I could work for the rest of my life," Topham says.

LARRY DAVIS: PIONEERING ARCHAEOLOGIST

At Anasazi State Park in Boulder, a modern museum building houses the office of the venerable and scholarly Larry Davis. Davis is something of Utah state treasure, an archaeologist who has devoted much of his adult life to ensuring that others have an opportunity to visit and understand ancient Anasazi Indian culture. For more than a thousand years these people farmed, built villages, and made pottery in the Four Corners area of Utah, Colorado, Arizona, and New Mexico, before mysteriously disappearing about A.D. 1300.

Unlike most Anasazi ruins, which tend to be located in defensible caves set in high desert canyon walls, the one at Boulder was built in open farmland. If you visit and you're fortunate enough to speak with Davis, he'll be able to tell you about the village and the meaning of the petroglyphs.

The first archaeologist to be hired by Utah's Division of Parks and Recreation, Davis has worked in ultra-conservative southern Utah since 1970. Life here, he says, offers him an opportunity to pursue two of his favorite pastimes: thinking and writing. An interesting mix of cynic, idealist, dreamer, and quiet philosopher, he occasionally puts pen to paper and expresses his feelings in the form of poetry. Thumbing through his book of poems, he recently pulled out a short piece to share with a visitor: It describes the solitude and magic of this wild region, and the satisfaction of taking the time to truly experience it.

"I've gained a tremendous appreciation for these ancient people," he says, "and their ability to adapt to an environment that is inhospitable to population increase and provides little food." No modern man, he feels, could survive on his own like the Anasazi.

Davis describes finding a shard of pottery and wondering about the human being who created it 1,000 years ago. He tells of a volunteer who helped to uncover an ancient burial site which contained a pot with the palm prints of an ancient pottery maker. Once the contents of the area were examined, bones and burial items were carefully replaced where they were found, as is customary, and the volunteer cried—feeling as if this reburial was a funeral.

Mostly, he says, he tries to use the park as a vehicle to teach people to respect the past. If occasionally he's been frustrated, and that frustration generates strong emotions, Davis turns those feelings into the poetry of the southern Utah desert—a place where there is time to contemplate the past and wonder about the future.

THE WASATCH FRONT

WHILE MUCH OF UTAH IS LARGELY RURAL, full of wide-open spaces, ranches, and splendid mountain scenery, the state possesses another, distinctly urban personality.

Eighty-percent of Utah's residents live along the roughly 175-mile (280-km) stretch of land called the Wasatch Front, which lies along the western base of the Wasatch Mountains, from Provo in the south to Ogden in the north. In 1990, U.S. Census bureau statisticians found this to be the 38th largest urban area in the United States.

Salt Lake City is the heart of a metropolitan area of more than a million people spread through the Salt Lake Valley. For over a hundred years, people from Wyoming, Idaho, Nevada, Utah, and parts of Montana and Colorado have traveled to Salt Lake City to shop, work, worship, make transport connections, and simply enjoy themselves. It has served as a hub of the Intermountain West ever since the Mormons founded it in 1847.

"From the time of its settlement, an air of the incredible has attended Salt Lake City," wrote one of the writers of the 1941 Work Project Administration's *Utah: A Guide to the State*. ". . . Travelers have forever been coming to see for themselves 'the New Jerusalem,' the 'Utah Zion,' 'the City of the Saints.' In all but a handful of the books written on Utah and the Mormons during the first 30 years of the city's existence, the Mormon capital *was* Utah, a way of thinking not yet entirely disposed of."

Naturally, many a citizen of the more sparsely populated southern and eastern portions of Utah have grumbled that Salt Lake City residents think the state ends at the city's southern boundary. It is, of course, the state's capital. Utah's major television and radio stations, and two of its three major newspapers, operate in the city. It is also the world headquarters for the Mormon Church, whose annual spring and fall conferences draw thousands into the city from all over the world, and whose Temple Square is easily Utah's top tourist attraction. Salt Lake City is the state's cultural center: people flock into the valley to enjoy the Utah Symphony, Pioneer Theatre Company, Ballet West, the Utah Opera Company, Ririe-Woodbury Dance Company, the Salt Lake Acting Company, the Repertory Dance Theatre, and the Mormon Tabernacle Choir. All of Utah's professional sports

teams—the Utah Jazz of the National Basketball Association, the Salt Lake Golden Eagles of the International Hockey League, and the Salt Lake Trappers baseball team—play in the capital. The largest state university, the venerable University of Utah, sits on the east bench of the city. (Its arch rival both in athletics and academics, the 27,000-student Mormon-owned Brigham Young University, is located less than 50 miles south in Provo.) The huge Salt Palace convention complex, the Delta Center sports arena, a large and continually expanding international airport, Utah's largest shopping centers, and its most important federal, state, and local government offices are found in Salt Lake City. Eleven major ski areas are located within a 90-mile (144-km) drive of the airport.

■ SALT LAKE CITY, OLD AND NEW

Modern-day Salt Lake City still reflects the vision of Brigham Young, the Mormon prophet who brought the small band of 143 men, three women, two children, 70 wagons, one boat, one cannon, 93 horses, 52 mules, 66 oxen, and 19 cows into the Salt Lake Valley on July 24, 1847.

Visitors to Salt Lake City can see the result of his early urban vision: first-timers usually comment on the width of the streets. After brief exploration, they marvel at the ease with which addresses are found. Most streets run north-south and east-west, and are numbered according to their direction and distance from the southeastern corner of Temple Square. Thus, the first street to the south of Temple Square is First South. Ninth East is nine blocks east of that corner. Nearly every Utah city is laid out in much the same manner.

When the U.S. government sent Captain Howard Stansbury to survey the Great Salt Lake in 1849, the city was already developing into an important urban area.

"A city has been laid out upon a magnificent scale, being nearly four miles in length and three in breadth," wrote Captain Stansbury. "Through the city itself flows an unfailing stream of pure, sweet water, which by an ingenious mode of irrigation, is made to traverse each side of every street, spreading life, verdure and beauty over what was heretofore a barren waste."

Though officially a part of the United States, for many years Salt Lake City operated largely as a kind of theocracy under Brigham Young. Greater cultural and religious diversity arrived in later years, starting with the California gold rush of

(previous pages) The Wasatch Range looms over the Capitol in downtown Salt Lake City.

1849, when many non-Mormons (referred to as "gentiles" by the Latter-day Saints) passed through the area. During the Civil War, soldiers were stationed in the city. The joining of the transcontinental railroad 80 miles (128 km) to the north in 1869, and the promise of silver, gold, and lead in the nearby mountains, brought more gentiles.

At times, the clash between the Mormons and non-Mormons became intense. In fact, many of the rivalries between the factions exist today, though they are certainly less evident than in the 1890s.

"The split between Mormon and non-Mormon communities was evident in the use of land in Salt Lake City," wrote Ted Wilson in his Utah Geographic Series book *The Wasatch Front.* "The Mormons dominated the north end of the city with Temple Square, Brigham Young's homes and offices, retail facilities and other buildings. Non-Mormon business leaders, including Samuel Newhouse, the Auerbach family, and Albert Fisher, built more than a dozen major buildings at the south end of the city's business district as a counter-weight to the Mormon influence at the north end. The area became the nucleus for the Auerbach Department Store, the Newhouse Hotel, the New Grand Hotel, the Salt Lake Stock Exchange (specially in mining stocks) and the Commercial Club, founded in 1902 to attract outside business to Utah."

Salt Lake City's present character began to take shape at that time. Buildings like the State Capitol and the Gothic Cathedral of the Madeline were completed. Residents of the new neighborhoods—the Avenues, Capitol Hill, Liberty Park, and Sugarhouse—rode trolley cars into the city. During the Great Depression, buses gradually replaced the trolleys and construction slowed.

Like many urban areas across the country, Salt Lake City seemed threatened in the 1960s when new malls and shopping centers opened in the suburbs, and the city retail district began to decline. That's when the Salt Palace, a downtown convention complex, keyed an urban renewal effort designed to bring people back into the heart of the city. The Mormon Church invested $40 million to develop a downtown shopping mall, the ZCMI Center, named for Zion's Cooperative Mercantile Institution, which claims to be the oldest department store in the United States. Shortly afterwards, the Crossroads Mall was built directly across the street from the ZCMI Center, effectively concentrating most of the retail trade on both sides of Main Street between South Temple and First South. A city-wide beautification project was completed at about the same time.

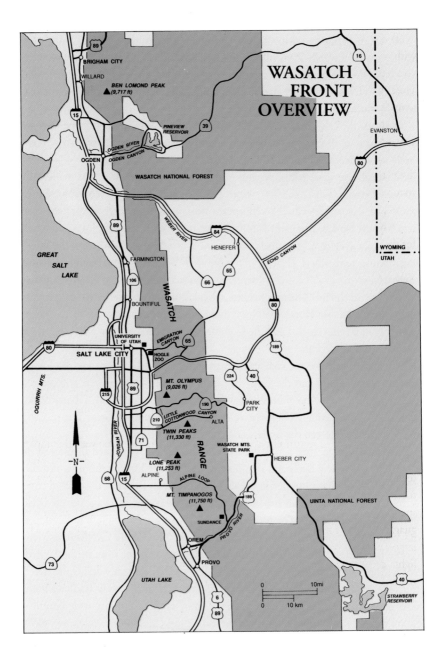

WASATCH FRONT OVERVIEW

The concentration of businesses on the north end of town did cause problems with the old "non-Mormon" district to the south. Famous old department stores like Auerbachs and the Paris Company went out of business. The Newhouse Hotel was razed. Now, the city fathers have begun to revitalize this area, first by completely restoring the Gothic-style City-County Building and then by constructing a combination of open spaces and new office buildings in the southern portion of downtown. Many of the city's older buildings located just south of the Salt Palace were tagged for redevelopment as part of a restaurant-entertainment district. The Peery Hotel Complex, containing two restaurants and an elegantly restored luxury hotel, is a good example of what can be done when older buildings are rehabilitated into useful, modern structures.

Despite their modern veneer, Salt Lakers still keep a warm spot in their hearts for the past. The state's biggest event is the **Days of '47** celebration, commemorating the day (July 24, 1847) when Mormon pioneers first entered the Salt Lake Valley. Every July 24, one of the largest parades in the United States marches through downtown Salt Lake, preceded by horse and children's parades, and drawing hundreds of thousands.

■ TEMPLE SQUARE

In much the same way that Trafalgar, Red, and St. Peter's squares reflect the personalities and histories of their respective cities, so is Temple Square the focal point of Salt Lake City.

Drawing close to four million visitors a year, the 10-acre stone-walled complex of gardens, statuary, and historic buildings fashioned in the last half of the nineteenth century by Brigham Young and the Mormon pioneers is Utah's premier tourist attraction. Over 1,100 volunteer guides, hosts, and hostesses—350 of whom speak one or more languages other than English, and some of whom use sign language—explain the history of Temple Square and the origins of Mormonism. The largest crowds come during the Christmas season, when some 300,000 twinkling lights draped on trees, bushes, and buildings turn Temple Square into a holiday treasure. A life-sized nativity scene, concerts, Christmas movies, and slide shows add to the festive atmosphere.

The majestic focal point of the square is the granite **Salt Lake Temple**, a cathedral-like building with six spires that took 40 years to complete. Designed by architect Truman O. Angell, this is the most famous of 43 such structures maintained throughout the world by the Latter-day Saints. Don't expect admission when you visit; entry is restricted to Latter-day Saints with passes, or written "recommends," from their bishops. (One of the two large visitors centers displays an exhibit giving non-Mormons a vicarious tour of the temple.) Mormon temples are not used for Sunday worship services, which take place instead in thousands of local churches. Temples are used on weekdays for marriages, baptisms, and other sacred ordinances.

According to author Quig Nelson in *Temple Square: The Crown Jewel of the Mormons*, the walls of the Temple are made of granite blocks, hewed to fit tightly together. At the base, the walls are nine feet (3 m) thick and taper to six feet (2 m) at the top. The granite was quarried in Little Cottonwood Canyon about 23 miles (37 km) from the Temple site. Until 1873, teams of oxen pulled the wagons loaded with the gargantuan blocks of granite from the quarry to the construction site. After 1873, the granite was shipped via a new railroad.

Perhaps the most distinctive feature of the temple is a 12-foot, 5 1/2-inch-tall (4-m) statue of the **Angel Moroni**, which stands on the middle spire on the east side of the structure. Mormons believe Moroni to be the last prophet of the Western

The Mormon Temple in Salt Lake City took 40 years to complete. (Utah State Historical Society)

Hemisphere, who finished compiling the writings of other ancient prophets in the Americas. Prior to his death, Moroni buried the plates on a hill. Upon resurrection, he returned to the earth, appeared to Mormon founder Joseph Smith, and showed him where the records were buried. The statue was constructed of hammered copper covered with glistening gold leaf. Nielsen writes that architects utilized a unique suspension system to keep the statue sturdy but flexible. Leverage action in the system allows the statue—which has stood on its spire for 85 years—to withstand wind storms of up to 90 miles per hour (144 kph).

With the exception of the Temple, all other buildings on Temple Square are open to the public. Next to the Temple, the most famous building on the square is the **Mormon Tabernacle**, an egg-shaped, silver-domed building completed in 1867. The building is 250 feet (75 m) long, 150 feet (45 m) wide, and 80 feet (24 m) high, and it sits on 44 cut sandstone buttresses.

"The roof is a great bridgework of timbers, with the wooden arches, beams and supports latticed and pinned together with wooden pegs and rawhide thongs," writes Nielsen. "Very few bolts or nails were used and what were available were homemade."

The Tabernacle was completed in 1867. When a balcony was added three years later, the seating capacity was increased from 4,500 to about 6,500. The original roof, which was replaced by metal in 1900 and aluminum in 1947, was covered with 400,000 wood shingles.

Noted for its fine acoustics, the Tabernacle served as the cultural center of Salt Lake City for over a century. Many Utah Symphony patrons remember sitting through concerts on the hard, wooden seats until the orchestra moved in 1979 to the new Symphony Hall less than a block away. The building still houses the world-renowned **Mormon Tabernacle Choir**, a 320-voice ensemble known for its weekly network radio and television broadcasts, top-selling records (five gold albums), and worldwide concert tours. When the choir is in town, the public can attend rehearsals at 7:30 p.m. each Thursday, and the Sunday CBS Radio broadcast at 9:30 a.m. (doors close at 9:15 a.m.).

The choir formed a few weeks after the arrival of the pioneers and sang in a quaint bowery constructed of adobe blocks, with poles supporting a roof of leaves and branches to hold back the warm August sun. Choir members are volunteers between 30 and 60 years of age and are limited to 20 years of service.

The giant 10,857-pipe **Tabernacle Organ** is another colorful part of Temple Square. The original, designed by an English carpenter named Joseph Ridges, was constructed before the coming of the railroad. Ridges had suitable lumber for the wooden pipes transported 300 miles by ox team from the southern part of the territory. Wind to operate the organ was furnished by four men pumping bellows. The organ was rebuilt by Niels Johnson in 1885, and again, several times in the present century: in 1901 by the Kimball Organ Company, in 1915 by the Austin Organ Company, in 1945 by the Aeolian-skiner Organ Company of Boston, and in 1948 by G. Donald Harrison. Its present configuration consists of eight divisions, played from five manuals and a pedal board, with 191 ranks, totaling 10,857 pipes. That is a far different instrument than the 32-rank, 1,600-pipe, 25-note pedal board and two 56-note manuals first designed by Ridges. After a cleaning of the pipes and installation of a new console to the organ in 1988, the president and tonal director of Schoenstein and Co. of San Francisco, Jack Bethards, wrote in *The American Organist* that the organ has a signature sound: "By this I mean an organ that is instantly recognizable, one with individual character. Creating a unique sound while staying well within the bounds of good taste and tradition is the work of genius. Achieving these things in an eclectic instrument is a miracle."

The **Assembly Hall**, a building with four gables that seats about 1,200, was completed in 1880 using leftover granite from the Temple construction. It now dominates the southwestern portion of Temple Square. Free concerts are presented every Friday and Saturday in this building, which is also used for funerals, lectures, musical programs, and summertime non-denominational services.

Temple Square's two **visitor centers**—one located on the north side of the square and the other on the south—house exhibits relating the history, beliefs, and programs of the 6.5-million-member Mormon Church. The focal point of the north visitors center is a large white marble statue of Jesus Christ, a reproduction of "The Christus," created in the nineteenth century by Danish master Bertel Thorvaldsen, whose original graces the Church of Our Lady in Copenhagen, Denmark. Other displays in the centers include giant murals and paintings on the life of Christ, automated dioramas, and a variety of audio-visual presentations. The **Nauvoo Bell**, a 782-pound (355 kg) bronze bell cast in England which once hung in the Nauvoo Temple in Illinois before the Mormons were forced to leave, can be seen and heard at Temple Square. The **Seagull Monument**, honoring the birds that Mormons believe were sent from God to eat a massive infestation of crickets which threatened to destroy crops planted by the pioneers, is also found inside the Square.

Admission to Temple Square and all activities is free.

As the Mormon Church has increased in size, other buildings surrounding Temple Square have been constructed. These include the Museum of Church History and Art, the Mormon Family History Library, and the 28-story office tower that is headquarters for the Mormon Church; it boasts the city's highest observation deck. The **Mormon Family History Library**, better known as the church genealogical library, is the largest of its kind in the world. Visitors come from all over the world to search out their family roots. There is no charge. Finding family roots is important to the Mormons, who hold a "baptism of the dead" for people not baptized in the LDS faith before the founding of the church. Many of the records are stored in tunnels carved into the granite near the mouth of Little Cottonwood Canyon.

Visitors can tour Brigham Young's primary residence, the **Beehive House**, as well as the **Lion House**. The latter now serves as a social center, but once was a sort of apartment complex for Young's wives and children. Both are located a block east of Temple Square at South Temple and State streets.

Salt Lake City, Utah, with the Wasatch Mountains beyond.

■ BEYOND THE SQUARE

It would be too much to say that non-Mormons—locally referred to as gentiles
—always get along or got along with the dominant Mormons in Salt Lake City.
People who move from other parts of the United States into Utah often complain
that government and culture in the state are dominated by the LDS Church. Still,
Catholics, Methodists, Buddhists, Baptists, Greek Orthodox, Jews, and most
major Christian denominations can be found in Salt Lake City. Many thrive on
their minority status. Although Mormons do dominate state and local elected
offices, Dee Dee Corradini, the first woman to be the city's mayor, is a non-
Mormon.

Early Mormon pioneers and the Catholic Church interacted cautiously, and
only when necessary. Bernice Maher Mooney, in her book *The Story of the Cathedral of the Madeleine*, discusses the association between Lawrence Scanlon, first
Catholic bishop of Salt Lake City, and high Mormon officials: "The reciprocal effort at peaceful association continued throughout the territory. In 1879, Apostle
Erastus Snow, leader of the Latter-day Saints at St. George, invited Bishop Scanlon
to offer High Mass in the Mormon Tabernacle there. The bishop did so on September 25, 1879. The Tabernacle Choir, conducted by John M. MacFarlane who
had become friends with Bishop Scanlon, obtained the music for the Kyrie, Gloria
and Credo and practiced diligently for some weeks."

The spirit of cooperation between the Mormons and the Catholics continues to
this day. Many prominent Mormons contributed to the $6.5 million drive to re-
store the interior of the historic and architecturally significant **Cathedral of the
Madeleine**, which is located on South Temple just east of Temple Square. Utah's
Catholic population, which has grown from 90 when Bishop Scanlon first arrived
from Ireland in 1873 to 60,000, regards the cathedral as the heart of its diocese.
Bishop Scanlon purchased the cathedral property, at 331 E. South Temple, for
$37,000 in 1890. The exterior of the building was finished in 1909, but the ornate
interior was not completed until 1926. The cathedral possesses some of the most
beautiful stained-glass windows in North America, created in 1906 by Zettler Stu-
dios of Munich, Germany.

St. Mark's Episcopal Cathedral, located at 100 South Street, was constructed in
1871 and is Utah's oldest non-Mormon church. The red sandstone exterior of the
First Presbyterian Church at East South Temple and C Street makes it stand out as
one of the most impressive structures on South Temple.

MARK TWAIN'S SALT LAKE CITY

Next day we strolled about everywhere through the broad, straight, level streets, and enjoyed the pleasant strangeness of a city of fifteen thousand inhabitants with no loafers perceptible in it; and no visible drunkards or noisy people; a limpid stream rippling and dancing through every street in place of a filthy gutter; block after block of trim dwellings, built of "frame" and sunburned brick—a great thriving orchard and garden behind every one of them, apparently—branches from the street stream winding and sparkling among the garden beds and fruit trees—and a grand general air of neatness, repair, thrift, and comfort, around and about and over the whole. And everywhere were workshops, factories, and all manner of industries; and intent faces and busy hands were to be seen wherever one looked; and in one's ears was the ceaseless clink of hammers, the buzz of trade and the contented hum of drums and fly-wheels.

❖ ❖ ❖

Salt Lake City was healthy—an extremely healthy city. They declared that there was only one physician in the place and he was arrested every week regularly and held to answer under the vagrant act for having "no visible means of support." They always give you a good substantial article of truth in Salt Lake, and good measure and good weight, too. Very often, if you wished to weigh one of their airiest little commonplace statements you would want the hay scales.

❖ ❖ ❖

It is a luscious country for thrilling evening stories about assassinations of intractable Gentiles. I cannot easily conceive of anything more cosy than the night in Salt Lake which we spent in a Gentile den, smoking pipes and listening to tales of how Burton galloped in among the pleading and defenseless "Morisites" and shot them down, men and women, like so many dogs. And how Bill Hickman, a Destroying Angel, shot Drown and Arnold dead for bringing suit against him for a debt. And how Porter Rockwell did this and that dreadful thing. And how heedless people often come to Utah and make remarks about Brigham, or polygamy, or some other sacred matter, and the very next morning at daylight such parties are sure to be found lying up some back alley, contentedly waiting for the hearse.

—Mark Twain, *Roughing It*, 1872

Some of the most impressive mansions in the state can be viewed when walking or driving along South Temple. These include the **Enos A. Wall Mansion**, which now serves as the headquarters for the LDS Business College, and the **Kearns Mansion** at 603 East South Temple, constructed by Thomas Kearns, an early mining baron who founded the state's largest daily newspaper, *The Salt Lake Tribune*. Kearns' heirs still own the newspaper, but his elegant 28-room residence now serves as the official residence of Utah's governor.

The morning *Tribune* and the *Deseret News*, which publishes on weekday evenings and weekend mornings, are long-time rivals, as evidenced by a debate the two had during a local election in the late 1800s. "The Peoples party represented the Mormon faction and Gentiles flocked to the liberal party," wrote Ted Wilson in his Utah Geographic Series book *The Wasatch Front*. "*The Deseret News*, owned and operated by the Mormon Church, became the feisty advocate of the People's party, while *The Salt Lake Tribune* held forth for the non-Mormons. The fight occasionally got tough. In 1876, the *Tribune* labeled the People's party ticket for city offices 'a Priesthood city ticket' made up of '1 President of the Church, 1 Apostle, 2 Bishops, 3 Bishop's Councilors, 2 sons-in-law of Brigham Young, and Brigham's private secretary.'"

The ornately decorated **Capitol** overlooks Salt Lake City from a hill atop State Street. Constructed of granite and capped by a copper dome, the building was completed in 1915 at a cost of $2,739,529. Housing the state legislature, governor's office, and Supreme Court, the building is certainly worth exploring. Don't miss the basement displays of Utah's history and industry.

Just south of the Capitol is **Council Hall**, a historical building that once served as city and territorial government offices. It was moved to the hilltop in 1960, where it now serves as the home of the Utah Travel Council, an excellent place to pick up travel literature.

The **Pioneer Memorial Museum**, found at 300 North Main, southwest of the Capitol, houses one of the West's most complete collections of authentic nineteenth-century pioneer memorabilia. Collections of dolls, Brigham Young's personal effects, paintings, pioneer fashions, a carriage house, and a children's playroom provide glimpses of early life in Salt Lake City. The Daughters of the Utah Pioneers, who operate the facility, are diligently seeking stories and histories concerning the people who settled Utah.

The Utah State Capitol in Salt Lake City, completed in 1915, was modelled after the Capitol in Washington, D.C.

Also located on State Street near the historic Eagle Gate, a scenic entrance to Capitol Hill, is **Hansen Planetarium**, a favorite of science buffs. Housed in what was once the Salt Lake City Library, the planetarium, with its laser shows, live stage plays, spectacular star shows, and science museum, is among the most innovative facilities of its kind anywhere. Especially popular is an outreach program teaching families how to use telescopes to view the evening sky.

Kids can't spend enough time at the **Children's Museum of Utah**, located just below Capitol Hill in the old Wasatch Baths building at 840 North 300 West. Museum exhibits allow young visitors to pilot a 727 training jet, excavate the skeleton of a sabertooth cat, control a robot, or broadcast on their own television station.

The **Salt Lake Art Center**, near the Salt Palace Convention complex, is a two-level gallery featuring traveling art displays and a small collection of locally significant pieces. The Salt Lake County Visitor and Convention building, located on the corner of 200 South and West Temple, is another good place to pick up tourist information and current details about cultural activities.

The Rio Grande Depot at 300 South Rio Grand Street not only serves as the Amtrak train depot, but also as home for the **Utah State Historical Society Museum** and research library. The library provides particularly fascinating glimpses at the past for those with time to spend rummaging through old books and magazines. We also like the Historical Society's bookstore, which has perhaps the most complete selection in the state of publications dealing with all Utah subjects. If a book has been published about Utah, chances are you can buy it there. (By the way, if you're waiting for the train, try the Rio Grande Mexican restaurant on the northern end of the building.)

Many Salt Lake City shopping trips begin at the Mormon-owned **Zion Cooperative Mercantile Institution** (ZCMI), which was founded by Brigham Young in 1868 while Macy's was still a specialty stop. Shoppers can find major department stores like Weinstock's and Nordstroms in the **Crossroads Mall** west of ZCMI on Main Street. But historic **Trolley Square**, at 550 South 700 East, provides the most interesting shopping atmosphere. This upscale complex of high fashion items, restaurants, and movie theaters once housed the city's trolley systems and is patterned after places like San Francisco's Ghirardelli Square. Take time to explore the winding, brick hallways and unusual antiques found in Utah's most unusual shopping center.

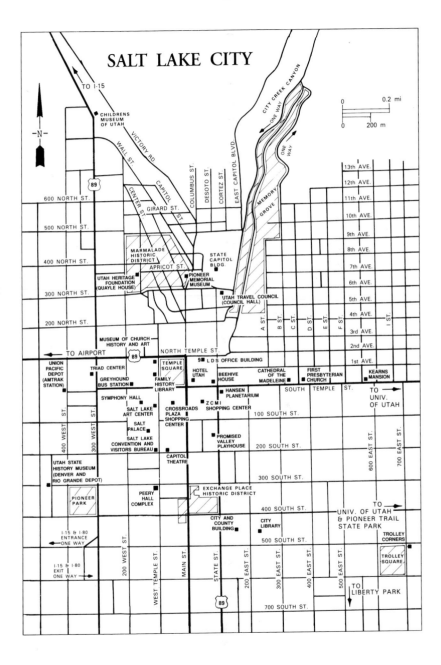

SALT LAKE CITY

Liberty Park, one of the oldest recreation areas in Salt Lake City, is located a few blocks south of Trolley Square. This is the city's answer to New York's Central Park. The venerable green space, four blocks long and two blocks wide, has served as a gathering place since Isaac Chase built a mill there in 1852. Free flour from the mill saved many families during the two-year famine of 1856-1857. The mill-stones and irons used at the mill—which still stands at Liberty Park—were brought across the plains by ox-team. A small amusement park, a modern children's playground, and landscaped gardens stand between the mill and Chase's yellow adobe brick home, which was constructed in 1853. The entrance to **Tracy Aviary** lies just to the north of the Chase Mill. Those strolling through the shaded grounds of the aviary watch golden and bald eagles, flamingos and peacocks, the hyacinithin macaw (world's largest parrot), Quaker parakeets, golden pheasants from China, and hundreds of other unusual birds. For the most part, though, Liberty Park serves as a quiet, shaded retreat. Just spending a fall afternoon walking through the manicured grounds or paddling a canoe on the pond delivers one from the hassles of the big city. Many Salt Lakers learned to play tennis in the large public complex on the west end of the park, and to swim in the nearby pool. The park is the site of community fairs, horseshoe contests, firework displays, and road races.

Although Liberty Park is the best-known recreational facility of its type in Salt Lake Valley, there are dozens other smaller parks, as well as public golf courses and tennis courts. **Sugarhouse Park**, now a quiet expanse of grass and hills, reveals a colorful chapter of Salt Lake City history. It was formerly the site of the old Utah State Prison, a facility surrounded by 18-foot-high red sandstone walls, which was finally closed down in the 1940s. Labor activist Joe Hill, made famous in a folk-song sung by John Baez, was executed here. So was a convicted murderer named John Deering, who was wired with an electro-cardiograph as a firing squad prepared to execute him. Seemingly unconcerned, his heart beat at the rate of 180 times per minute shortly before he was shot. The heart of a man doing violent exercise seldom beats faster than 120 times a minute. The prison physician said Deering would have died even if no bullet had been fired. A monument at Sugarhouse Park is a reminder of its grim past.

Joggers and bicyclists also enjoy **Memory Grove** and **City Creek Canyon**, located directly behind the state Capitol. The road up the canyon is often closed to automobile traffic, making it an excellent place to walk, run, or ride.

A movement is afoot in Salt Lake Valley to preserve natural areas. The **Parleys Gulch Nature Center**, at the mouth of Parleys Canyon, and the **Dimple Dell Regional Park**, near Sandy in the southeast corner of the valley, have been preserved as such. Planners hope some day to have a trail system in place along the entire length of the Jordan River, which almost cuts the valley in half as it flows from Utah Lake into the Great Salt Lake. Portions of that trail system are already in place. The best part begins at the Utah State Fairgrounds on North Temple and runs for two miles (3.2 km) along the river. We enjoy taking canoe trips from the Raging Waters waterslide complex at 1700 South, past Jordan Park and the International Peace Gardens, through the fairgrounds, to the Northwest Community Center. Despite its situation in the midst of a bustling city, this is a surprisingly scenic and quiet float trip.

The **Raging Waters** complex itself comprising a wave pool and a number of twisting, turning waterslides is one of Salt Lake City's many commercially operated recreation centers. Another is the **49th Street Galleria**, an indoor menagerie consisting of miniature golf courses, batting cages, a bowling alley, and video games center. The **Lagoon** theme park (see pp. 101-104) is located just off I-15 north of Salt Lake City and features many rides, games, and other attractions, as well as another big water slide park.

Utah affords ample opportunities for outdoor recreation. (Photo by Steve Griffin)

■ THE UNIVERSITY OF UTAH

The University of Utah's roots date back to 1850 when the Territorial Legislature established the University of Deseret and placed it under the control of a chancellor and board of 12 regents. A month after the passage of the act, the regents solemnly announced: *PATRONS OF LEARNING: The citizens of the State of Deseret have established a University at Great Salt Lake City. . . . It . . . will teach all nations all useful arts and sciences. . . . instruction by means of lectures or otherwise will be brought to the level of the laboring classes. . . . It is neither arrogant nor extravagant to say this institution is forthwith prepared to teach more living languages classically than any other University on the face of the earth. . . . as to the matter of dead languages, we leave them mostly to the dead. Facilities for acquiring intelligence from every portion of the globe will be more perfectly secured to this institution than to any other of our acquaintance. Correspondence will be kept up with persons in the service of the University, living at London, Edinburg, Paris, Rome, Copenhagen and Calcutta. Whatever is valuable in the laws and usages of nations . . . diversified languages . . . practical mechanism . . . fabrics of governments . . . physical laws . . . will be copiously poured into the lap of this institution.*

These lofty early aspirations were not, however, matched by available facilities or teachers. The home of the first "university" was the parlor of an adobe cabin owned by John Pack. Unfortunately, the $5,000 grant that the Legislature of 1851 appropriated for the school came from an empty treasury. The original venture into higher education lapsed into almost non-existence until 1867. Although the school lacked early success, it remains the oldest university west of the Missouri River.

The revival of the University of Deseret came in 1869 when Dr. John Park took over. He established a department and a training school. Although most of the institution's students were of high school ability, the schools of law, medicine, education, and mining were nonetheless quickly established. The name was changed to the University of Utah in 1892 and, in 1900, the institution was moved to its present site on the east bench of Salt Lake City, overlooking the valley. The university headquarters, located on a U-shaped road students call "The Circle," is called the Park Building, in honor of the man who helped revive the institution.

From those humble beginnings, the University of Utah has grown into a visually appealing architectural mix of traditional and contemporary buildings located in a lush, park-like setting. The campus consists of 1,500 acres and 230 buildings. It boasts a faculty of 3,400 and a student body of 25,000. In addition, the University of Utah Research Park, with 56 tenants in 21 buildings, is located on 320 acres adjacent to the campus. The institution offers majors in 63 undergraduate and 90 graduate subjects, as well as more than 50 teaching majors and minors. Several interdisciplinary degree programs enable students to design their own majors while working closely with faculty advisors.

While some of its recent scientific research has been controversial, the University of Utah continues to enjoy a reputation as one of the finest state-run institutions of higher learning in the country. Edward B. Fiske, the education editor for the *New York Times*, said the school's special academic programs "place the U. in the ranks of the most distinguished colleges."

The university continues to be a leader in the studies of technology, Middle Eastern culture, computer science, artificial limbs and organs, modern dance, genetics, and mining; and the culmination of two major research projects in the 1980s brought it international notoriety. The first artificial heart transplant and the announcement of a cold fusion experiment exemplified what University of Utah President Chase Peterson says brings many "highly promising as well as established scholars to the University for a sense of freedom that allows them to get things done."

The transplant of the Jarvik 7 artificial heart into retired dentist Barney Clark in December of 1982 by a team headed by surgeon William DeVries at the University of Utah Medical Center was the culmination of 15 years of research. Developed by Dr. Robert K. Jarvik, a design engineer who completed medical school at the U. in 1976, the heart consisted of two pumps that replaced Clark's right and left ventricles. The artificial heart was powered by an external air compressor linked to the patient by two hoses. Clark survived for 112 days.

The research project toward an artificial heart began with the establishment of the Division of Artificial Organs by Dr. Willem J. Kolff, a Dutch-born scientist, in 1967. He was appointed professor of surgery, research professor of engineering, and finally director of the Institute of Biomedical Engineering. The critical link for Kolff was the opportunity to join medical research with engineering disciplines.

Although the artificial heart has been used with mixed results and is now utilized primarily as a stop-gap measure for patients until a live transplant becomes available, artificial heart research is on-going at the University. It's possible that one day, tens of thousands of lives will be sustained with permanent totally artificial hearts, and many thousands of patients will lead more productive and gratifying lives with artificial hearing. "Our efforts to make these technologies widely available to the public and to build a large and profitable business are based on technological excellence and the early establishment of a strong position in the marketplace," noted Jarvik.

The second major research announcement to come from the University of Utah also made the front pages of newspapers throughout the world. In March of 1989, Dr. B. Stanley Pons, chairman of the Department of Chemistry at the University of Utah, and Dr. Martin Fleischmann, professor of electrochemistry at the University of Southampton, England, announced their creation of a sustained nuclear fusion reaction at room temperature in a chemistry laboratory at the University of Utah. The experiment used electrochemical techniques to fuse some of the components of heavy water.

Heavy water contains deuterium which is found in sea water. Nuclear fusion offers the promise of providing humanity with a nearly unlimited supply of energy. It creates a minimum of radioactive waste, gives off much more energy, and is

The Jarvik heart.

a virtually unlimited fuel source in the earth's oceans.

Pons called the experiment extremely simple. "Observations of the phenomenon required patient and detailed examination of very small effects," he said. "Once characterized and understood, it was a simple matter to scale the effects up to the levels we have attained."

The idea to attempt the innovative experiment started in the late 1960s when Fleischmann conducted research on the separation of hydrogen and deuterium isotopes. The results were odd, but indicated that he should look further for nuclear fusion reactions. Pons also looked at isotopic separation and remained puzzled as well. The two discussed their findings on a drive through Texas, and later, during a hike up Millcreek Canyon on the outskirts of Salt Lake City.

"Stan and I often talked of doing impossible experiments," Fleischmann said at the time. "We each had a good track record of getting them to work. The stakes were so high with this one we decided we had to try it."

The actual research strategy was concocted in the Pons' family kitchen. It was performed mainly to satisfy scientific curiosity.

"It had a one in a billion chance of working although it made perfectly good scientific sense," said Pons, who worked with Fleischmann for five and a half years without outside funding because "we thought we wouldn't be able to raise any money since the experiment was so farfetched."

The state of Utah invested $5 million in cold fusion shortly after Pons and Fleischmann made their announcement, but that money was soon spent. Both scientists have now left the University of Utah to work in France.

No significant cold fusion research project is now going forward at the University, but it is still spending roughly $200,000 annually in legal fees in an attempt to secure patents on the Pons/Fleischmann work.

The scientific establishment remains profoundly skeptical of cold fusion, but a handful of researchers worldwide still claim startling results.

The University of Utah is not only a place where important research is conducted and where students attend class—it is an educational gathering place for the community, as well. The State Arboretum, the Utah Museum of Natural History, and the Utah Museum of Fine Arts are located on campus. The 15,000-seat Jon M. Huntsman Special Events Center and the 35,000-seat Robert L. Rice Stadium host cultural, artistic, and athletic events throughout the year.

The **Utah Museum of Natural History**, located in the old university library building, houses more than 200 exhibits. These portray ancient Indian life in the

West, explain the geologic forces which shape the earth, and feature Utah wildlife. Mounted skeletons of Jurassic period dinosaurs in combat and lifelike dioramas of animals in natural settings delight the youngsters who venture into the museum. Special events and exhibitions are held at the museum throughout the year. Perhaps the most important of these are educational outreach programs designed to introduce different aspects of the natural world to adults, families, and children. Our sons and daughter have enjoyed Junior Science Academy programs at the museum. The winter lecture series sponsored by the museum brings experts from all over Utah and the United States to address such themes as Wasatch Front geology, the importance of the Colorado Plateau, and ancient Indian culture.

Though small in size, the **Utah Museum of Fine Arts** is a small but fine facility for the visual arts. Among the museum collections are works that range from ancient Egyptian objects and examples of Italian Renaissance painting to European and American art from the seventeenth century to the present. The collections include sculptures from Southeast Asia, screens and prints from Japan, ceramics from China, Navajo textiles, and objects from African, Oceanic, and Pre-Columbian cultures.

When you walk through the well-landscaped grounds of the University of Utah campus, it is difficult not to notice the collection of 8,000 trees. Three hundred varieties of trees were planted as a part of the state arboretum, including collections of hybrid oaks in Sotto Grove, beeches in Chapel Glen, conifers along North Campus Drive, and a California sequoia. Pick up a self-guiding tour map at the Arboretum Office located one block south of the Jon M. Huntsman Center in Building 436. Two additional arboretum collections can be enjoyed at the mouth of Red Butte Canyon east of the university near Fort Douglas. There, the conservatory houses plants from tropical rain forests and deserts of the world, ranging from common plants to rare and endangered species. Enjoy a quiet stroll through the adjacent gardens—a place where the city seems to meet the forest. A meandering stream and waterfalls, quiet ponds, plant collections with accompanying explanatory signs, and rolling lawns add to the experience.

■ ALONG THE EASTERN BENCH

The University of Utah sits on the eastern bench of Salt Lake City, a rise between the urbanized valley and the higher Wasatch Mountains. Some of the city's most interesting attractions are located on the bench.

Historic **Fort Douglas** dominates a site just east of the University of Utah, a position chosen by Colonel Patrick Connor for its commanding views over the defiant Mormon capital—defiant in Washington's view, at any rate. Fort Douglas has been deactivated as a military base and has become a part of the university campus.

Five different examples of military architecture can be viewed at the fort. A museum on the grounds contains exhibits tracing military activities from the Escalante Expedition in 1776 to the present. The original cemetery on the fort's grounds dates back to 1862.

Hogle Zoo, located nearby at the mouth of Emigration Canyon, is the largest and best animal park of its type in the state. It contains over 1,000 animals representing more than 300 species. Each visitor seems to have his or her favorite exhibit. Kids thrill at touching the variety of critters at the petting zoo and at wandering through the recently constructed pioneer fort. Most children eventually con their parents into taking them for a ride on a replica of an 1869 steam train. Our favorite exhibit is a solarium full of exotic plants where tropical birds fly freely. Like many Utah institutions, Hogle Zoo has an aggressive outreach program which extends to more than 20,000 students and adults annually throughout the state. There are few school children in the Salt Lake Valley who haven't enjoyed a lecture from a zoo docent. Our kids will never forget the time the zoo teamed up with the Utah Symphony for a youth concert dedicated to animals that featured a musical piece built around "walk talk," and a classical rendition of "Pop Goes the Weasel." If you plan to be in Salt Lake City during the summer, check out one of the Hogle Zoo's summer educational programs.

For a look back at pioneer times in the Salt Lake Valley, from its 1847 settlement to the coming of the railroad in 1869, spend a few hours roaming through **Pioneer Trail State Park,** located directly north of Hogle Zoo. This park portrays pioneer living as it developed from temporary dugouts to the comforts of substantial adobe homes. A town called Old Deseret has been established here. Original buildings have been moved to the site from all over the state. Allow a guide dressed in pioneer garb to take you on a tour of Brigham Young's Forest Farm House. Our kids are especially fond of the story of how the Mormon leaders' wives and children used silk worms at the farm to produce silk cloth. During the summer months, a variety of living history demonstrations are set up. Blacksmiths, adobe brickmakers, and various craftsmen encourage visitors to ask questions and even to join in the work. Special events are held during holidays.

For a state its size, Utah is home to an unusual number of large and successful international businesses. The Marriott Hotel chain was based here, until it was sold recently. Mrs. Fields Cookies (left) still thrives in Park City. Computer wizard Ray J. Noorda of Novell Inc. poses with some of his software (right). The control room of Utah Power and Light is representative of the valley's many high-tech enterprises.
(Photos by Tim Kelly)

Nearby stands the **This Is The Place Monument**, where visitors can hear the story of the Mormons' coming into the Salt Lake Valley. Sections of the last 35 miles (56 km) of the Mormon Pioneer National Historic Trail from Henefer to the Salt Lake Valley can be viewed.

Wheeler Farm, at 6351 South 900 East, is a place where time stopped at the turn of the century. Most of the activities are free, but a nominal fee is charged for extras like hayrides, storytime, and special classes. Kids especially enjoy joining the farmer on his evening round of chores when they can help him gather eggs and milk cows. For those who like to fish but aren't particularly adept at it, the ponds in the back of the farm are stocked with rainbow trout. Expect to pay by the inch for the fish you catch. For those looking to spend a leisurely afternoon, rowboats can be rented at the ponds. Holidays are celebrated in the old-fashioned way on the farm. At Halloween, for example, the woods surrounding the old house become "haunted" as creatures suddenly appear on the trail. Visitors during the Christmas season are welcomed by the aroma of home-made goodies.

■ THE SALT LAKE STAGE

From the beginning of the pioneer era in Salt Lake City, cultural events played a major role in society. Carl Arrington, writing in a 1977 issue of *New Era* magazine, observed that the Mormons had plenty of drama to provide them with inspiration.

"If we are actors in a drama, as the Bard would have us believe, then certainly Latter-day Saints have produced a script and players as dramatic as there have ever been," wrote Arrington. "The Mormon story is a complete drama with characters, conflicts, action, morality, tragedy, and comedy. Persecutions and hardships, combined with a yearning for that which is ennobling and uplifting, created a strong appreciation for culture and drama among the saints as they sought a place where they could establish a complete social experience centered around the gospel of Jesus Christ."

The first cultural organization in Utah was the Deseret Musical and Dramatic Society, organized in 1849 at the request of Brigham Young. It presented musicals, concerts, and pageants in the Old Bowery Building on Temple Square. The group's initial dramatic performances occurred in 1851 and included the melodramatic comedy, *Robert McCaire*, and the farce, *Dead Shot*.

"Theater continued to flourish," wrote Arrington, "and in the late 1850s a company called the Mechanics Dramatic Association was formed. The name was appropriately titled since all its members were busy giving their days to intensive physical labor and were committed to the fine arts in the evening. . . . In the early theater days, it was common practice to accept goods for the price of a ticket. One night the theater took in 20 bushels of wheat, five of corn, four of potatoes, two of oats, four of salt, plus two hams, one live pig, one wolf skin, one set of children's embroidered undergarments, one keg of applesauce, a dog, and a German silver coffin plate."

In 1862, when the Salt Lake Theatre opened, dramatic productions had become increasingly important to the cultural life of the community. Brigham Young had decided to build a real theater, the only one between the Comstock and the Mississippi at the time. A resident stock company started presenting productions. The company was so successful that, after starting with two performances a week, it was soon playing almost every weeknight. Its attractions were heightened by the traveling stars who stopped between Chicago and San Francisco to present their famous roles with the support of the local company.

That tradition was nourished when Maud May Babcock came to the University of Deseret as a part-time elocution and physical education teacher. When she retired 44 years later, she had founded two departments, a college, a professional theater company, and a university community theater. Her first major production, *Eleusinia*, was presented in 1895 in the Salt Lake Theatre. From 1918 to 1921, the first American professional company at a university, The Varsity Players, presented an ambitious series of plays in the Social Hall. Kingsbury Hall, a large performing hall on the University of Utah campus still used today, opened in 1930, two years after the final program was presented on the stage of the Salt Lake Theatre. When Dr. C. Lowell Lees came to the University of Utah in 1943 to chair the Theater Department, he also brought with him two dreams: to build a replica of the old Salt Lake Theatre and to form a theater company with a nucleus of professional actors. As chairman of the Drama Section of the Utah Centennial Pageant Committee, Dr. Lees brought internationally known actors, choreographers, dancers, singers, and conductors to Utah. He joined with the American National Theatre Association, a New York-based organization founded to decentralize theater, and within one season brought Judith Evelyn, Orson Wells, Jeanette Nolan, and Roddy McDowell to perform at Kingsbury Hall.

Finally, in 1962, the **Pioneer Memorial Theatre** was dedicated on the University of Utah campus, a full century since the dedication of its progenitor, the Salt Lake Theatre. Now, with an annual budget of close to $2 million and a full-time staff of 31, the Pioneer Theatre Company ranks in the top 25 percent of non-profit theaters nationally. Those familiar with the national "regional theater" scene compare the company's work favorably with the best that is being produced by the nation's top theaters. The company operates on a League of Resident Theatres contract with Actors' Equity Association, the same contract as major non-profit theaters in the country like Arena Stage, the Guthrie, Long Wharf, ACT, and Seattle Rep. The company stages seven productions a year, usually two musicals and five plays, as well as a Young Peoples' Theatre season. Actors working in the productions often come from Broadway, off-Broadway, television, and films. Lees Main Stage, named after C. Lowell Lees, seats 1,000 patrons. The large stage, with its 48-foot proscenium opening, is equipped with a state-of-the-art computer lighting system, an excellent sound system, a full "fly loft," and two stage elevators. The downstairs Babcock Theatre, a 200-seat facility, features performances by the University of Utah Theater Department.

While Pioneer Theatre Company stages more traditional and mainstream productions, the **Salt Lake Acting Company,** with an annual operating budget of $800,000, offers lesser known, more contemporary plays, which many might not expect to see in a town the size of Salt Lake City. Located in a small 200-seat theater on Marmalade Hill at 168 West 500 North, the Salt Lake Acting Company supports and develops new works by Utah playwrights, particularly those of national caliber. Patrons might expect to see examples of contemporary theater not available elsewhere in the region, including the works of such major writers as David Mamet, Emily Mann, Sam Shepard, John Patrick Stanley, Christopher Durang, and Wendy Hammond. In 1982, SLAC'S original production of Utah playwright Al Brown's *Back to Back* received the San Francisco Bay Area Theatre Critics' Circle Award for Best Touring Production. The theater isn't afraid to produce plays with controversial themes and hard language, which sometimes challenge traditional conservative Utah values. A popular offering is *Saturday's Voyeur* (the title is a play on words taken from a popular Mormon musical called *Saturday's Warrior*). The play, which is sometimes offered in the summer and is offered during the Christmas season other years, satirizes all aspects of Utah life and is updated yearly. If you plan to attend, call ahead to check dates and be sure to reserve seats well in advance.

Though these are the major professional theater companies in the Salt Lake area, several other smaller groups, including City Rep, the Desert Star Playhouse, and the Hale Center Theatre produce plays on a regular basis.

The Promised Valley Playhouse, a showplace at the turn of the century, has been restored to its former glory by the Mormon Church as a stage for live theater productions and special programs. Other smaller, community theaters also thrive throughout the valley.

One of the more recent, and most popular, additions to the Utah arts scene is the **Utah Opera Company.** Founded in 1978 by Glade Peterson, a Utah native who has performed for the Metropolitan Opera in New York City, this company stages three fully costumed grand operas a year at the Capitol Theatre. It often enlists some of the great stars in American opera for its performances. The Utah Opera Company was one of the first of its size to use English super-titles to allow newcomers to opera to understand the words being sung in foreign operas. Some 70,000 Utah school children a year are introduced to grand opera as the company makes an effort to educate students about the pleasures of opera. Get your tickets well in advance since many operas in Salt Lake City sell out.

Sculptor Karl Momen stands in front of the desert construction site of his controversial "The Metaphor, Tree of Utah." (photo by Tim Kelly)

ROBERT REDFORD'S SUNDANCE INSTITUTE

"The first year," recalls Robert Redford, Sundance Institute's founder and all-around guru, "I couldn't get a loan from the banks. The waiters didn't show up so the owners had to wait on tables. The stablemaster was more interested in the female customers than in the horses, and horses from our stables wandered in confusion all over the canyon. The Sundance Summer Theatre was launched with a misfired rocket that lay fizzling on the stage.

"Vehicles stalled, sewers backed up, we were robbed, and the tree in the Tree Room died. A potential early investor who spoke eloquently about his belief in our concept was hauled away by men in white shirts.

"But we endured."

Sundance Institute did more than endure. Redford's extravagant vision of a combined resort, film workshop, artist colony, and environmental field laboratory in the mountains of Utah has prospered over the years. Recently, as Sundance has had to prune back some of its film-related activities, Utah's nascent environmental movement is looking to it more and more for guidance and inspiration. And the Sundance U.S. Film Festival, held each winter in Park City, has burgeoned into a full-scale entertainment industry phenomenon, attracting product-hungry media buyers from all over the world.

In fact, Sundance's present predicament has everything to do with its success. Redford's dream was always of an intimate, intense group of filmmakers, writers, and producers, working outside the relentlessly commercial purview of Hollywood, a "small colony of the saved," to use the poet Robert Bly's phrase. Provo, which was the Oscar-winning star's home base anyway, was a perfect venue.

The Sundance Institute was born in 1980 under the less-than-ideal conditions Redford described. In the beginning, it had a makeshift, improvisational feel to it, which both spurred artistic innovation and served to separate it from the slick, conformist feel of Hollywood. Sundance was to be a mecca for the rebels, for the independents, for the ones chafing at the restrictive yoke of commercialism. There, films would be talked about as art, and the bottom-line mentality of the box office would be banished.

The idea was to bring novice movie-makers to Utah and cross-polinate them with movie professionals. "The filmmakers' lab brings some of the most talented and successful filmmakers to Sundance to act as resource advisors," says John Genette, the institute's general manager. "It gets you away from the marketplace and the pressures of the marketplace. It could be done in some other remote place. But it takes the leadership of a person with vision."

And that person just happens to live in Utah. So Utah it was; specifically, a down-at-the-heels ski resort in the Wasatch Range east of Salt Lake City. As Redford cajoled funds from contributors or poured in his own money from million-dollar acting fees, the place was transformed. Each year, the institute sifts through some 1,000 film proposals, project ideas, and inchoate dreams to select a baker's dozen (some years more, some years less) as official institute projects. Sundance supports its babies in a variety of ways, from helping punch up a script to making the right connections with a producer.

The intermontane paradise at Sundance attracts movie industry heavy-hitters, desperate to leave behind another smog-filled L.A. summer, and the Redford name can pull its share of rabbits out of the hat, too. Actors Alan Alda and Sam Waterson, directors Oliver (*Platoon*) Stone and Sidney (*Tootsie*) Pollack, screenwriters Ring Lardner and the late Waldo Salt have all been Sundance participants at one time or another.

El Norte is a perfect example of the type of film produced by the innovative process. Nurtured and developed at Sundance, it most definitely is not a mainstream movie. Tracing the painful, arduous journey of a fragmented Hispanic family displaced by an earthquake and emigrating to America, it is socially trenchant, compassionate, and moving. It was extremely well-received by the critics, mildly successful at the ticket office, and is still seen on the art house circuit.

As the concerns and obsessions of Robert Redford change, so does Sundance. Perhaps a bit betrayed by their own success, the institute and the U.S. Film Festival are no longer purely artistic fringe endeavors. They have been co-opted into the heart of Hollywood—where the Sundance Institute now has its main office. Although the festival is still the nation's prestige launching pad for independent films, the success of some of its vehicles—most notably Steven Soderburgh's *sex, lies and videotape* and Whit Stillman's *Metropolitan*, shown at the festival in 1988 and 1989, respectively—have attracted exactly the type of crowd Redford is most uncomfortable with: the slick Hollywood deal-makers. In 1989, he did not even attend the festival. The official reason was that he was on location, but the absence of the institute's prime mover and shaker was a telling sign.

The cancellation of a few aspects of the institute's summer program—the writers' lab, for example—is probably more of an example of necessary retrenchment than any disillusionment on the part of the founder. But Redford is increasingly drawn to environmental concerns, and Sundance has gone along with him. Research projects and ecological studies have now moved to the front of the institute's agenda. Perhaps, in the future, the nation's environmentalists will speak of Sundance in the same reverential tones now used by the country's young filmmakers.

—Gil Reavill

The **Capitol Theatre** at 50 West 200 South serves as the home for Ballet West, Repertory Dance Theatre, Ririe-Woodbury Dance Company, and the Utah Opera Company as well as a venue where touring national theater companies regularly perform. It was built in 1912 to host touring vaudeville shows, but fell into disrepair in the early 1970s when it was used as a huge movie house. When Salt Lake County voters approved the construction of the Symphony Hall in the seventies, they also elected to restore the Capitol Theatre to its former elegance so it could be used as a performing arts center.

■ SALT LAKE MUSIC

There is evidence of musical instruments and singing in pioneer times, but the classical musical tradition formed later. The first performance of Handel's *Messiah* took place in 1875 at the Salt Lake Theatre with a choir of 200 and a "full orchestra" of 45 members, making it the largest group of musicians ever brought together in Utah at that time. The *Messiah* is now performed by the Salt Lake Oratorio Society in the Salt Lake Mormon Tabernacle each Christmas season.

The Salt Lake Symphony Orchestra Association was organized in the late 1800s. Most historians credit George Careless with conducting Utah's first symphony concert on May 17, 1892. Unfortunately, the orchestra disbanded at the end of that year, and it took 10 years for another symphony orchestra to be organized in Salt Lake City. In 1902, 22-year-old Arthur Shepherd put together an orchestra of 32 members. That group disbanded when Shepherd left the state. He would later be a two-time winner of the Society of American Composers' awards for musical compositions. The symphony was revived again in 1912 as the Salt Lake Philharmonic Orchestra by Anton Pederson. Two weeks after the first concert was given in 1914, Pederson died and his son, Arthur Pederson Freber, filled the vacancy. In 1924, the Philharmonic Orchestra was replaced by the Salt Lake Symphony Orchestra, which disbanded after two seasons. The forerunner to the current Utah Symphony was the Utah Works Progress Administration Orchestra, which was formed in 1935.

The **Utah Symphony**'s first season consisted of five concerts performed by 52 part-time musicians in 1940. The orchestra now numbers 85 members, tours internationally, releases acclaimed recordings, and plays year-round, performing more than 250 times annually in Salt Lake City. In in its first seven years under the direction of Hans Heniot and Werner Janssen, however, the Utah Symphony struggled artistically and financially. The most important event in its rise to prominence was the hiring of Maurice Abravanel as musical director in 1947.

"When President Fred Smith and the Utah Symphony board went after a new conductor in 1947," wrote Conrad B. Harrison in his book *Five Thousand Concerts, A Commemorative History of the Utah Symphony,* "they found, by some stroke of good fortune, not only what the orchestra needed at the moment, but just what it was going to need in the continuous battle for its very life as a major symphony organization. Maurice Abravanel had been fighting for music ever since he was a youngster, and he was prepared and equipped for the job, on and off the podium. Ordinarily, an orchestra conductor of such skill and opportunities as this experienced cosmopolite might have chucked the local symphony's financial storms and moved on to milder climes. But he had loyalty, tenacity, and honesty as well as music in his temperament, and he remained to finish the job he had taken on."

Soon after Janssen resigned, the board compiled an impressive list of 40 applicants for the job of musical director. One story concerned the consideration of a brilliant 28-year-old conductor who was in the midst of a three-year whirl at the helm of the New York WPA Symphony. Smith and another symphony board member interviewed the young musician in New York City, but wrote off the prospective candidate as "too young and inexperienced." The prospect's name was Leonard Bernstein.

Still, Abravanel proved to be just the tonic the Utah Symphony needed.

"Abravanel made it clear," wrote Harrison, "that he intended to build the Utah Symphony with Utah musicians and gave the assurance that he would stay on and complete the task he had undertaken. It was not until 32 years later, after giving Utah an internationally acclaimed major symphony, that he retired."

In a typical season, over a half million people enjoy Utah Symphony performances, including over 73,000 children. Audiences have ranged in size from 350 in Duchesne, Utah—about one-third the town's population—to close to 50,000 people who filled the University of Utah's Rice Stadium to hear a July Fourth concert in 1985. In addition to the 19 pairs of concerts performed at Symphony Hall each season, the Utah Symphony holds Pops and Classical summer series at both Symphony Hall and the Deer Valley and Snowbird ski resorts. There is a chamber orchestra series, special holiday concerts, and 65 performances a year in Utah schools. The symphony visits each school district at least once every two years and performs to nearly half of the state's public school enrollment. The orchestra also provides music for Ballet West and Utah Opera Company productions.

Perhaps the crowning moment for Abravanel came when Salt Lake County voters approved the funding for a new Symphony Hall and for the transformation of the old Capitol Theatre into a performing arts center. Though Abravanel retired for health reasons in 1979, the same year Symphony Hall opened, he was the inspiration for what *Time* magazine called "the most impressive of all (concert halls) in the country" in a 1983 article. Finally, after years of playing in the Salt Lake Mormon Tabernacle, the symphony moved into its stunning new home. The $12 million hall measures 160 feet (48 m) in length, 90 feet (27 m) in width, and 55 feet (17 m) in height, with 2,811 seats. Six geometric chandeliers with 18,000 beads of hand-cut crystal imported from Austria and Czechoslovakia grace the interior. The exterior consists of a massive three-story wedge of glass and granite-like brick, enhanced by a 100-foot (30-m) long diagonal fountain. The interior is a dramatic combination of brass, gold leaf, natural oak, and forest-green carpet. Dr. Cyril Harris, who was acoustical designer for the Metropolitan Opera House, Kennedy Center, and the remodeled Avery Fisher Hall in New York's Lincoln Center, was the acoustical consultant.

■ SALT LAKE DANCE

If Abravanel was the guiding force behind classical music in Salt Lake City, then William Christensen was a pioneer in bringing ballet to the western United States. Christensen joined with Salt Lake City arts benefactor Glenn Walker Wallace in 1963 to establish the Utah Civic Ballet. The first fully professional ballet company in the Intermountain West originated in the classrooms of the University of Utah and performed at Kingsbury Hall on campus. The company was renamed **Ballet West** in 1968 to represent the western United States as the region's designated ballet company. Christensen, who served as the company's first artistic director, is recognized as one of the pioneers of American dance and is also noted for establishing the first ballet department at an American university—the University of Utah in 1951. He was the first American to stage full-length versions of *The Nutcracker*, *Coppelia*, and *Cinderella*.

When Christensen retired in 1976, he was replaced by Bruce Marks, an internationally acclaimed dancer and choreographer who had served as co-Artistic Director since 1976. Under Marks' direction, Ballet West received national acclaim for its production of *The Sleeping Beauty* and the re-created Bournoville classic *Abdallah*. "Only a truly classical company, which is what Ballet West has become, could carry this feat off," wrote *New York Times* critic Anna Kisselgoff after watching *Abdallah*. "Ballet West's young dancers bring the ballet back to life on new and valid terms."

Marks was replaced by England's John Hart as Artistic Director in 1985. Hart is a former Principal Dancer, Ballet Master, Assistant Director, and Artistic Administrator of the Royal Ballet of England. He added many new works to the company's repertory. With 40 members, Ballet West has transcended its regional status to become one of America's leading companies.

Classical ballet isn't the only form of dance Utah audiences enjoy. Salt Lake City is also a center for modern dance and boasts of two professional companies—the Repertory Dance Theatre and the Ririe-Woodbury Dance Company—in addition to the Children's Dance Workshop founded by Virginia Tanner.

The **Repertory Dance Theatre**, known locally as RDT, was founded by Kay Clark and Linda Smith in 1966 with a grant from the Rockefeller Foundation. Members of the foundation with a love for modern dance sought a place where a modern dance company could preserve the work of the nation's top choreographers. With Virginia Tanner established as a modern dance instructor at the University of Utah, Salt Lake City was selected, and RDT was born. The 10-member professional company performs a variety of dance forms but does not use its own choreographers. It is one of the few modern dance companies of its size in the world currently operating without a budget deficit. In addition to two annual concert series at the Capitol Theatre in downtown Salt Lake City, RDT performs at the University of Utah and throughout the state. Like most of Utah's major art groups, it brings its specialty to school children and to rural areas. RDT also tours extensively in the United States.

Established in 1964 by University of Utah dance instructors Shirley Ririe and Joan Woodbury, the **Ririe-Woodbury Dance Company** combines performances at the Capitol Theatre with educational and performing tours. The two dancers take particular pride in the pioneering activities that have helped integrate dance and movement into children's curricula throughout the United States.

We can attest to the magic of Shirley Ririe's teaching abilities. As students at the University of Utah in the early 1970s, we enjoyed a class called "The Artist in Each of Us," which was partially taught by Ms. Ririe. She soon had inhibited college students—most with little coordination or feel for modern dance—leaping around a dance studio waving long pieces of sheer cloth in the air and thoroughly enjoying the experience. The company, which employs six full-time professional dancers, is noted for its light shows which combine dance with lights and projections. In addition to performing the works of its co-founders, Ririe-Woodbury has performed works choreographed by dance innovators as diverse as Tandy Beal, Alison Chase, Bill Evans, Murray Louis, and Alwin Nikolais. The company's concert with pop singer Bobby McFerrin of "Don't Worry, Be Happy" fame was a recent Salt Lake City offering. The company has performed throughout the world and in all 50 states, including three seasons in New York City and the Kennedy Center in Washington, D.C.

■ THE MOUNTAINS

The cultural and urbane amenities of the Wasatch Front cities satisfy the demands of an increasingly sophisticated population, but Utahns and visitors still feel an occasional urge to escape into the nearby mountains to ski, hike, picnic, fish, or hunt. Of these mountains, the most compelling is the Wasatch Range.

Stretching from the Idaho border in the north to the southern summit of Mt. Nebo, its highest point at 11,877 feet (3,620-m), the Wasatch Range endows one of the most spectacular urban settings on earth. A first-time visitor to the Salt Lake International Airport marvels at the peaks that seem to dwarf the city's modern skyline. Photographers use the reflection of the mountains in the windows of modern skyscrapers to illustrate the beauty of the contrast between urban and natural worlds. The mountains are dear to Wasatch Front residents because they provide water for the body and peace for the soul.

The Wasatch Mountains have always been a source of life to the Salt Lake Valley, providing the game that drew both the Indian and the early trappers into the area. Mormon pioneers used the water flowing from their snowcapped peaks to drink and to irrigate their crops. The early settlers quarried granite from the mountains to build their fine temple and cut wood from the forests to construct

(opposite) Mt. Timpanogos rises from one of Utah's most popular wilderness areas, just north of Provo.

their homes. Members of Johnston's Army camped at their base and prospected for precious metals in the Wasatch canyons. Today, the mountains bring skiers from all over the world to experience the thrill of skiing on what Utah's car license plates proclaim to be "The Greatest Snow on Earth." Campgrounds, picnic areas, hiking trails, babbling brooks, small lakes, large manmade reservoirs, and seven Congressionally designated wilderness areas provide places both to escape urban life and to renew one's spirit.

A friend who is an avid outdoorsman points out that, on a typical Utah weekend, more cars, campers, and trucks pour out of Salt Lake City and into the mountains than come into the city. Salt Lake City is one of the few urban regions in the United States where residents can reach the trailhead of a 16,000-acre designated wilderness by driving 10 minutes from their home, or leave work at noon and be skiing at a world-class resort by 1 p.m. The numerous hiking trails, picnic areas, streams and lakes filled with trout, cozy little restaurants and country inns provide an easy escape from the hurry of urban life. John Veranth, author of *Hiking the Wasatch*, lists 207 hiking trails in his book without even leaving Salt Lake County!

Hikers can explore seven wilderness areas found along the Front. These include the 30,088-acre **Lone Peak**, 44,350-acre **Mt. Naomi**, 28,000-acre **Mt. Nebo**, 16,000-acre **Mt. Olympus**, 10,750-acre **Mt. Timpanogos**, 13,100-acre **Twin Peaks**, and 23,850-acre **Wellsville Mountains**. These wild places draw an amazing mixture of people—don't be surprised to see grandmothers at the top of mountains and fathers carrying babies.

Each canyon of the Wasatch, and there are many, holds its own secret. Hiking and fishing are the major summer activities in the canyons east of Salt Lake City. The Snowbird Tram in **Little Cottonwood Canyon** whisks visitors to the top of 11,000-foot (3,548-m) Hidden Peak. Some ride it back down, while others choose to walk. When the snow finally leaves the area around mid-July, the high alpine meadows are covered with wildflowers. When we've ridden the tram to the top, we've hiked over to nearby Mt. Baldy, enjoying the clear mountain air and spectacular views. And, speaking of views, the hike to the top of 9,026-foot (2,912-m) **Mt. Olympus**, much of which lies in wilderness, is both difficult and rewarding —as are dozens of other hikes along the Wasatch Front.

The drive to the hamlet of Henefer through **Emigration Canyon** basically follows the route that the Mormons took into the Salt Lake Valley. Later, the Pony

Express trail traversed this canyon. Markers along the way depict the progress the pioneers made as they completed their 1,500-mile (2,400-km) journey.

Heading farther north, a scenic loop drive connects the towns of Farmington and Bountiful. Forest campgrounds and picnic areas are available along the steep, winding road.

■ UTAH COUNTY

In many ways, Utah County and its county seat, **Provo**, serve as the quintessential models for a modern Mormon community. Where a considerable spectrum of influences exist in Salt Lake City and Ogden, the population of Utah County is primarily white, middle class, politically conservative, and of the Mormon faith. The influence and culture of the modern Mormon religion is more keenly felt here than in any other urban area of the world.

Ironically, two *Catholic* priests—Francisco Silvestre Velez de Escalante and Francisco Atanasio Dominguez arriving in September of 1776—are believed to be the first white men to visit Utah Valley. In his journal, Father Escalante noted that the group "ascended a low hill and beheld the lake and extended valley of Nuestra Senora de la Merced de los Timpanogotzis (as they called it) . . . surrounded by the peaks of the Sierra." Escalante noted that the river (later named the Provo) running through the valley watered plains sufficient to support, if irrigated, "two and even three large villages."

Provo is named after Etienne Provot, a young French-Canadian who explored the valley with a group of trappers in 1825. Though the Mormon pioneers explored Utah Valley three days after reaching the Salt Lake Valley, the first settlers didn't arrive until March of 1849, when John S. Higbee brought 30 families to establish a Mormon colony. As the story is told, the white men were greeted by members of the Ute Indian tribe. After promising not to drive the native Americans from their land, the Mormons constructed a fort, plowed 225 acres of land, and planted rye, wheat, and corn.

When **Brigham Young University** was founded (as Brigham Young Academy) in 1875 with the goal of turning its first 29 students into teachers, few could have imagined its modern scope of influence. Yet today, the Provo-based institution and its current enrollment of 27,000 students play a dominant role not only in Utah

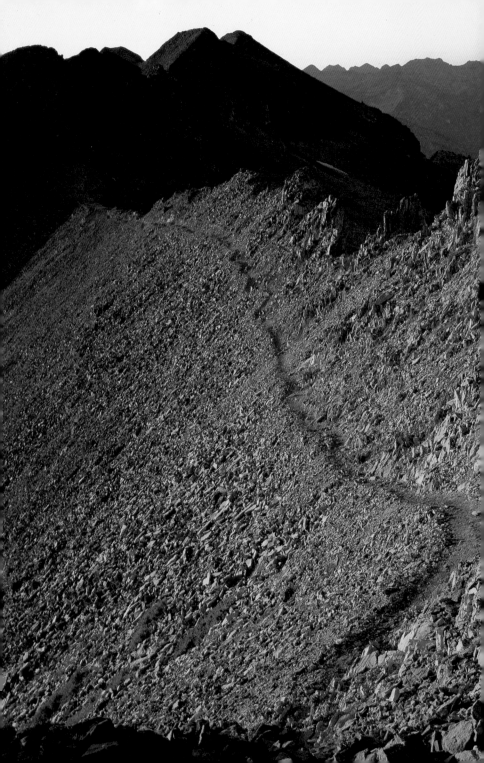

County, but around the country. It is no accident that the bumper stickers on the cars of a few of BYU's thousands of athletic fans declare the school to be "*The* University of Utah," a dig at the Provo school's arch rival to the north.

Brigham Young set the tone for the university he founded when, in 1876, he declared to students: "I want you to remember that you ought not to teach even the alphabet or the multiplication tables without the spirit of God." Dr. Jeffrey R. Holland, a modern BYU president, put things another way. "We want our students value-laden and moral," he said. "We want them to be a veritable rod of iron in what is too often a dark and misty ethical void. . . . There's a spiritual power here that goes out into the world. It is a result of our determination to place academic excellence in the context of committed religious faith and wholesome, broad development of the total person. It comes from our insistence on linking Virtue with Truth."

There are few gray areas in BYU's honor code, which students entering the university agree to obey. This includes following Mormon Church rules that encourage pride in maintaining a clean, strong, healthy body as a temple for the intellect and the spirit. The school's code of honor includes such commitments as being honest, observing university regulations, following the dress and grooming standards, refraining from sexual relations outside of marriage, avoiding drug abuse, and abstaining from alcohol, tobacco, tea, and coffee. Dress codes require students to be "modest, neat and clean in their grooming. Shorts, swimming suits, gym clothes and other extremely casual or grubby attire are not considered acceptable wear on campus. Beards are not permitted."

The beauty of the BYU campus setting is in keeping with the neatness of the students. The 646-acre campus, with more than 450 mostly modern buildings, is cradled between the lofty Wasatch Mountain peaks and the placid waters of Utah Lake. Facilities include an 837-acre farm, a motion picture studio, a 462-acre preserve in southern Utah, a 6,200-acre ranch in southern Idaho, radio and television stations, and a mountaintop observatory. Because Mormon leaders feel healthy bodies lead to healthy minds, some of the finest physical education and athletic facilities found on any campus in the world can be seen scattered through a campus dominated by grass and wide walkways.

Game day—be it basketball, football, track and field, or baseball—is a major event at BYU. The university's 65,000-seat football stadium fills for fall events or the fantastic July 4th Freedom Festival. The school used its pass-oriented offense to win the national football championship in 1984 and is regularly ranked among the

(previous pages) A crestline trail affords spectacular views of the Wasatch Range from Mt. Timpanogos.

top 20 college teams in the United States. The 23,000-seat Marriott Center serves as the home for the BYU basketball team, a place for cultural events, and a setting for the regular Sunday meetings of students with Mormon church spiritual leaders. The modern track, one of the finest in the United States, is host to many major track and field events. The spring BYU Invitational, which dates back to 1915, brings high school athletes from all over the Intermountain West to compete.

Academically, BYU offers 150 undergraduate subject areas in 12 schools and colleges, along with a continuing education program. Master's degrees are available in more than 150 disciplines through 57 graduate departments. Doctoral degrees are awarded in 55 subjects. In addition, researchers at BYU tackle such challenges as alleviating the world's food shortage through more efficient agriculture, developing synthetic antitumor agents in the fight against cancer, finding low-pollutant energy alternatives, and breaking language barriers with computer-assisted translation. The school's language program, which assists in training the thousands of young Mormon men and women who volunteer to serve on two-year missions all over the world for their church, teaches 45 languages and boasts one of the largest enrollments in Korean and Japanese of any American university. Live-in language experience is available in 16 different language houses, and Spanish- and French-language television is broadcast on campus cable 24 hours a day.

BYU also serves as a cultural center for much of the Wasatch Front. Its dozen performing groups, including International and American Folk Dance ensembles, perform throughout the world. Theater-goers enjoy seeing live plays and musicals on campus.

Visitors to BYU can browse through four museums. The **Monte L. Bean Life Science Museum** exhibits a wide array of natural history scenes, mounted animals, insects, and plants, and also stores scientific collections. Artifacts of ancient Indian cultures from the United States, Central America, and South America can be seen at the **Museum of Peoples and Cultures** in Allen Hall. A major addition to the Harris Fine Arts Center, the **Museum of Fine Arts**, is scheduled to open in the early 1990s. It will safeguard a collection of more than 12,000 works by Rembrandt, Durer, and Daumier. The **Earth Sciences Museum** displays several full and partial dinosaur skeletons. Visitors can watch as paleotologists work on BYU's nearly 100 tons of fossils.

Though BYU dominates the list of places to see in the urbanized part of Utah County, there are other cultural and recreational attractions to enjoy.

Provo's **McCurdy Historical Doll Museum** features a collection of more than 3,000 dolls. Changing monthly exhibits spotlight dolls in such themes as folk dress of the world, dramatic episodes in history, provincial dress of Spain, or first ladies of the United States, both delighting and educating visitors. A doll shop and doll repair facility add a finishing touch to the museum.

The **Pioneer Memorial Museum**, also located in Provo, contains an extensive display of pioneer and Indian relics. The highlight of a trip here is seeing the Pioneer Cabin, a replica of an early Utah home furnished with rustic furniture. The **Springville Museum of Art**, just south of Provo, is among the finest in the state. If you happen to be in Utah during April, try to find time to see the museum's national art exhibit.

Utah Lake, the state's largest natural freshwater lake, dominates the western portion of Utah County. Due to the murkiness of the water, the lake receives mixed reviews from boaters and fishermen. Three marinas—including a state park west of Provo, a marina west of Lindon, and another south of American Fork—provide places to launch boats, fish, or camp. A state park also has a beautiful ice skating rink.

North of Provo, **American Fork** and **Provo canyons** provide many more recreational possibilities. The two canyons are connected by a narrow, winding road called the **Alpine Loop**. Take time to hike one of the trails found along the way, or to stop at a turnout and enjoy the view of the canyon. Our family likes to ski and fish at Tibble Fork Reservoir in the North Fork of American Fork Canyon. The Uinta National Forest operates a number of picnic areas and campgrounds in the area. Another nice side trip off the Alpine Loop will take you to **Cascade Springs**, a natural area where flowing water appears and then disappears out of the side of a mountain. Interpretive signs along a boardwalk trail explain the flora and fauna of the area. Kids like to look at the brown trout swimming in the clear water. The Provo River, flowing through Provo Canyon, is one of the top wild brown trout fisheries in the state. Since much of the stretch is governed by special fishing regulations, knowledge of the rules is a must. Another interesting attraction in Provo Canyon is **Bridal Veil Falls**, which drop 607 feet (184 m) in two cascades. A sky tram, climbing 1,228 feet (372 m) in a single 1,753-foot span (531 m), is one of the steeper of the world's tram lines. The view from the top is stupendous.

The most famous attraction of American Fork Canyon probably is **Timpanogos Cave National Monument**. The steep, 1.5-mile (2.4-km) hike from the visitor

Prickly pear cactus blooms along the shoreline of the Great Salt Lake in late spring.

center at the bottom of the canyon to the entrance of the cave entails an elevation gain of 1,065 feet (323 m), and is a summer tradition for many Utah families. The cave itself rewards those who make the hike on a summer day, both with its 43-degree temperature and the many limestone formations found inside. These include flowstone formations in subtle shades of green, yellow, red, and white. Martin Hansen discovered the first of three separate caves (tunnels now connect all the caverns) in 1887 while tracking a mountain lion. The other two weren't discovered until 1921 and 1922. The cave received both its lighting and national monument status shortly thereafter. Though a normal cave tour takes between 45 minutes and an hour to complete, plan three to four hours both for the hike and the cave tour. On busy weekends, it's an excellent idea to arrive at the visitor center early to purchase your tickets. No reservations are taken and tours do sell out. If you are in the mood for a little more adventure, try taking the special candlelight, flashlight, and historic tours offered occasionally through the summer. Call ahead to learn more about these tours.

■ SOUTH OF PROVO

The mountains behind Provo are particularly beautiful. At the top of **Payson Canyon**, to the south of the city, are a series of little lakes stocked with trout. Fine Uinta National Forest campgrounds are at hand, some with facilities for people who bring horses. A paved nature trail, two small beaches, and some grassy day-use areas are found at the edge of Payson Lake.

If you have time, drive the entire length of the **Nebo Loop**, which rambles from Payson around the east side of magnificent Mt. Nebo, passing what looks like a miniature Bryce Canyon along the way, and ends near the town of Nephi on the southern boundary of the Wasatch Front.

With the exception of the comparatively modern Snow Junior College in Ephraim and a few new subdivisions, the towns along the northern portion of Highway 89 seem largely unchanged from pioneer times. These quiet farming communities are perhaps best described as the Utah equivalent of Garrison Keillor's Lake Woebegon.

One well-known figure in part of the state is a retired basketball coach/philosopher/grocery store owner named Wilbur Braithwaite. Braithwaite coached at

Manti High School for over 30 years, and though he won but a single state championship, his emphasis on old-fashioned sportsmanship and his love for the pure, amateur ideals of high school athletics influenced countless students and peers throughout the nation. He exchanged ideas and letters with well-known college coaches like UCLA's John Wooden and Indiana's Bobby Knight, and mailed poetry and letters to friends, former students, and newspaper writers all over the world. Braithwaite's soft-spoken commitment to youth has been acknowledged. He was elected to the National High School Hall of Fame.

Wilbur also took the time to operate the Manti Grocery where he started working at age 10 as a delivery boy, packing bags of flour, sugar, and produce to nearly every household in town. By the 1980s, Wilbur's bag boys only delivered to the elderly and the home-bound, so the rest of the town's 2,080 residents turned Manti Grocery into something of a gathering place.

Although Braithwaite's old Manti Grocery store was recently torn down and replaced with a modern supermarket, the town's Main Street has retained much of its charm. It resembles something out of the fictional town of Mayberry of Andy Griffith Show fame. The quiet town does come alive in mid-July each year when thousands of people come from all over the United States to watch the highly dramatic and spectacular Mormon Miracle Pageant on the grounds of the Manti Temple.

The center of **Manti** and, in fact, all of Sanpete County, is the stately **Mormon Temple,** which sits on the top of a hill at the north end of town. Brigham Young dedicated the site just three months before his death in 1877. It took workers 11 years to complete the magnificent structure. The highlight of the Sanpete County tourist season comes in July when church leaders, using the same story from the *Book of Mormon,* perform the Mormon Miracle Pageant.

For year-round recreation, locals and a few savvy out-of-state visitors venture east into the **Manti-La Sal National Forest.** Small canyons east of Ephraim, Manti, Fairview, and Mayfield lead to tiny fishing lakes, U.S. Forest Service campgrounds, and some fine nordic skiing and snowmobiling. **Palisade State Park,** located in the lower part of Manti Canyon on the edge of the forest, provides perhaps the nicest public camping, with fishing, swimming on a pretty beach, and golf on the adjacent nine-hole golf course. Owners of four-wheel-drive vehicles—and the brave drivers of two-wheel drive vehicles with high clearance—enjoy negotiating the 150-mile (240 km) **Skyline Drive,** on the top of the Manti Range, in summer and fall. The autumn leaf displays make this drive appealing.

■ OGDEN

Though Mormon pioneers settled Ogden, Utah's third largest city is named after a trapper. It possesses an exciting history shaped by the 1869 coming of the transcontinental railroad, and some awfully colorful characters.

It seems somehow appropriate that Ogden honors the memory of trapper Peter Skene Ogden, because the mountain men were the first non-Indian residents in the area. The current site of the city, built on the deltas of the Ogden and Weber rivers, served as a winter rendezvous site for six or seven years in the 1820s. A particularly memorable gathering took place in the summer of 1826, when General William H. Ashley arrived from St. Louis with a hundred well-laden pack animals. "It may well be supposed that the arrival of such a vast amount of luxuries from the East did not pass off without a general celebration," noted Jim Beckwourth, one of the mountain men. "Mirth, songs, dancing, shouting, trading, running, jumping, singing, racing, target shooting, yarns, frolic, with all sorts of extravagances that white men or Indians could invent, were freely indulged in. The unpacking of the medicine water contributed not a little to the heightening of our festivities."

Miles Goodyear became the first pioneer to settle in the Ogden Valley in 1841. The **Goodyear cabin**, oldest known dwelling constructed by a non-Indian in Utah, still stands at 2141 Grant Avenue. Goodyear moved out when the Mormons bought his property. Brigham Young sent a group of 100 families to settle the area in 1849. The community suffered through floods, drought, early frosts, insects, cholera, and Indian attacks. They supplemented their harvests with thistles and other wild plants. The sego lily, Utah's state flower, helped to save many pioneers from starvation.

The arrival of the transcontinental railroad in 1869 changed the character of the town and also created friction with Mormons who disapproved of the saloons and gambling halls that began to spring up.

Those animosities slowly dwindled as Ogden became an important railroad, manufacturing, milling, canning, livestock, and agricultural center. The increasing importance of nearby Hill Air Force Base as an employer helped the city continue to grow well into the 1980s. Established in 1939, the base occupies 6,600 acres just south of Ogden, and employs more than 20,000 people. Airplane buffs might want to stop at the **Hill Air Force Base Museum** and examine the thousands of aviation artifacts and numerous old airplanes.

Another important event in the development of modern Ogden came on January 7, 1889, when 98 students gathered at the old Second LDS Ward meeting house on the corner of Grant and 26th streets for the first day of class at the Weber State Academy. In those lean times, school founders mortgaged their own homes to ensure that classes could be held. The school became Weber Academy in 1908 and broke into the college ranks in 1916 when two years of college work were added to the regular four-year high school curriculum. The name was changed again in 1918 to Weber Normal College and again in 1923 to Weber College, when the high school department was discontinued. The LDS Church transferred title of the college to Utah in 1933. Shortly after the college was moved from downtown to its present site in 1954, Weber State College became a four-year institution. The first senior class graduated in 1964 on the 75th anniversary of the school's founding. Now, 13,000 attend **Weber State University;** a modern institution offering undergraduate degrees in 98 fields of study. With its spacious Dee Events Center, Museum of Natural Science, Collett Art Gallery, Val A. Browning Center for the Performing Arts, and the Layton P. Ott Planetarium, all found on campus, Weber State serves as a center for culture in Ogden.

John Browning, the foremost American inventor of firearms (building his first gun at the age of thirteen), helped shape the character of Ogden. Visitors to the city can see his collection of guns and learn about his life by visiting the **Union Station Museum** at 25th and Wall Avenue. Built inside the old railroad depot, the museum houses an auto collection and traces the history of the railroad. A parkway along the Ogden River includes a rose garden, dinosaur park for children, and an outdoor convention center. Parks line the river as it winds its way through the middle of town. Bicyclists, hikers, and joggers enjoy a trail system while anglers catch wild brown and planted rainbow trout.

Fishing in the Weber and Ogden rivers can be excellent. Pine View Reservoir in **Ogden Canyon** is extremely popular with local boaters. The beaches are an ideal place to cool off when the temperature climbs in the valley.

One final note about Ogden. Don't be surprised if **Ben Lomond Peak**, which dominates the view to the east of the city, looks familiar. It served as the inspiration for the Paramount Pictures logo.

North of Ogden stands the venerable town of Brigham City. Settled in 1851, this town of 20,000 people was originally named Box Elder Creek, but was later renamed to honor Mormon leader Brigham Young. Historic displays at the

Brigham City Museum and Gallery show how residents lived in the nineteenth century. We like to visit the **Crystal Hot Springs resort** in neighboring Honeyville to soak in the naturally heated outdoor pools after a day of downhill or cross-country skiing in the nearby mountains. During harvest time, Wasatch Front residents visit the fruit and vegetable stands located along old US Route 89 between Ogden and Brigham City, near the town of Willard. **Fruit Way**, as it is called, is a place where local farmers sell apples, apricots, peaches, pears, squash, corn, and pumpkins as they come into season.

■ CACHE COUNTY

The Wellsville Mountains separate Cache Valley from Brigham City to the west. Cache Valley takes its name from the beaver trappers, who liked to cache their pelts here in the early 1820s.

Some may travel to **Logan**, in the heart of Cache Valley, to attend a summer professional theater performance at the old Lyric Theater. Others might marvel at the beauty of Logan Peak, the 9,713-foot (3,133-m) summit rising above the picturesque Mormon Temple.

We enjoy coming to Logan and Cache Valley because of the cheese.

Cheese? The dairy industry is one of the major employers in this part of Utah, and some of the best cheese to be found is produced here. We like to tour the **Cache Valley Cheese Plant** in the tiny town of Amalga north of Logan and treat ourselves to samples of different kinds of dairy products. Or, we've been known to go out of our way to visit the **Gosner Factory** or the Mountain Farms processing plant in Logan so we can take home boxes full of discounted cheeses for cooking or munching.

It is not surprising that the agricultural industry still plays a key role in Logan's economy. **Utah State University**, a land grant institution established in 1888, is one of the leading agricultural research institutions in the United States! As a land grant school, Utah State supports basic and applied research. The school ranks 52 among public universities and colleges receiving contract and grant funds from the U.S. Government. With an enrollment of around 14,000 students, the school consists of 100 buildings located on 400 acres, with an additional 7,000 acres used for agricultural and other research. Colleges include agriculture, business, education, engineering, family life, natural resources, humanities, social sciences, arts, and science. The university influences Beehive State life because of its Extension Service, which administers classes and gives advice to farmers and homemakers at locations throughout Utah. Old Main Hill, where construction started on Utah State's historic administration building in 1889, was planned by the same landscape architects who laid out New York's Central Park.

More important to visitors, Utah State University contributes to the culture of the Beehive State by way of a variety of museums and performing arts centers. The **Daryl Chase Fine Arts Center** houses a theater and concert hall. The **Nora Eccles Harrison Museum of Art**, designed by the internationally acclaimed architect Edward Larabee Barnes, exhibits a fine collection of twentieth-century American art, examples of native American art, and fine ceramics.

The **Logan Mormon Temple**, designed by Truman O. Angell, dominates the skyline of downtown Logan. Completed in 1885 after Brigham Young selected the site in 1877, the limestone temple found on beautifully manicured grounds ranks with the Salt Lake, Manti, and St. George temples for its striking appearance.

No Utah event celebrates the heritage of the American West and the trappers better than Logan's eight-day **Festival of the American West**. Some 50,000 people attend this event which traditionally opens the last Friday of July and continues through the first week of August. The festival gives visitors a chance to pan for gold, visit a military camp, see a Wild West show in a saloon, purchase Indian crafts, and get a feeling for what it was like to live in a mountain man camp. A pageant featuring dramatic action combined with music and dance helps bring to life the drama of the settling of the American West.

The Cache Valley Cheese Plant at Amalga. (Photo by Tim Kelly)

The **Jensen Living Historical Farm,** located six miles (9 km) southwest of Logan on US Route 91, is a different kind of museum. It is used as a laboratory in outdoor museum studies and living history for students who may go on to work as interpreters in state or national parks throughout the country. Graduate students operate the farm while completing master's degrees in history or American studies. Activity at the living history farm mirrors rural life circa 1917. Workers use farm equipment and techniques from that era. Kids especially enjoy helping workers cut, bind, and stack wheat and barley. Threshing time usually takes place the first week of August, when farmers use a steam-engine tractor. Depending on the time

Waterfall, Deep Creek Mountains.

of year, visitors can watch historic plowing demonstrations, sheep-shearing, the thinning of sugar beets, a traditional wedding, fruit and vegetable canning, and cider pressing.

South of Logan, **Blacksmith Fork Canyon** strikes due east of Hyrum. It is one of our favorite canyons. Ducks and geese can be seen in the river and big game is common throughout the canyon. On one winter drive, a white weasel scampered across the road. At the end of the road sprawls the **Hardware Ranch,** an elk preserve owned and operated by the Utah Division of Wildlife Resource. Workers at the site feed up to 700 elk every winter to prevent the animals from either starving or doing damage to farmers' lands in the valley below. Many families drive up to see the elk in winter when sleighs pulled by Clydesdale horses bring visitors right up next to the hulking beasts.

From Logan, you can also drive up **Logan Canyon** to marvel at the view of **Bear Lake** from the summit. Straddling the Utah-Idaho line at the extreme north end of the state, Bear Lake supports a state park and several private campgrounds and recreation areas. The lake contains four distinct kinds of fish thought to be the descendents of species found in ancient Lake Bonneville: the Bonneville cisco, Bear Lake whitefish, Bonneville whitefish, and Bear Lake sculpin. Most fishermen, however, would rather catch the larger lake trout and Bear Lake cutthroat. In the summer, power boaters and sailboaters take over the lake. If you're in the Bear Lake area in July or August, stop at one of the little drive-in restaurants in Garden City to enjoy a fresh raspberry malt or sundae. The area is famous for its crops of big berries. Many Salt Lakers make a special trip up to Bear Lake to pick or purchase raspberries for jams, jellies, and just munching.

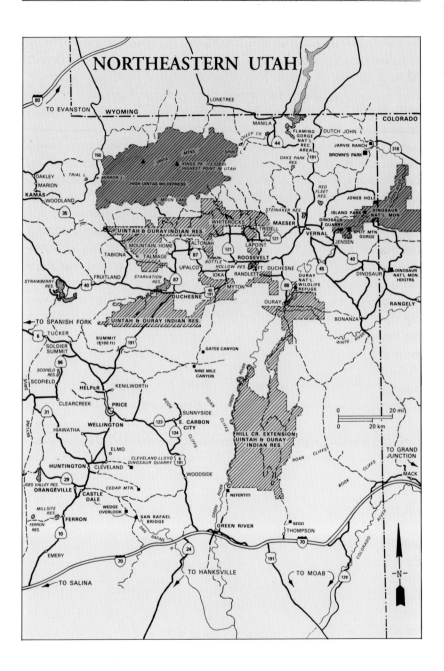

NORTHEASTERN UTAH

NORTHEASTERN UTAH
MOUNTAINS AND DINOSAURS

THE WIND ROARED FIERCELY THROUGH THE PINE TREES above our cheap pup tent, bringing lightning, thunder, and rain. We huddled next to one another, for warmth and to keep from brushing against the side of the tent. Doing so would have brought a downpour of water on our heads. Eight miles (13 km) from our automobile, we had no other choice but to hunker down for a long, frightful night. We had, of course, been seeking a wilderness experience, but this wasn't exactly what we had in mind.

We had come to climb 13,528-foot (4,099-m) King's Peak, Utah's highest. Our attempted ascent earlier that day had failed a few feet from the summit when descending clouds turned the boulders slippery and clammy, and the frigid rain drenched us.

Now, as a storm raged around us, a small rivulet of water slowly started trickling through the middle of the tent. By the time it was light, we were soaked. So was the firewood. Fortunately, a Peruvian sheepherder who had set up camp over the next hill spotted us and, in broken English, invited us to share a cup of hot chocolate and a cake he had baked the evening before. It was the kind of gesture strangers make to one another in such situations.

We packed our backpacks and began making our way down the muddy trail, certain that the adventures were over— until we noticed moose tracks in the mud. Fresh moose tracks. It wasn't long before we spotted a majestic bull browsing in a meadow about 40 yards (36 m) away. Confident we'd seen the last of the moose, we sauntered down the trail, only to be confronted by a cow and her calf. Mother moose wasn't pleased to have strangers around, and we quickly scrambled up a side hill, giving the huge animal and her baby the right-of-way.

When people ask what there is to do in northeastern Utah, we think back to trips like this one and know that anything is possible. We've paddled canoes down the remote White River in the springtime, watching geese and goslings scramble for cover. We've been drenched by white-water rapids when rafting down the Green River through Dinosaur National Monument's Split Mountain. We've spent a day bird-watching at the Ouray National Wildlife Refuge, and basked in the sun at remote Antelope Flat beach in the Flaming Gorge National Recreation Area.

The Uinta Mountains, the only major range in the lower 48 states which runs east and west, dominate northeastern Utah. Visitors can escape to rocky peaks, grassy alpine meadows, and thick, lodgepole forests in the 460,000-acre High Uintas Wilderness Area; it's Utah's largest designated wilderness, and the 17th biggest in the United States. Four of Utah's larger rivers—the Bear, Weber, Provo, and Duchesne—spring from 20 drainages and a thousand-odd lakes in the range. Small towns and remote highways surround the Uintas, providing a touch of comfort amidst the beauty of the outdoors and a place to enjoy the Western charms of rural America.

■ THE HIGH UINTAS

The Uintas look much the same today as they did in the days of the early pioneers. A passage from the book *Utah: A Guide to the State*, written in 1940 as part of Utah Writers Project under the Federal Works Projects Administration, tells part of their story:

"Wandering prospectors, cowboys and sheepherders penetrated the forests and climbed the peaks, leaving only burnt sticks and tin cans to mark their passing. A Swedish prospector was working with his partner in the Rock Creek country. The Swede felt that he had found what he always wanted—gold near running water, lakes, trees, flowers, and a fishing stream right in camp, but his partner yearned for the fleshpots of the mining camps. After many heated quarrels, the partnership was broken up in a fierce fight. The winner—the peace-loving Swede—sucked his bruised knuckles and yelled after his ex-partner: 'Yah, now run qvick to Park City vit its hussies and saloons. Anyhow! You are yust a snoose-chewing, coffee-grinding, visky-drinking, ski-yumping, fisk-eating yackass, anyhow!' Homesteading pioneers preferred better land in lower valleys, irrigable with water from these mountains. Some logging was done, but the roads were too rough and the distance to the large centers too far to make it profitable. All factors seemed to conspire to leave the High Uintas a primitive area. . . ."

The Uintas remain wild and undeveloped. Visitors searching for nightlife, ski lifts, and fine hotels can find them if they drive out of the Uinta Basin to Park City on the eastern side of the Wasatch Front. Though a few rustic alpine lodges on the edge of the wilderness area (like Moon Lake, Defas Dude Ranch, or Spirit

Northern Utah's mountains are among the most rugged and wild in the West.

Lake) supply bedding and shelter, the Uintas are really for hikers, anglers, campers, and hunters. One doesn't need to backpack to enjoy the Uintas, however. The wilderness is surrounded by developed U.S. Forest Service campgrounds, which are easily accessible by car.

The best known and most popular of roads to the Uintas is State Highway 150, known to locals as the **Mirror Lake Highway**. The road connects the town of Kamas, Utah, with Evanston, Wyoming. Closed by snow from late October until mid-June in most years, the highway climbs from 6,500 feet (1,970 m) at Kamas to the 10,678-foot (3,236-m) Bald Mountain Pass, and leads to dozens of developed campsites. Some of the campgrounds are located near lakes regularly stocked with rainbow trout by the Division of Wildlife Resources. Trails off both sides of Mirror Lake Highway lead to popular backpacking areas. Most hikers are drawn by the wilderness designation on the east side of the road, but the west side (though not a congressionally designated wilderness) possesses many of the same qualities without the crowds. Wise backpackers check with rangers at the Kamas Ranger Station or the Mirror Lake Guard Station to find the least visited lakes and routes.

Mirror Lake at dawn in the High Uintas Wilderness Area.

Most Wasatch Front families seem to have a favorite lake or campground situated along the Mirror Lake Highway, and many make it a tradition to camp there at least once a summer. One of the largest campgrounds surrounds **Mirror Lake**, located only 80 miles (130 km) from the heart of Salt Lake City. The lodge on the lake burned down a few years ago, but the lake remains popular.

Campers willing to drive slightly farther can discover less crowded conditions at North Slope sites like Bridger Lake, China Meadows, and Hoop Lake. Located just south of Mountain View, Wyoming, these quiet places are tucked under some of the highest peaks in the range. Fishing for trout along the creek that flows through **China Meadows**, or just lying in the tall grass, can be a fine alternative to battling the crowds at better-known places.

The same can be said for the camping areas at **Browne** and **Sheep Creek lakes**, on the eastern edge of the Uintas, located on dirt roads leading west from the Flaming Gorge National Recreation Area. Streams flowing from these small alpine lakes are teeming with cutthroat trout. Those willing to take a hike from **Spirit Lake** into the nearby wilderness area can be rewarded with excellent fishing.

We've spent many pleasant vacations camped near the **Moon Lake Lodge** on the South Slope of the Uintas in a developed U.S. Forest Service campground. As youngsters, we'd rise earlier than our parents and head for the stream flowing into Moon Lake to catch whitefish and trout for breakfast. We'd beg our parents to rent horses for an hour so we could ride into the forest or we'd paddle a canoe along the shoreline. Similar experiences were available at Defas Dude Ranch on the north fork of the Duchesne River. We would fish in Rock Creek or the Duchesne or Uinta rivers after our fathers had finished deer hunting. We enjoyed catching fish much more than "bushwhacking" through the aspens trying to scare a big buck into a hunter with a rifle.

The Uintas are one of Utah's premier fishing regions. Anglers tell stories of walking to a nondescript, unnamed alpine lake and catching hungry trout on each cast. The simple technique of using a fly that imitates a mosquito, a plastic bubble for weight, and a traditional spinning rod works well here. Anglers soon get wise to the fact there are many lakes in each drainage. If one lake isn't producing, hiking 100 yards (30 m) to the next can often change a fisherman's luck in a matter of seconds.

The Division of Wildlife Resources manages 650 of these lakes, most of which contain either cutthroat or brook trout planted by airplane. That agency sells a series of 10 booklets called *Lakes of the High Uintas* ($1 each), which give detailed descriptions of lakes, types of fish stocked, trail access, and camping. Each book covers a different drainage. They are available from the Salt Lake and Vernal offices of the Division of Wildlife Resources, or by writing the Division of Wildlife Resources. (See "PRACTICAL INFORMATION.")

"We always suggest going into an area with more than one lake," says Glenn Davis, a fisheries biologist with the Division of Wildlife Resources. "That gives you some alternatives. The lakes closest to the highway get fished heavily. The Provo River drainage gets hit particularly hard. On the North Slope, there is high use on Henry's Fork (the trailhead to King's Peak) and Red Castle." Davis generally recommends fishing the east end of the Uintas where use is lighter.

Hikers seeking information on backpacking in the Uintas will find plenty of resources. Topographical and hiking maps of the areas can be obtained from the Wasatch National Forest headquarters in Salt Lake City, or the Ashley National Forest headquarters in Vernal. U.S. Forest Service district offices can be found along the roads into the mountains near Flaming Gorge, Vernal, Roosevelt, Duchesne, and Kamas in Utah, as well as Evanston and Mountain View in Wyoming. Bait shops and fishing guides sell other maps. A 1974 publication written by Mel Davis, *High Uintas Trails*, gives information on trailheads and lengths of hikes.

Exploring the High Uintas Wilderness Area in the winter is difficult, if not impossible. Poor access, heavy snow, and extreme cold discourage visitation. The Mirror Lake Highway is cleared to a snowmobile trailhead near Soapstone Basin and groomed on a regular basis by the Division of Parks and Recreation (see "Greatest Snow on Earth" chapter).

■ RESERVOIR RECREATION

Since Utah is one of the most arid states in the country, Wasatch Front residents rely on storage reservoirs to supply much of their water needs. One of the most complicated and expensive components of this water supply system is the Central Utah Project, a huge water-capture and delivery project conceived in 1956 to bring water from the eastern part of the Uinta Basin to the Wasatch Front. The large reservoirs of northeastern Utah, which provide drinking and irrigation water, also possess great recreational value for boaters, fishermen, and campers.

Strawberry Reservoir, for example, is one of the premier trout fisheries of the Western United States. The huge reservoir, located 23 miles (37 km) southeast of

Heber City near US Route 40, was originally built in 1906 as one of the nation's first reclamation reservoirs. It was expanded to 17,000 acres with the completion of the Soldier Creek Dam in 1973 and the joining with Soldier Creek Reservoir a few years later. Three immense U.S. Forest Service campgrounds give the thousands of fishermen who flock to Strawberry a place to spend the night. We've spent many a summer afternoon fishing for the large cutthroat trout that have made this place a popular angling spot for generations of Utahns.

Deer Creek Reservoir, located just west of Heber City, is also popular with anglers seeking trout, bass, perch, and walleye. Sailboarders and sailboaters have discovered the afternoon wind, which blows regularly at the reservoir. The relatively low elevation also draws waterskiers and swimmers. Two private marinas and a state park cater to the needs of all.

Located near the town of Duchesne, **Starvation Reservoir** is a quiet alternative for Wasatch Front boaters. The fishing here is often poor, but the beautiful state park, complete with showers, a grassy beach, and children's playground, make the two-hour drive worth the effort.

Currant Creek Reservoir, 19 miles (30 km) off US Route 40 on a bumpy dirt road, is a scenic, relatively new Central Utah Project lake, surrounded by pines and aspens. Fishing can be spotty, but the campground, offering a children's playground and some specially designed units for campers with horses, is one of Utah's best.

On the eastern side of the Uintas, south of Flaming Gorge, a handful of smaller reservoirs provide some interesting side trips from US Route 191. Bass and trout fishing, camping, and boating facilities can be found at **Steinaker** and **Red Fleet Reservoir** state parks. Calder, Crouse, and Matt Warner reservoirs on Diamond Mountain are also full of trout. The scenic 74-mile (118-km) Red Cloud Loop leads to several small reservoirs, some beautiful forest, and Indian petroglyphs in Dry Fork Canyon.

■ FLAMING GORGE

The problem with visiting Flaming Gorge National Recreation Area is that there are almost too many interesting outdoor recreational possibilities. That's why families from all over the United States travel to Utah's northeast corner, again and again.

Flaming Gorge anglers tell stories about catching and releasing 30-pound (14-kg) lake trout. Below the Flaming Gorge Dam, fly fishermen cast nymphs, streamers, and dry flies to catch beautiful trout on the Green River, as rafters float down the gentle rapids on lazy summer afternoons. Boaters travel to remote campgrounds on the reservoir shore to spend a quiet evening under the stars and away from the sound of automobiles. As waterskiers zig and zag on the reservoir beneath 1,500-foot (454-m) red-rock cliffs, swimmers bask in the sun on sandy beaches at Antelope Flat and Mustang Ridge. Hikers climb to the top of Bear Top Mountain in search of views across the canyons, enjoying close encounters with bighorn sheep. Children lead their parents on self-guided tours of the **Flaming Gorge Dam**, dropping 502 feet (152 m) down in an elevator to the interior of the huge concrete structure, where they see the turbines, generators, and transformers, which turn flowing water into electric power.

Best of all, visitors to Flaming Gorge can simply find a quiet, shaded campground, and spend their vacation *relaxing*. Our family will never forget a day spent at Antelope Flat beach. As the youngsters enjoyed swimming in the warm waters and building sand castles, two of us fished for smallmouth bass by casting spinners from the shoreline. We all marveled at the antelope and deer that wandered within a few feet of us. As we began to fry the fish we had caught, a surprise thunderstorm blew through the gorge. Lightning flashed on the red cliffs across the reservoir as we huddled in a sheltered picnic area. Then, as the storm blew over, a magnificent rainbow stretched from one side of the reservoir to the other. As the rain clouds dissipated, the sunset turned the entire surroundings into flaming orange embers. We watched the sun set and the sky turn dark before driving back to our campsite.

First-time visitors to this national recreation area would do well to stop at the **Red Canyon Visitor Center**, located west of Dutch John on Utah State Highway 44. In addition to receiving information on things to do and places to camp, the interpretive display informs travelers about local plants, animal life, geology, and cultural history. The view of Flaming Gorge Reservoir, 1,360 feet (412 m) below the plate glass window at the Red Canyon facility, gives a feeling for the massive beauty of the gorge itself. Try to take some time to walk around the self-guided nature trail, an easy stroll designed to introduce visitors to the ecology of the area.

A second visitor center at Flaming Gorge Dam provides yet more local information. Visitors can view the movie *Flaming Gorge: A Story Written in Water*,

Strawberry Pinnacles along their namesake river in Uinta Mountains.

which explains the natural and human history of Flaming Gorge from ancient times.

Though the main recreation season at Flaming Gorge runs from Memorial Day to Labor Day, you can fish on both the Green River and the reservoir itself year-round. Flaming Gorge Reservoir is famous for producing large lake and brown trout; lake trout of over 50 pounds (23 kg) are occasionally caught. Guide services and boat rentals are available at Cedar Springs Marina near the dam, Lucerne Valley near the Utah-Wyoming border, and Buckboard Marina in Wyoming. A number of Salt Lake City-based guides also take clients down the Green, which is easily Utah's best river fishery and one of the top trout waters of its kind in the United States. Nine ramps service the power boats and fishing crafts that ply the 66 square miles (171 sq km) of the 91-mile-long (146-km) reservoir. When you visit the Flaming Gorge Lodge near Dutch John, you can see the huge fish caught in the reservoir and often talk to anglers who have been out trying their luck. (Because of the complicated regulations designed to protect and produce trophy trout, anglers should study a Utah fishing proclamation closely.)

One of our favorite summer activities in the national recreation area is to rent a raft, either from the Flaming Gorge Lodge or the Dutch John Service, and take it down the Green. The river's small rapids provide thrills for experienced adventurers willing to guide their own rafts, as well as a good introduction for beginners with guides. Most enter the river at a ramp below the Flaming Gorge Dam and travel to the Little Hole pullout, just over seven miles (11 km) downstream. A few ride the river all the way down to Brown's Park, a trip that takes the better part of a day, especially if you stop to fish. Concessionaires who rent the rafts will pick up clients. If you have two cars, it is less expensive to shuttle them back and forth, leaving one driver behind to travel the short distance over a dirt road between the dam and Little Hole to pick up rafters. If you have a shuttle vehicle available, the distances are short enough so you can make two or three trips from the dam to Little Hole in a single day, giving everyone a chance to enjoy the ride. Hikers also enjoy strolling along the **Little Hole National Recreation Trail**, which parallels the Green River.

Developed campgrounds abound at Flaming Gorge. Some of the best include Firefighters Memorial, Lucerne Valley, Buckboard Crossing, and Firehole. Most camping sites are nestled in aspen and pine forests, while a few are found in sagebrush flats. Those who enjoy swimming might consider staying at Mustang Ridge or Antelope Flat, two campgrounds with beaches located nearby.

See how early foresters used lookout towers to detect forest fires at the **Ute Mountain Lookout Tower.** The only structure of its kind remaining in Utah, it has earned a place on the National Register of Historic Places. Visitors who climb the stairs to the top of the tower can see clear into Wyoming. Check with one of the visitor centers to see whether the tower is open, and to ask directions.

There is also much to learn about geology at Flaming Gorge. The loop road in **Sheep Creek Canyon,** on the west side of the reservoir, gives travelers an opportunity to view tremendous numbers of geological layers and formations exposed by erosion. An alternative is the 30-mile (50-km) **"Drive Through the Ages"** on US Route 191 between Flaming Gorge and Vernal. As you proceed along the highway, you will drive across the edges of exposed layers, ranging in age from the one- billion-year-old Uinta Mountain Group to the 80-million-year-old Mancos Formation. Interpretive signs along the way point out the exposed formation. (For more information, pick up a free booklet from the Utah Field House of Natural History in Vernal or from any Bureau of Land Management or U.S. Forest Service office.)

■ BROWN'S PARK

Brown's Park is a remote valley lying across the borders of Utah and Colorado, just below the Wyoming boundary. It received its name from Baptiste Brown, an early fur trader. The area was frequently visited by the mountain men in earlier days. Today, the various parts of Brown's Park are managed by the U.S. Fish and Wildlife Service, the Utah Division of Wildlife Resources, the BLM, and the National Park Service.

A point of historical interest in Brown's Park is the **John Jarvie Ranch,** on BLM property. In the late 1800s, the ranch contained a store, post office, river ferry, and cemetery, and was a regular stopping place for anyone traveling through this section of Utah, Colorado, and Wyoming. John Jarvie, a Scotsman, settled in the Brown's Park area in 1880. A colorful character, the well-educated Scotsman ran a ferry across the Green River, prospected in the nearby mountains, and entertained the locals by playing both the organ and the concertina. He knew, and occasionally hosted, outlaws like Butch Cassidy, the Sundance Kid, Matt Warner, Isom Dart, and Ann Bassett, who was known as the Queen of the Rustlers. Jarvie was murdered on July 6, 1909, by a pair of transient workers from Rock Springs, Wyoming, who were never captured. His body was placed in a boat and pushed out into the Green River. It was found a few days later, just above the Gates of Lodore in the eastern end of Brown's Park. Today, the property consists of the stone house and dugout that served as Jarvie's homes, a blacksmith shop, and corrals built of hand-hewn railroad ties that drifted down the river from Green River, Wyoming, in the 1870s.

Local legend has it that the dugout, which was Jarvie's first home, was often used as a secret meeting place for outlaws. John Bennett, a member of the Wild Bunch gang who was later hanged by vigilantes for his part in a local murder, built the stone house in 1888.

Only one paved road leads into this area—from Maybell, Colorado. Dirt roads, however, lead from Dutch John to Clay Basin Creek, and from Vernal to the Brown's Park Waterfowl Management Area.

■ DINOSAUR NATIONAL MONUMENT

The lush, alpine forests of the Uintas and Flaming Gorge contrast with the stark, barren landscapes in the valleys of the Uinta Basin and Carbon County to the south. As one looks over these desolate landscapes of tan, red, and white rock, it is hard to imagine this as a once-verdant land of ferns, cycads, club mosses, and clumps of tall conifers, where dinosaurs roamed. Yet fossils remain to attest to that history.

Giant vegetarians, like the *Apatosaurus* (once better known as *Brontosaurus*), *Stegosaurus, Diplodocus,* and *Camptosaurus,* as well as sharp-toothed and clawed carnivores like the *Allosaurus,* roamed this land 145 million years ago. When these dinosaurs died, some were washed by river floodwaters onto sandbars, where their bones mixed with the remains of turtles, crocodiles, clams, and other animals that lived in the river. Thick sediments piled up on top of them during later centuries. As the sea crept in and out, silica dissolved and percolated through the strata, turning the ancient riverbed into a hard sandstone, and mineralizing the bones buried within it. When the Rocky Mountains began to form to the east, the mountain building at what is now Dinosaur National Monument did not push the rock layers from below, but squeezed them from the sides. This action warped and tilted the rock. When rain, frost, and wind wore away the layers of sediment, a bit of the long-buried river bed—and its fossil treasure—began to appear at the top of a jagged ridge.

Thousands of tourists flock to Dinosaur National Monument each year to see this fossilized history of a time no man knew. Although hiking trails, river running, and some fine campgrounds can be enjoyed by visitors to the monument, most folks come to watch National Park Service paleontologists chip away at fossilized dinosaurs in a covered quarry. Remains of these ancient creatures dominate famous museums in New York, Washington, Chicago, Denver, and other cities throughout the world. Some of the earliest dinosaur skeletons ever assembled were excavated here in 1909 for the Carnegie Museum in Pittsburgh.

Earl Douglass, a Carnegie Museum paleontologist, was one of the first scientists to search for fossilized bones in the area. "I saw eight of the tail bones of a *Brontosaurus* in exact position," he wrote on August 7, 1909. "It was a beautiful sight."

Woodrow Wilson designated the place as Dinosaur National Monument in 1915. The national monument, which is now being considered for national park status, thus became America's most important natural display of fossilized dinosaur bones. It was increased in size by Franklin Roosevelt in 1938 to about 78 square miles (202 sq km). Additional land acquisitions since then have increased

The Green River cuts through Whirlpool Canyon in Dinosaur National Monument.

its size to about 325 square miles (841 sq km).

Douglass dreamed of the day when a museum could be built next to the quarry where he dug out so many unique dinosaur specimens. Visitors today enjoy the realization of that vision when they drive seven miles (11 km) north of US Route 40 from Jensen to a dinosaur quarry enclosed in an architecturally novel building. Paleontologists use tools ranging in size from jackhammers to dentist picks to expose the fossils. These scientists also serve as interpreters who are more than willing to answer visitors' queries. During the summer, rangers invite children to become "junior paleontologists," to get a behind-the-scenes look at the quarry. The kids can examine fossilized bones stored at the quarry, use tools to dig bones out of a dirt pit, or take a walk with the paleontologist through the museum.

Tourists often spend too little time at Dinosaur National Monument. Take the time to contemplate and study the dinosaur bones entombed in the quarry rocks. Walk to the balcony overlooking the quarry and attempt to piece together the potpourri of fossilized bones into a single dinosaur, while imagining the giant creatures wandering through lush vegetation. Then spend an evening camped at Split Mountain watching the Green River roll slowly through the colorful canyon. Take a walk on the short, self-guided nature trail. You might be inspired to recall the words of John Wesley Powell, who stood near here on a bluff above the Green, 12 years after his 1869 expedition: "We are standing three thousand feet above its waters, which are troubled with billows, and white with foam. Its walls are set with crags and peaks, and buttressed towers, and overhanging domes. Turning to the right, the park is below us, with its island groves reflected by the deep, quiet water. Rich meadows stretch out on either hand, to the verge of a sloping plain that comes down from the distant mountains. These plains are almost naked rocks, in strange contrast to the meadows; blue and lilac colored rocks, buff and pink, vermilion and brown, all these colors clear and bright. . . . We are tempted to call this Rainbow Park."

The **Utah Field House of Natural History** in nearby Vernal is an excellent place to learn more about dinosaurs. The outdoor Dinosaur Garden features 13 replicas placed in a natural setting, allowing visitors to view the creatures as something more than fossilized bones. In addition, skeletal reproductions, archaeological and geological exhibits, fluorescent minerals, and other natural history aspects of the Uinta Basin are found here. Pick up a free dinosaur hunting license from the visitor center. Our kids like to purchase souvenirs, such as fossils, children's books, or pieces of dinosaur bone, at the museum shop.

UTAH'S JURASSIC PARK

Dinosaur National Monument provides us with a grand view of the Jurassic landscape of 145 million years ago, when the earth's continents were joined together in a single land mass now referred to as "Pangaea." As you look about you at the subtle greys and browns of the desert, try to imagine the brilliant green ferns, conifers, and mosses which once grew here, and the behemoth dinosaurs that wandered among them. One of these was *Apatosaurus* (a.k.a., Brontosaurus), a long-necked and long-tailed vegetarian—measuring over 70 feet in length and tipping the scales at 35 tons. Because *Apatosaurus's* brain was smaller than ours, though given the job of directing a body as big as 18 station wagons, some people assumed it was dull-witted and spent most of its time sloshing around in swamps. Yet, now we know from studying rock strata in such places as Dinosaur National Monument that *Apatosaurus* galloped around in herds, probably with its young in the middle, kicking up dust and trampling trees. The smell must have been awful, but they may have been fairly smart. After all, *Apatosaurus* belongs to one of the most successful groups of animals ever to live on the earth.

Other smaller dinosaurs shared Jurassic Park with these monsters, among them the comely *Stegosaurus* ("roofed reptile"), known for the bony knobs and bumps all over its body, the upright plates on its back and its tail spikes. These animals grew to 20 feet in length and weighed about one-and-a-half tons. Early researchers thought that the back plates served as a defensive weapon, but more recently scientists have suggested that they served as solar panels and radiators regulating *Stegosaurus's* body temperature.

Roaming around with these oversized vegetarians were meat-eating carnosaurs, who packed their weight behind large heads, powerful necks, stout hind limbs, and small forearms. These included *Allosaurus* ("strange reptile") and *Ceratosaurus* ("horned reptile"). Adult *Allosaurus* was close to 40 feet long with a skull that reached nearly three feet in length; it had sharp, recurved daggers for teeth—serrated on both sides—lining its jaws. Possibly, it sped around Jurrasic Park on its long, powerful hind limbs and grabbed its prey in the claws on its small, muscular forelimbs. *Allosaurus* probably fed on whip-tailed *Apatosaurus*.

As you climb into your two-ton station wagon to leave Dinosaur National Monument, you may feel vaguely relieved to return to the twentieth century, where the descendants of *Allosaurus* (birds) prey on insects and worms.

—Mark Goodwin, scientist at the U.C. Berkeley Museum of Paleontology

(following pages) This famous mural of the Jurassic Period from Yale University gives an imaginative view of a world dominated by dinosaurs. (Peabody Museum)

DINOSAUR NATIONAL MONUMENT

Dinosaur's Human History

The colors of the rocks vary from a rich red-brown to vermilion, from gray to almost sugar-white, with many shades of pink and buff and salmon in between. The cliffs and sculptured forms are sometimes smooth, sometimes fantastically craggy, always massive, and they have a peculiar capacity to excite the imagination; the effect on the human spirit is neither numbing nor awesome, but warm and infinitely peaceful.

❖ ❖ ❖

There passed nearly a thousand years after the last of the Fremont people departed during which, as far as history knows, these canyons were only wind and water and stone, space and sky and the slow sandpapering of erosion, the unheard scurry of lizard and scream of mountain lion, the unseen stiff-legged caution of deer, the unnoted roar of rapids in the dark slot of Lodore and the unrecorded blaze of canyon color darkening with rain and whitening with snow and glaring in the high sun of solstice.

❖ ❖ ❖

A place is nothing in itself. It has no meaning, it can hardly be said to exist, except in terms of human perception, use, and response. The wealth and resources and usefulness of any region are only inert potential until man's hands and brain have gone to work; and natural beauty is nothing until it comes to the eye of the beholder. The natural world, actually, is the test by which each man proves himself: I see, I feel, I love, I use, I alter, I appropriate, therefore I am. Or the natural world is a screen onto which we project our own images; without our images there, it is as blank as the cold screen of an empty movie house. We cannot even describe a place except in terms of its human uses.

And as the essential history of Dinosaur is its human history, the only possible destruction of Dinosaur will be a human destruction. Admittedly it would be idiotic to preach conservation of such a wilderness in perpetuity, just to keep it safe from all human use. It is only the human use that it has any meaning, or is worth preserving. . . .

❖ ❖ ❖

And so it is plain that there is more to looking at a canyon or a mountain than merely filling the eye with scenery. The more we know about canyons and cliffs, buttes and ridges, valleys and terraces—their origin and their structure and the history of the strata that compose them—the more satisfying the scenery itself becomes. The further our curiosity probes back into the story of the rocks, openly revealed but in a language strange to most of us, the further our imagination is stretched by new revelations, and by a new concept of time.

—Wallace Stegner, "The Marks of Human Passage," *This Is Dinosaur*

Eden in the Desert
You follow a stream course, now in it, now on a rock shelf above. After a time it will suddenly strike you: what happened to the desert? This surely doesn't belong—this sudden chill twilight, these firs and maples and birches and bowers of orchids and ferns. No rustle of cottonwoods or rasp of cicadas here—only the flute call of a hermit thrush and the tinkle of water under the sedges.

Some light shows through dark boughs up ahead. In a moment you emerge into a vast room, as high-walled as it is wide. Now the barrier is behind you and you're really on Split Mountain—not in the split itself, for that's where the noisy river is, but face to face with the naked castellated wall that hides it. If you are a climber, you'll be glad to find the rock firm and not slick. You will see that for all the depth of these massive formations, they run in layers, criss-crossed with ledges that will lead you to the top of the ridge high above the rushing Green. From this vantage point you can look into Dinosaur's Zion—more spiry than Zion but a true counterpart in color: chocolate and red, pink and purple and white and golden tan, its lower talus overgrown with sage and dotted with junipers, its heights dark with conifers.

And here on top you can stride along the wind-swept plateau past towering columns and steeples, past gulf after gulf of the kind by which you climbed from the valley. It has been a long climb, but the mountains always save their greatest rewards for climbers.

—David Bradley, "A Short Look at Eden," *This is Dinosaur*

■ TOWNS AROUND THE UINTAS

Little towns like Kamas, Oakley, Manila, Dutch John, Vernal, Roosevelt, Duchesne, Tabiona, Hanna, Altamont, Coalville, and Heber City surround the High Uintas. Each offers its own special taste of Utah life for those willing to take the time to look beyond the gas stations and franchises.

We like to visit, for example, the little drugstore in Kamas to enjoy a freshly made malt with real ice cream. The drive-in restaurants in Heber City also serve great milk shakes and sundaes.

Heber City is the home of the **Heber Creeper Steam Railroad**, which takes travelers across the western part of Deer Creek Reservoir and down into Provo Canyon. Don't be surprised if train robbers attack the old steam engine somewhere along the way. (Call ahead as it is not always in operation.)

The Homestead Resort, founded on hot springs in 1895, is located in Midway, west of Heber City. It has recently undergone a multi-million-dollar modernization program, which included construction of an 18-hole golf course. You can climb the miniature volcano which produces the hot water for the swimming pool and peer down into the crater.

Nearby **Wasatch Mountain State Park**, with its 27-hole golf course and fine campground, is surrounded by scrub oak trees that turn a blazing orange in the fall.

Oakley hosts one of the finest small-town rodeos in Utah on the Fourth of July weekend each year.

When we visit Roosevelt, we like to stop in at the mill in the center of town to purchase pancake flour. It's the only place in the state where we can find this particular blend.

Towns off the main highways, like tiny Tabiona at the base of the Uintas, or Altamont, still possess a Western charm. Stop in at the general store in one of these hamlets to chat with the proprietor about local history.

This is a wild, hard land, away from the culture of the Wasatch Front's big cities and the fame of southern Utah's red-rock national parks. The lure of the Uintas and of Flaming Gorge, Dinosaur National Monument, and the small towns dotting eastern Utah's landscape draws those in search of solitude, wildlife, and a place still waiting to be discovered.

■ HELPER AND PRICE

Moving west of Vernal to the town of Duchesne, and then southwest on US 191 to the settlement of Helper and the city of Price, travelers can discover another active dinosaur quarry and museum, and some colorful mining and railroad towns. Summer festivals, like Price's **Greek Days** during the second weekend in July, and

(previous pages) The Green River exits Dinosaur National Monument and enters the Uinta Basin at Split Mountain Canyon.

International Days during the second week in August (in conjunction with the county fair), celebrate Carbon County's ethnic diversity.

Local railroad and mining industries have left Carbon County with a distinctive religious and ethnic flavor that can still be felt in downtown Helper. Though many of the old stores and hotels are boarded up, enough remain to provide glimpses of this coal-mining town's interesting past. With almost 3,000 present-day residents, Helper was named after the locomotives called "helpers," which were stored here in the late 1800s to help pull trains over the steep grade of nearby Soldier Summit and into the Wasatch Front. The **Western Railroading and Mining Museum**, located on Main Street, uses old photographs and memorabilia to trace Carbon County's roots. People from other parts of the state enjoy searching payroll lists to find old friends and relatives who once worked here. Other visitors may browse through the exhibits to get a feel both for the diversity of the region and for the hardships endured by miners.

A city of nearly 10,000 residents, nearby Price was named after Bishop William Price of the Latter-day Saints who led an exploring party through Spanish Fork Canyon in 1869. The city serves as a gateway to the canyonlands country to the southeast. The **College of Eastern Utah Prehistoric Museum**, in the rear of the Price City Hall, contains a skeleton of an allosaurus, dinosaur footprints collected from nearby coal mines, and Indian artifacts found in the area. Most of the fossils came from the Cleveland-Lloyd Dinosaur Quarry, south of Price. (See "Stories in Stone" chapter.)

Northeast of Price, the 50-mile-long (80-km) **Nine-Mile Canyon** contains some of the finest examples of Fremont rock art. Why is a 50-mile-long canyon called Nine-Mile Canyon? According to one story, when John Wesley Powell headed a government expedition through this part of the state in 1869, a mapmaker charting the area made a nine-mile triangulation drawing which he named Nine-Mile Creek. The name stuck with the canyon. Another tale states that the canyon got its name when the Miles family settled the area in the 1880s. Seven daughters and two parents added up to "nine Miles." Free guides to Nine-Mile Canyon are available from the Price Chamber of Commerce or the local BLM office. The brochures point out the locations of rock art panels. Archaeologists say the writing on the rock is the remains of the Fremont culture. These Indian tribes may have inhabited Nine-Mile Canyon as early as A.D. 300. The rock art itself depicts both humans and animals. No one knows exactly what the Indians were trying to say with their etchings, but part of the fun of visiting such a site is interpreting the writing yourself.

Price also serves as a gateway to the eastern edge of the Manti Mountains. State parks at Millsite, Huntington, and Scofield offer fine camping facilities, as do U.S. Forest Service sites near Joe's Valley, Ferron, and Electric Lake reservoirs. Utah's nicest and least-visited alpine scenery is set away from the Wasatch Front population centers.

A tough customer prepares for another day at work. (Utah State Historical Society)

(opposite) Pioneer barn near Capitol Reef National Park.

G R E A T   B A S I N

UTAH'S GREAT BASIN IS A LAND OF ISLANDS AND ILLUSIONS. Totally barren or covered with sagebrush and other desert-loving plants, often it is dismissed as wasteland. Yet in many places, water lies just beneath the surface. Alpine forests on the high mountain peaks and marshes around the Great Salt Lake sustain exuberant islands of life amidst the desolate mud and salt flats.

Mirages are among the first illusions encountered in the Great Basin. Motorists crossing the Great Salt Lake Desert see mountain ranges which seem to float on sky-colored water. Or are the mountains floating on air? But in approaching the mountains, the water slowly, mysteriously disappears. In other directions, where there are no mountains, the sky is indistiguishable from the horizon. All is bright and shimmering.

Closer to Salt Lake City, a strong ocean smell assails the nostrils. Seagulls fly overhead. Sailboats race across the bright blue water. Sun seekers wander along white sand beaches. It appears as if one has reached the coast. Yet, Utah's largest city is 500 miles (800 km) from the Pacific, almost 1,500 (2,400 km) from the Gulf of Mexico, and about 2,000 (3,200 km) from the Atlantic.

Through the years, this great, nearly deserted wilderness has seduced thousands with the richness of her mineral deposits. Great Basin names like Disappointment Hills, Confusion Mountains, Skull Valley, and Little Sahara sound like the most uninviting spots on earth. This too, is illusory. Today Utah's western desert beckons with an extraordinary wealth of beautiful scenery and fascinating history.

While the masses of people living in Wasatch Front communities are inclined to avoid the Great Basin as much as possible, we have been increasingly drawn to the solitude. The view from the top of 11,031-foot (3,640-m) Deseret Peak is breathtaking. Farther east rise the peaks of the Wasatch Range, and on most days, a light gray haze veils the buildings of Salt Lake City. The Great Salt Lake stretches to the north. To the west and southwest, countless basins and ranges, mostly uninhabited, drift off toward the horizon. One spring, we were lucky to follow cougar tracks down the mountain in the snow.

There are a handful of popular tourist destinations scattered around the Great Salt Lake, but to appreciate the rest of the Basin, it is necessary to explore with an adventurous attitude. Many a pioneer cursed the heat and the barren landscape of

SHERLOCK HOLMES IN UTAH

In the central portion of the great North American Continent there lies an arid and repulsive desert, which for many a long year served as a barrier against the advance of civilization. From the Sierra Nevada to Nebraska, and from the Yellowstone River in the north to the Colorado upon the south, is a region of desolation and silence. Nor is Nature always in one mood throughout this grim district. It comprises snow-capped and lofty mountains, and dark and gloomy valleys. There are swift-flowing rivers which dash through jagged cañons; and there are enormous plains, which in winter are white with snow, and in summer are gray with the saline alkali dust. They all preserve, however, the common characteristics of barrenness, inhospitality, and misery.

There are no inhabitants of this land of despair. A band of Pawnee or Blackfeet may occasionally traverse it in order to reach other hunting-grounds, but the hardiest of the braves are glad to lose sight of those awesome plains, and to find themselves once more upon their prairies. The coyote skulks among the scrub, the buzzard flaps heavily through the air, and the clumsy grizzly bear lumbers through the dark ravines and picks up such sustenance as it can amongst the rocks. These are the sole dwellers in the wilderness.

In the whole world there can be no more dreary view than that from the northern slope of the Sierra Blanco. As far as the eye can reach stretches the great flat plain-land, all dusted over with patches of alkali, and intersected by clumps of the dwarfish chaparral bushes. On the extreme verge of the horizon lie a long chain of mountain peaks, with their rugged summits flecked with snow. In this great stretch of country there is no sign of life, nor of anything appertaining to life. There is no bird in the steel-blue heaven, no movement upon the dull, gray earth—above all, there is absolute silence. Listen as one may, there is no shadow of a sound in all that mighty wilderness, nothing but silence—complete and heart-subduing silence.

It has been said there is nothing appertaining to life upon the broad plain. That is hardly true. Looking down from the Sierra Blanco, one sees a pathway traced out across the desert, which winds away and is lost in the extreme distance. It is rutted with wheels and trodden down by the feet of many adventurers. Here and there are scattered white objects which glisten in the sun, and stand out against the dull deposit of alkali. Approach, then examine them! They are bones: some large and coarse, others smaller and more delicate. The former have belonged to oxen, and the latter to men. For fifteen hundred miles one may trace this ghastly caravan route by these scattered remains of those who had fallen by the wayside.

—Arthur Conan Doyle, "A Study in Scarlet," from *The Adventures of Sherlock Holmes*, 1902

the salt flats and refreshed himself in the cool canyons of the mountains. With air-conditioned cars, modern tourists have the chance to appreciate the beauty of the desert in relative comfort.

About 12,000 years ago, humans lived in caves around the edges of Lake Bonneville, precursor of the Great Salt Lake. The lake at that time was freshwater. Its salinity increased as the lake diminished in size.

The Great Salt Lake reached its present level about 9,000 years ago. The Shoshone, Utes, and Goshutes may have collected salt on its shores. Mountain men explored the lake for a water route to the Pacific, but found none.

Immigrants bypassed the lake and salt deserts immediately to its west because they lacked water for their livestock. One hapless exception was the Donner-Reed party, which decided to cross after a California politician, Lansford Hastings, assured them it was a shortcut to the Golden State. Hastings himself had traversed the territory on horseback. What everyone failed to recognize was that the immigrants' heavily laden wagons would sink into the sludge, and their oxen would need more frequent water and pasture than did Hasting's horse. Delays in crossing caused the Donner-Reed party to reach the Sierra Nevada late in the season. They were stranded by the winter's first blizzard, bringing horrible suffering, starvation, and cannibalism. Forty of the original 87 members of the party died, making it the worst disaster of the California Trail.

The story of their ordeal is told in the Donner-Reed Museum in Grantsville, northwest of Tooele and on the edge of the salt flats. The museum houses guns and relics abandoned by the party as it struggled to lighten its loads.

■ THE PONY EXPRESS

The increasing wealth and population of gold-rich California, coupled with the threat of Civil War, convinced leaders in Washington of the necessity of improving communications between the East and West coasts. The Pony Express helped to ensure this. For 18 months between 1860 and 1861, young men (preferably orphans because of the risks involved) rode from one station to the next in stretches of approximately 11 miles (18 km) each, linking the continent. At its peak, the Pony Express route incorporated 190 stations, 420 horses, and 80 riders. The fastest crossing took seven and a half days to carry Lincoln's Inaugural Message

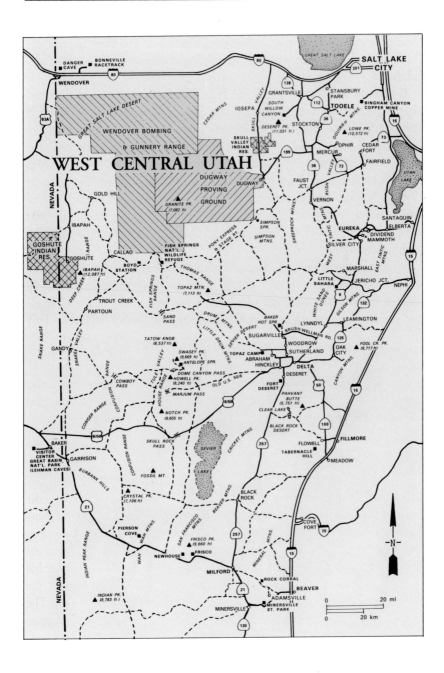

WEST CENTRAL UTAH

SALT LAKE CITY

DANGER CAVE
BONNEVILLE RACETRACK
WENDOVER
GREAT SALT LAKE
GREAT SALT LAKE DESERT
WENDOVER BOMBING & GUNNERY RANGE
GRANTSVILLE
STANSBURY PARK
TOOELE
BINGHAM CANYON COPPER MINE
IOSEPA
SOUTH WILLOW CANYON
STOCKTON
LOWE PK. (10,572 ft.)
CEDAR MTNS.
SKULL VALLEY
DESERET PK. (11,031 ft.)
SKULL VALLEY INDIAN RES.
OPHIR
CEDAR FORT
MERCUR
FAIRFIELD
UTAH LAKE
DUGWAY PROVING GROUND
DUGWAY
GOLD HILL
FAUST JCT.
GRANITE PK. (7,082 ft)
VERNON
NEVADA
IBAPAH
SIMPSON SPR.
SANTAQUIN
GOSHUTE INDIAN RES.
GOSHUTE
CALLAO
FISH SPRINGS NAT'L WILDLIFE REFUGE
PONY EXPRESS STAGE RT.
SIMPSON MTNS.
SHEEPROCK MTNS.
EUREKA
SILVER CITY
ELBERTA
DIVIDEND
MAMMOTH
IBAPAH (12,087 ft)
BOYD STATION
THOMAS RANGE
WEST TINTIC MTNS.
MARSHALL
EAST TINTIC MTNS.
TROUT CREEK
TOPAZ MTN. (7,113 ft)
LITTLE SAHARA
JERICHO JCT.
NEPHI
PARTOUN
WHITE SAND DUNES
SAND PASS
DRUM MTNS.
BAKER HOT SPR.
LYNNDYL
GILSON MTNS.
LEAMINGTON
TATOW KNOB (8,537 ft)
SUGARVILLE
BRUSH
WELLMAN RD.
WOODROW
FOOL CR. PK. (9,717 ft)
SWASEY PK. (9,669 ft)
ANTELOPE SPR.
TOPAZ CAMP
ABRAHAM
SUTHERLAND
OAK CITY
COWBOY PASS
DOME CANYON PASS
HOWELL PK. (8,240 ft)
OLD U.S. 50/6
HINCKLEY
DELTA
DESERET
CANYON MTNS.
MARJUM PASS
FORT DESERET
NOTCH PK. (9,655 ft)
PAHVANT BUTTE (5,751 ft)
SKULL ROCK PASS
CLEAR LAKE
BAKER
VISITOR CENTER GREAT BASIN NAT'L. PARK (LEHMAN CAVES)
GARRISON
SEVIER LAKE
BLACK ROCK DESERT
FLOWELL
FILLMORE
FOSSIL MT.
TABERNACLE HILL
MEADOW
CRYSTAL PK. (7,106 ft)
BLACK ROCK
COVE FORT
PIERSON COVE
FRISCO PK. (9,660 ft)
NEWHOUSE
FRISCO
MILFORD
ROCK CORRAL
BEAVER
INDIAN PK. (9,783 ft)
ADAMSVILLE
MINERSVILLE ST. PARK
MINERSVILLE

0   20 mi
0   20 km

N

from St. Joseph, Missouri, to Sacramento, California. The Pony Express was thrust into sudden obscurity with the completion of the first transcontinental telegraph line.

Besides the daring mail carriers, the Pony Express route was also used by passenger stagecoaches and wagons hauling freight. Later, portions of the first transcontinental roadway, the old Lincoln Highway, would be built along the Pony Express route. Today a gravel road follows the trail through a hundred miles of Utah's Great Basin. Drivers can follow the Bureau of Land Management's (BLM's) interpretive signs along the route from Faust Junction (south of Tooele) through Simpson Springs Station and Boyd Station to Canyon Station, each in varying stages of reconstruction or disintegration. Before going, write to the BLM for information, or pick up the Utah Travel Council's maps that show Pony Express stations.

Better yet, start at Fairfield's **Stagecoach Inn State Park**, 25 miles (40 km) west of Lehi, where you can obtain a printed guide describing the route and telling some of the wild tales associated with it. Here you can explore the Pony Express and stagecoach station where Mark Twain and Horace Greeley stopped on their

The Pony Express. (Utah State Historical Society)

journeys west. Fairfield was also the site of **Camp Floyd**, the army bivouac built by Colonel Albert Johnston when he was sent to put down a rumored Mormon rebellion that never materialized.

As you head farther west, you can sometimes see wild mustangs grazing in the valleys along the road. Ancestors of these animals were captured and broken to carry the riders through this unfriendly desert.

Captain James Hervey Simpson described the desert around his namesake outpost, **Simpson Springs Station**, as a "somber, dreary wasteland, where neither man nor beast can live for want of the necessary food and over which a bird is scarcely seen to fly." In later decades, the spring water refreshed freighters hauling supplies to nearby mining towns such as Gold Hill.

■ THE RAILROAD

On May 10, 1869, at Promontory, Utah, the United States started on its way to becoming a world power. The American continent had been linked by rail!

The railway lines from East and West finally met at Promontory on May 10, 1869. (Utah State Historical Society)

Golden Spike National Historic Site preserves this important piece of our history.

Before the railroad, land routes to the Pacific shore stretched over vast and often hostile terrain, a journey that took wagon trains months to make. The fastest voyage by clipper ship around the tip of South America still required at least a hundred days. With increased migration, Congress began to recognize the pressing need for a rail link between the East and West coasts. Quarrels between the North and the South over which route the railroad should take kept it from being built until the outbreak of the Civil War. President Lincoln and Congress then decided to commence the job with a northern route in order to keep California with the Republic and to keep the war chest filled with California gold.

To spur interest in the construction project, Congress promised free use of building materials from the public lands, cash subsidies of $16,000 per mile of track on the plains and from $32,000 to $48,000 per mile through the mountains, and an outright bonus of every alternate, odd-numbered section of public land, which stretched checker-board fashion for 20 miles (32 km) on each side of the tracks.

Employing mostly Irish workers to lay the tracks, the Union Pacific raced across the plains from Omaha. The Central Pacific snaked its way through the Sierra Nevada, employing workers mainly from China. Just as many modern contractors seek to bilk the federal government, the railroad companies, too, found ways to get rich. The most blatant example was the laying of 225 miles (360 km) of parallel track in northern Utah before the government demanded that they bring the rails together at Promontory, joining a total of 1,776 miles (2,841 km) of track. Completed in fewer than four years, the first transcontinental railroad is an engineering feat unequalled in American history.

Trains no longer pass through Promontory. Politicians and businessmen arranged to have it moved closer to established commercial centers, specifically Ogden, 45 miles (72 km) to the south.

Visitors to **Golden Spike National Historic Site** can glean the significance of this momentous event through visitor center film shows and displays. The most riveting exhibition takes place outdoors on the anniversary of the event, May 10, and during the Railroaders Festival, usually the second Saturday in August. On those occasions, two full-sized replicas of the engines used in the original ceremony, the *199* and the *Jupiter*, recreate the historical meeting. Shiny and impressive, with thick, black smoke billowing from their stacks, they dwarf onlookers. Puffing and tooting, the engines ease together, head to head, to a squeaking, hissing stop. Engineers dressed in authentic uniforms jump from their cabs and take turns addressing the crowd, telling the tale of the joining of the rails and answering questions.

The original event was not without some humor. "California's Leland Stanford raised his hammer and swung a mighty blow," relates the WPA version from *Utah: A Guide to the State.* "He missed entirely, but the telegraph operator (a line was connected to the last spike to record the blow), a man of practical foresight, simulated the blow with his key and let tumult loose upon the cities of the country; fire

Train replicas at Golden Spike National Historic Site.

bells, cannon, and factory whistles joined with shouting human voices to signalize the linkage of a continent. At Promontory the two locomotives gingerly nosed their cowcatchers together. To the world the telegrapher tapped out the historic message to the world:

> *The last rail is laid*
> *The last spike is driven.*
> *The Pacific road is finished.*

Within two weeks of the joining of the rails, more than 300 frame buildings, shanties, and tents were erected at Promontory and nearby **Corinne**. The rough and lusty population grew to 7,500, including 5,000 Chinese railroad workers, and a temporary city government was set up to handle them. Colonel Patrick Connor, who had set out to weaken the Mormons' stronghold by bringing mining to the Utah Territory, headed the Liberal Political Party, based in Corinne.

Brigham City, 32 miles (51 km) to the east of Promontory, tried to maintain its status as a quiet religious community by ignoring its unholy neighbors. Mormons took advantage of the railroad, however, to obtain jobs. They were not allowed to work on the trains themselves but kept busy grading the roadbeds.

In 1872, a diphtheria epidemic swept Corinne. Hundreds died. Many deserted the city. Indians surrounded the town and helped themselves to the ranches of the remaining inhabitants until soldiers from Fort Douglas drove them out.

In 1903, the Lucin Cutoff moved the rails across the Great Salt Lake to shorten the line, and Corinne was struck a crippling blow.

Present-day Brigham City celebrates the anniversary of the driving of the golden spike with many Chamber of Commerce promotions and community activities. Brigham Young's curse on Corinne for its lawlessness has been fulfilled. It is the tiny unprosperous place he prophesized it would become. The old railroad bed is abandoned in many places, and is used by off-road-vehicle and mountain-biking enthusiasts.

■ BOOMS AND BUSTS

With the coming of the railroad, mining became a more lucrative business. Brigham Young had discouraged his followers from prospecting, but gold and silver fever spread wherever the precious metals could be found. Boomtowns like Ophir, Mercur, Gold Hill, Eureka, Mammoth, and Frisco sprang up in the Great Basin seemingly overnight. Many still stand in various states of disrepair—fascinating and picturesque, they appeal to historians, antique collectors, photographers, painters, solitude seekers and dreamers. Rockhounds can use guides available in bookstores to help them locate specimens of fossils and minerals from sites all around the Great Basin.

The adventurous are invited to try their own hand at prospecting. There is treasure to be found if the searcher gets lucky. The treasure might be an ancient gold pan or century-old whiskey bottle. More often, it is a quiet day spent contemplating the past preserved in rusting machinery and dilapidated shacks. Visitors, however, should respect property rights and make sure buildings are safe and truly abandoned before entering.

As market conditions and milling methods changed, Great Basin towns repeatedly boomed and died. As new methods for extracting metals and minerals from the rocks are developed, some may be resurrected in the future. Until then, they struggle along and wait for better times, shadows of their former thriving communities.

One of the first discoveries of precious metals was made in 1863 at Bingham Canyon, in the Oquirrh Mountains west of Salt Lake City. Although gold, silver, and lead first drew miners here, the modern quest is for copper. Today, the **Bingham Copper Mine** is the world's largest and most productive. Since 1906, when the open-pit method was first used, several towns have been bulldozed to make way for its ever-enlarging spirals.

Visitors on the lip of the Bingham copper pit look out across uncounted spiraling cuts in the rock, which drop dramatically from a few remaining peaks to the rust-red, damp earth at the mine's lowest level. At 2.5 miles (4-km) wide and a half mile (.75-km) deep, the pit could easily hold all of downtown Salt Lake City; the tops of the city's tallest buildings would barely reach one-eighth the way up the walls of the mine.

The owner of the mine, Utah Copper Division (formerly Kennecott), was, at one time, the major employer of Salt Lake City residents (making the city a "boomtown"). Fluctuations in the copper market and the import of less costly ores from South America resulted in layoffs. Salt Lake City was forced to diversify its employment base, but mining continues to bring in 3.4 percent of Utah's industrial dollars.

Bingham Canyon has been designated a National Historic Landmark by the United States Department of the Interior. The visitor center is open daily from 8 a.m. to dusk, April through October.

Bingham Canyon and other mining towns throughout the state attracted people from all over the world: Scandanavia, the Balkan States, Western and Central Europe, Asia, and even, during World War II, the Navajo lands to the south. Each nationality settled into a separate neighborhood in the narrow canyon.

The immigrants kept a tight hold onto their old-world languages and customs. Since mining at Bingham Canyon in those times meant dark tunnels, poor working conditions, and low pay, there were labor disputes and strikes. The old-world dislikes and prejudices crept into the new neighborhoods and there were fights. But as time passed, the disasters of fire, flood, and snowslide forced people of different nationalities to help each other and the old boundaries dissolved. Over time, the canyon evolved into a cohesive community.

John R. Wharton, principal of Copperton Elementary in the 1950s, had an unusual job heading a school with such an international makeup. "I thought I knew what a PTA meeting was like, but this one was different. I was told I didn't need to do anything except be there at a certain time and have a specific number of tables and chairs set up. I walked in as some women were setting up a big coffee pot. Shortly, parents arrived bringing specialties from their native countries. There was Italian food, Chinese food, Mexican food, everything you could imagine!"

West of Bingham Canyon stands the town of Tooele and the **Tooele County Museum.** (One of the tests of native Utahns is whether or not they can pronounce the name of Tooele: TOO-ill-uh.) The museum houses a collection of railroad and mining artifacts, including a scale railway and simulated mine. The town also has a **Daughter of the Utah Pioneers museum.** The log cabin next door to the museum, built in 1856, was one of the first houses in Tooele.

Another of Utah's richest mining towns was **Ophir,** south of Tooele, named after King Solomon's fabled mines. By 1900, the town had produced $13 million, including $1 million from the Kearsarge Mine alone. Even as it dimmed, Ophir's fabulous legacy was carried on beyond the boundaries of Utah by Marcus Daly, founder of Anaconda Copper, who earned his grubstake, and much of his know-how, while working at his Zella mine in Ophir. Although a few diehards still inhabit Ophir, it is a favorite of photographers because so much of the old appearance remains. Ophir Canyon is also an excellent place to view bald eagles during the winter months.

Few old buildings survive in **Mercur**, just south of Ophir on Utah State Highway 73. The old town has been bulldozed to make room for the ever enlarging mine. This will be Mercur's fourth reincarnation. A fire on Statehood Day, January 4, 1876, burned the town completely. Rebuilt, it burned again in 1902 in a fire originating at a Chinese lunch counter. Flash floods rolling down the bare hills finished the job of ruining the city.

Mercur was named for the mercury ore mined there, which also contained large amounts of gold. In 1898, the Golden Gate Mill in Mercur became the world's first all-steel, non-ferrous mining plant and the first metallurgical plant in the Western Hemisphere to use transmitted electric power. Gold profits fell, however, and by 1917 Mercur became a ghost town. Seventy years later, mining began again. This time, however, the miners do not live in town but commute from Tooele and other towns.

Farther south, **Eureka** has been called a living ghost town, not only because many of the buildings and mining paraphernalia have been kept intact for a century, but because a small population of old-timers still call it home. In 1868 it was the center of the Tintic mining district, one of Utah's biggest and richest. By the end of its first hundred years, the Tintic's production of silver, gold, and other metals and minerals exceeded $500 million. Eureka's

Inside the Anchor Mine.
(Utah State Historical Society)

fortunes faded along with those of many other boomtowns, but 700 residents remain.

About 100 miles (160 km) west of Eureka along the old Pony Express route, **Gold Hill** is one of the most picturesque and complete ghost towns in Utah. Gold Hill started as a gold boomtown in 1892. It died and was rebuilt during World War I when tungsten and other minerals were needed for the war effort. One former prospector who didn't strike it rich in Gold Hill but knocked out enough opponents to become the heavyweight champion of the world was Jack Dempsey. The town is 23 miles (37 km) north of Callao on a dirt road.

A ghost town of a different nature was **Topaz**. In the wartime hysteria of 1942, about 9,000 Japanese, most of them American citizens, were brought to a camp hastily constructed here. The ghosts of the wrongly imprisoned souls can be felt around remaining streets and foundations. A monument to the injustice has been erected on the northwest corner of Topaz. To reach Topaz, drive six miles (10 km) from Delta on US Route 50/6 to the small town of Hinckley, turn north, and continue 4.5 miles (7 km) on a partly paved, partly graveled road to its end. Turning left (west), go 2.5 miles (4 km) on a paved road to its end in Abraham, then turn right (north) and drive 1.5 miles (2.5 km) on a gravel road to a stop sign. From there, turn left and drive 3 miles (5 km) to Topaz on a gravel road.

West of Delta, you can search for souvenirs in the trilobite fossil beds in the House Range. South of town you can find the crumbling remains of **Fort Deseret**, an adobe-walled fort quickly built during the Black Hawk War of 1865. The **Gunnison Massacre Monument**, about six miles (10 km) southwest of Fort Deseret, marks the spot where Captain John W. Gunnison and seven of his men were killed by Indians while working on a federal railroad survey during the Walker War.

■ ISLAND RANGES, INLAND SEA

One of the greatest illusions of the Great Basin is that it is a deserted wasteland that must be crossed in haste as a traveler heads for California. The striking beauty of the mountains of the Great Basin are a well-kept secret. The magnificent desert, marsh, and alpine scenery of Utah's Great Basin is showcased in two designated and 19 proposed wilderness areas and seven wildlife refuges.

AMERICA'S MOST IN-DEBT BUSINESSMAN

E. Sterling Hunsaker is $613 billion in the red. Or is he? The slippery Utahn filed this staggering listing of debts in 1981 (at *that* time comparable to two-thirds of the national debt); meanwhile, his assets were listed as a meager $7,310. In doing so, he became the largest debtor in U.S. history. Those were the figures given in the October 27, 1986, issue of *Forbes 400*. But maybe things have changed—one way or the other—for Hunsaker. The state of his fortune (or misfortune) remains a mystery as he is unavailable for questioning. Rumor has it that he is somewhere in Europe or South America "peddling his wares." Have you seen this man? . . .

How did it happen? Laura Jereski of *Forbes* explains: "Hunsaker wanted to extract gold and oil from the tar sand of eastern Utah at a cost per barrel of $60. Unable to find local investors, Hunsaker looked overseas. He transferred his mining leases to a Panamanian trust and, unfortunately, committed his personal assets to it, thereby making himself liable for the trust's obligations."

Apparently, those trust certificates (bought by the tar sand deposits), along with similar paper produced by the dubious Cambridge International Fiduciary Trust, were decisive in pushing the teetering Hunsaker into a $613 billion pit. Hunsaker filed these liabilities after he caught on to the untrustworthy activities of the trust officers. The man was unmistakably getting short-shrifted—he was paying for the certificates but, *FUND*amentally speaking, nothing was coming back his way. On the other side of things, however, as was indicated in *Forbes 400*, "very little of the paper had ever actually been sold."

In April 1986 (five years after the filing), Hunsaker thought he would once more break into the world of big business using a whole new approach (with some very familiar elements); but by May, the break went "bust" and Hunsaker's operation was closed down by the Utah Financial Institutions Commission. Here's what happened: As if from out of the blue, Hunsaker's "John Hancock" began turning up on some rather airy documents called "irrevocable letter[s] of credit."

Writes Jereski, "These instruments, ranging in face value from $11.5 million to $30 million, were issued by a bogus bank whose capital consisted of—you guessed it—oil and gold certificates collateralized by an assay valuation of eastern Utah tar sands."

Seems that those darn tar sands just wouldn't pan out for E. Sterling Hunsaker.

—Holly Cratty

The mountain ranges of the Great Basin have been called islands of ecological diversity because slightly different species of plants and animals have developed on each. The intervening mud and salt flats and broad dry valleys kept the plant and animal species from migrating and interbreeding.

The upper reaches of the Stansbury and Deep Creek mountains are untouched wilderness areas. Deseret Peak in the Stansburys, Notch Peak in the House Range, and Haystack Peak in the Deep Creek Range provide fantastic views of the salt and mud flats of the Great Basin. The mountain ranges looming in the distance are home to thousand-year-old bristlecone pines. Miners, pioneers, and outlaws frequented their peaks and canyons. While hiking in the ranges, deer, pronghorn antelope, chukar partridge, bald and golden eagles, and peregrine falcons can be sighted. Obtain detailed topographical maps from the U.S. Forest Service offices listed in the Practicalities section of this book to help you explore these mountains.

US Route 50/6 which, from Delta, skirts the House Range to Baker, Nevada, has been called the loneliest highway in the United States. Just over the Nevada border, it passes **Great Basin National Park**, which preserves a spectacular stretch of mountain and high desert including 13,063-foot (3,958-m) Wheeler Peak. Starting in a dry desert valley near Baker, where temperatures often soar over 100 degrees F in the summer, the park road switchbacks up through desert woodlands of mountain mahogany, pinyon pine, and juniper to alpine forests of Douglas fir, where it's always cool.

No streams or rivers leave the Great Basin. The water running off from the mountain ranges ends up mainly in marshes. In the middle of seemingly barren desert, the United States government has established wildlife refuges to act as sanctuaries for migrating birds, as well as local wildlife. **Fish Springs National Wildlife Refuge** is located on the old Pony Express and Stage Route. A self-guiding auto tour makes an 11 1/2 mile (18 km) loop motorists may follow using a brochure that they can pick up at the entrance. The brochure describes various birds that inhabit the refuge seasonally or year-round.

Locomotive Springs State Waterfowl Management Area is west of Golden Spike National Historic Site. **Bear River Migratory Bird Refuge, Harold S. Crane State Waterfowl Management Area**, and **Ogden Bay State Waterfowl Management Area** border the Great Salt Lake where the fresh water of the Bear and other rivers enters the salt water. **Clear Lake State Waterfowl Management Area** is the

(previous pages) The House Range, which straddles the Utah-Nevada state line, is typical of Great Basin limestone formations.

southernmost of them, over 20 miles (32 km) from Delta in the Black Rock Desert. Bird watching in these areas takes patience but can be rewarding. A variety of birds frequent the refuges.

The Great Salt Lake, dominating the Basin, appears worthless since its high salt content makes it impossible to use for culinary or agricultural purposes. Yet a political war for the future of the lake is raging between environmentalists and chemical companies. Environmentalists contend that the salt flats, a unique natural feature, are being harmed by the harvesting of potash by the evaporation of ponds on the flats. The potash companies disagree.

The islands of the Great Salt Lake are always changing in relation to the lake's water levels. Stansbury Island closely resembles a peninsula now, but may, once again, be an island should the lake rise. All of the islands in the Great Salt Lake are actually extensions of the Oquirrh and Stansbury mountains. Bison, placed by early pioneers, inhabit Antelope Island. The diverse gene pool of this herd is utilized to keep bison herds elsewhere in the country healthy.

Remnants of sandbars deposited by Lake Bonneville have accumulated in white dunes in the **Little Sahara Recreation Area**, managed by the BLM. Winds pushed the sands 180 miles (288 km) to the northeast until they were deflected by Sand Mountain. Off-road vehicles and motorcycles can ply the sands but a separate area is set aside for foot traffic. The three campgrounds in the area have water.

■ LAKESIDE RESORTS

A trip to Utah is not complete without trying out the greatest illusion of them all, walking on water. While no one exactly "walks" on the lake, sitting in water where it is impossible to sink is a fascinating sensation. So is leaving the water and having your skin slowly turn white with salt crystals as you dry. Innocents who try swimming underwater in the Great Salt Lake come up spluttering, with stinging eyes and throats. Look in the water for the tiny orange brine shrimp, the solitary inhabitants of water six to eight times as salty as the ocean. Tropical fish food companies harvest these creatures.

The sand on the beaches of the Great Salt Lake is also an illusion. Unlike most sand, it is not made of tiny pieces of rock, but, rather, pellets cast out by the brine shrimp digestive system. Small crystals of calcium carbonate, a mineral found in the water, grow around each pellet to form rounded gray or yellowish-gray grains of sand. Each grain is called an oolite, meaning fish egg, because of its shiny spherical shape.

The Utah Division of Parks and Recreation manages a large beach facility with freshwater showers and restrooms on the south shore of the Great Salt Lake. Take time to visit the visitor center and museum exhibits near the entrance to the park. The beaches are accessible from Salt Lake City by taking the Great Salt Lake Beaches exit off Interstate 80.

Past entrepreneurs have built elaborate bathhouses and pavilions to capitalize on this unusual natural wonder. Unfortunately for them, lake levels fluctuate too radically for anyone to operate a permanent structure successfully.

Antelope Island, largest in the Great Salt Lake, is protected as a state park.

The first attempt to promote tourism on the Great Salt Lake was made by John W. Young, the third of Brigham's 25 sons. He had taken advantage of the railroad by subcontracting for the Central Pacific and Union Pacific. For a decade, he financed all the railroads in Utah. Near the railroad stop of Farmington, he built a resort which he named Lake Side. Within the year, Jeter Clinton opened a competing resort on the south shore called Lake Point. Both resorts offered steamboat rides. A skipper of one of the steamboats soon built another lake resort, Lake Park, to the north. It boasted a large dance pavilion and covered pier, elegant dressing rooms, a restaurant, and a saloon. It also had the best sandy beach. Unfortunately, after 50 years of massaging by thousands of tourist's feet, the sand turned to mud, and Lake Park failed.

In 1893, Saltair was born. "Saltair," writes Dale Morgan in *The Great Salt Lake*, "caught everybody's imagination. The train was run on pile-supported track 4,000 feet out into the lake to reach the pile-driven, crescent-shaped platform. The 2,500 10-inch pilings were driven into the lake bottom through salt dissolved by steam. Upon this platform was built a large two-story pavilion, with picnic tables

Saltair was Salt Lake City's answer to Coney Island. (Utah State Historical Society)

and restaurant overlooking the lake on the ground floor, and an immense ballroom, locally thought to be the largest in the world, on the upper floor." Rows of bathrooms served thousands at a time. Because there was no beach, bathers descended directly into the waters of the lake. Amusement park rides assured that everyone had a good time. The other resorts faded. When Lake Park burned to the ground in 1904, Saltair was the only one remaining until lake levels dropped in the early 1930s and two new resorts were built closer to the lake: J.O. Griffith's Black Rock Beach a few miles south of Saltair, and Ira Dern's Sunset Beach a short distance east of Black Rock.

Despite fluctuations in the lake levels, the three resorts continued to entertain tourists transported to them by railroad and automobile through World War II. In those years, hundreds of people came to the large Moorish-styled pavilion for ballroom dancing. But ballroom dancing went out of style and the lake level dropped. Saltair burned down in the sixties, and no one came along to replace it until 1981.

This last attempt to capture the tourist trade on the Great Salt Lake was made by John Silver and Wally Wright. They built a large Moorish structure similar to the old Saltair resort pavilion of 1898 in a new location.

No sooner had Mr. Silver started a new era of recreation on the lake than Salt Lake City had record floods. The lake rose and flooded the new pavilion as well as the airport, railroad line, and the interstate highway to Nevada. Following two years of record floods came two years of drought. The Great Salt Lake receded, leaving Silver's pavilion high, dry, *and* waterlogged. It still stands at the **Great Salt Lake Beaches State Park.**

■ THE BONNEVILLE SPEEDWAY

The Great Salt Lake Desert once impeded transportation between the cities of Salt Lake City and San Francisco. Now the fastest men on earth come to the Bonneville Speedway portion of the Great Salt Lake Desert to race their machines. The unwary amateurs, curious to see what it is like on the vast expanse of seemingly hard, flat prehistoric lake bottom, sometimes drive off the road and become mired in gray-green mud.

Travelers to Nevada along Interstate 80 can stop at the rest area next to the Salt Flats and walk out on the salt. Displays explain the history of the Bonneville

Speedway where many land speed records have been set. The first trials began in 1896 when W.D. Rishel, a bicycle racer and promoter out of Salt Lake City, rode and carried his bicycle across the flats. The Bonneville Salt Flats International Speedway is only nine miles (14 km) long and 80 feet (24 m) wide. Most of the Salt Flats' approximately 44,000 acres is managed by the Bureau of Land Management.

In spring and winter, the salt flats are usually covered with water because surface moisture at this time neither penetrates nor evaporates readily. The water is, rather, blown about the surface by the wind until it evaporates. Water moving over the surface smoothes the salt, making it almost perfectly flat. The salt flats are said to be one of the only places in the United States where one can see the curvature of the earth over dry land.

Tourists to Utah should not be fooled by the illusions of the Great Basin. It is a desert filled with surprises. History has been preserved in countless small towns and ghost towns. High, forested mountains can be enjoyed without the crowds that usually flock to wilderness areas like the Sierra or the Great Smokies and the views from the peaks are unparalled. Wildlife of the desert, marsh, or forest is abundant. The Great Salt Lake is truly one of the wonders of the natural world and the Great Basin is a place of adventure.

The Mormon Meteor III set 81 new speed records in 1940 in the hands of the "world's greatest racing driver and mayor of Salt Lake City," Ab Jenkins. (Utah State Historical Society)

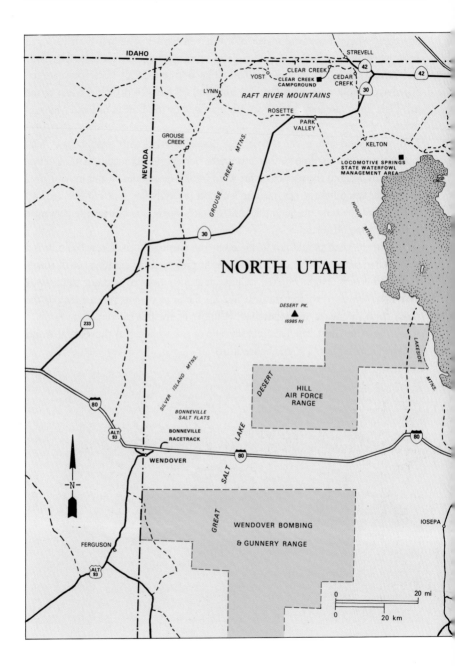

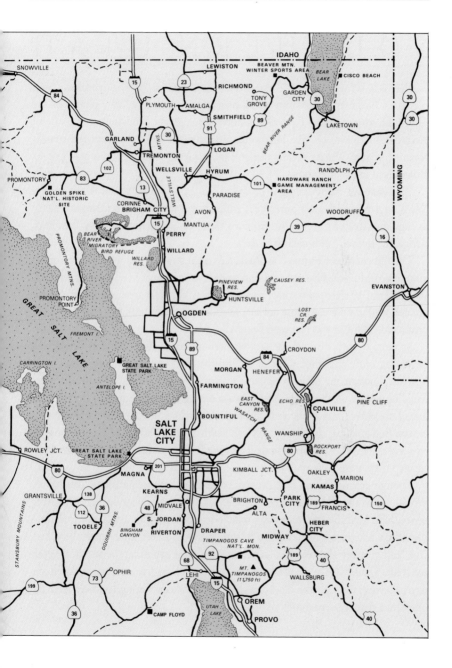

SOUTHERN UTAH

SOUTHERN UTAH IS A PLACE FULL OF INCREDIBLE SURPRISES, contrasts, and pleasures. Summer tourists can watch Shakespeare performed in a replica of the Globe Theatre in Cedar City, ride a horse amongst the sandstone monoliths of Kodachrome Basin, or hike into a remote canyon miles away from the nearest town or person. Winter visitors can golf in St. George in the morning and ski at Brian Head in the afternoon.

"By whatever name it might be called," once wrote long-time Utah author Ward Roylance, "this great province is as distinctive in its own peculiar personality as, say, the Alps of Europe, the Amazon Basin of South America, the Sahara of Africa, the steppes or Himalayas of Asia."

The "Enchanted Country," as Roylance called it, is indeed a unique, magical, almost surreal place. Five national parks preserve a hunk of it; so do four national monuments, 19 state parks, three national forests, three ski areas, six currently designated wilderness areas (more are sure to follow in the future), two BLM primitive areas, and Glen Canyon National Recreation Area.

As more tourists discover the famous national parks, like Zion and Bryce, it is becoming more and more difficult to find the kind of solitude enjoyed by early visitors. Though the scenery remains essentially the same as in pioneer times, avoiding people on the trails and roadways can be difficult. But even the popular areas host secret times of the year and remote canyons, which modern-day explorers can find and cherish. People who visit south-central Utah often become possessive and secretive and try to hide their favorite spots from others, hoping somehow to keep them unspoiled.

Though getting lost on backcountry roads does have its pleasures, this region should not be toured by automobile alone. Take time to explore the many nuances of southern Utah by raft, mountain bike, horseback, jeep, or airplane. More simply, take a hike in a lonely canyon. In some ways, southern Utah might be called "the land of many choices." You can spend a lifetime exploring the area and never see it all. Visitors make a mistake when they try to see five national parks in six days, blowing through the landscape like tumbleweeds. Seeing less here actually provides a chance to see more.

WHAT ARE PARKS FOR?

The Park Service, established by Congress in 1916, was directed not only to administer the parks but also to "provide for the enjoyment of same in such manner and by such means as will leave them unimpaired for the enjoyment of future generations." This appropriately ambiguous language, employed long before the onslaught of the automobile, has been understood in various and often opposing ways ever since. The Park Service, like any other big organization, includes factions and factions. The Developers, the dominant faction, place their emphasis on the words *"provide for the enjoyment."* The Preservers, a minority but also strong, emphasize the words *"leave them unimpaired."* It is apparent, then, that we cannot decide the question of development versus preservation by a simple referral to holy writ or an attempt to guess the intention of the founding fathers; we must make up our own minds and decide for ourselves what the national parks are and what purpose they should serve.

—Edward Abbey, *Desert Solitaire,* 1968

❖ ❖ ❖

There persists an old confusion between the National Parks and the National Forests—two very different things. The Forests provide the people, all the people, with magnificent facilities for recreation, and with vital watershed protection, and so do the Parks. But there the similarity ends. For the Forests are consistently put to economic use under policies prescribed by Congress and administered by the National Forest Service, a bureau of the Department of Agriculture. The Forests sell lumber and grazing, and can be developed for mining, irrigation, and power. The Parks sell nothing, although, like the Forests, they contract with concessioners to supply food and lodging and services to visitors. The Forests are open to grazing, under permit, and as a result have their troubles with some cattlemen. The same cattlemen yearn for grazing permits in the Parks, but there, in principle at least, they do not get them. Where cattle are seen in what appear to be Park lands, these are lands still held in private ownership within the Park's borders, and the Service is making every effort to eliminate them. Or the stock-owners are holders of pre-park permits which will not be renewed after their lifetime.

—Alfred A. Knopf, "The National Park Idea," *This is Dinosaur,* 1955

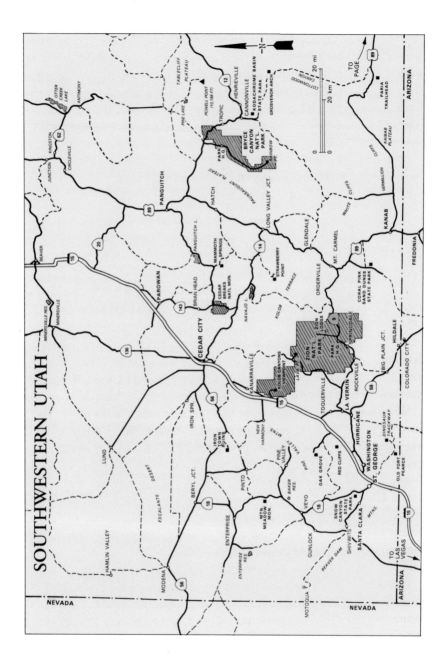

SOUTHWESTERN UTAH

This country challenges all five senses. Smell the sagebrush after a fall rainstorm. Feel the cool waters of the Green River as you enjoy a moonlight swim after a day of canoeing. Listen to the howl of a coyote on a dark night in Horse Pasture Canyon. Taste the dust stirred up after driving a four-wheel-drive vehicle over the challenging bumps of Canyonlands' Elephant Hill. Watch the sun set from the edge of Grandview Point on a late December afternoon, casting shadows over three mountain ranges and the canyons of the Colorado River.

Southern Utah can intimidate first-time visitors. Though civilization in the form of towns, gas stations, grocery stores, restaurants, and motels is seldom more than a few miles away, the dry desert and lonely roads can scare off the uninitiated.

■ FILLMORE TO CEDAR CITY

Interstate 15 leads south 160 miles (256 km) from Salt Lake City to Fillmore, a town of over 2,000 residents. Because the site is near the geographical center of the state, Brigham Young designated Fillmore as Utah's original territorial capital in 1851, even though no town then existed. Visitors can tour the **Territorial Statehouse**, Utah's oldest government building, pioneer living quarters, and a jail. The first of four planned wings was completed in 1855, and several territorial legislatures met here. Lack of facilities, and antagonism between the U.S. government and the Mormons, eventually caused the legislature to move to Salt Lake City.

When traveling south along the interstate, we like to detour along the old Utah State Highway 133 into towns like **Meadow** and **Kanosh**. This is a part of Utah where getting off the beaten track pays dividends. There are few museums or tourist facilities; instead, visitors can stop at an old general store to enjoy a soft drink and some pleasant conversation with a local merchant, who often has the time to talk about the history of his city. Old pioneer homes, many restored to their original condition, dot either side of the four-lane main streets decreed by Brigham Young. The old pioneer cemeteries reveal interesting bits of history and family names. In the Kanosh cemetery, look for the headstone marking the burial place of old Chief Kanosh, the Paiute leader when the pioneers first settled this area.

Corn Creek Canyon leads into the Fishlake National Forest, east of Kanosh. A small, developed campground—ideal for family reunions—sits next to a clear mountain stream full of wild brown trout. Mule deer roam in the oak brush, and a few pieces of ruddy-colored stone jut out above the canyon, hinting at the redrock grandeur farther south.

Beaver is a good town to explore. There are more than 200 historic houses of architectural interest scattered around town. Beaver began as an agricultural community. When gold and silver were found in the San Francisco Mountains to the west, non-Mormon miners rushed to Beaver. Tensions between the two groups, and threats of Indian attack, prompted the army to build Fort Cameron. One stone building from the fort still stands on the east edge of town, across the highway from the golf course.

The ornate **Beaver County Courthouse** now houses a historical museum of pioneer and mining exhibits, as well as the courtroom and a dungeon-like jail in the basement.

■ CEDAR CITY

After passing through Beaver and Parowan, visitors reach Cedar City. With 11,000 residents, it's the second largest settlement in southern Utah. Boosters call it "The Festival City," because of numerous special activities built around Southern Utah University. The **Summer Games**, an athletic extravaganza where athletes representing many different sports compete in an Olympic-type atmosphere, ushers in the summer festivities at Cedar City. But the main event of summer is the **Shakespearean Festival**, which runs from early July through the first week of September.

At present, theater goers choose from three Shakespearean plays in the Adams Memorial Theatre, on the SUU campus, and three other classical or contemporary productions in the Randall L. Jones Theatre. The **Adams Memorial Theatre** is one of the world's most accurate reproductions of Shakespeare's Globe Theatre. "We searched worldwide to find a replica of Shakespeare's theater and found it in Utah," said Peter Wineman, a producer at the British Broadcasting Corporation. The 700-seat Randall Jones Theatre is the cornerstone of the planned Utah Shakespearean Festival Center for the Performing Arts. Planners proclaim that the center will provide "exquisite landscaping, ambling walks, idyllic streams of water, fountains, statuary and a central plaza complete with one of the most ambitious bronze pieces to be found in our state. This plaza will be surrounded by three theaters, each serving as a venue for its own unique theatrical offerings. A replicated old English village will feature shops, tea room, clock tower, and the Utah Shakespearean Theatre Administration Center. This entire complex will be walled in to shut out all 20th Century intrusions and will become a mecca for thousands of students, theatre patrons and tourists."

Literary and production seminars, special workshops, backstage tours, foyer entertainments, and an orientation to the evening's performance are also presented during the Shakespearean Festival. The nightly **Greenshow** adds to the festivities with jugglers, puppeteers, and vendors dressed in Elizabethan costumes. The audience is invited to join skits and impromptu plays. In addition, the popular **Renaissance Feaste** tempts tourists to dine in the lively manner of Elizabethan England. Patrons attending an outdoor play at the Globe replica can watch the sky change from blue to red to black. During the rare summer thunderstorms, they may be forced to move inside the adjacent auditorium until the storm passes over.

Southern Utah's love of Shakespeare actually dates back to pioneer times. According to R. Scott Phillips, marketing director for the Utah Shakespearean Festival, Mormons who settled nearby Parowan staged a Shakespearean play three weeks after moving in from the north.

Fred Adams, who left New York City to come West, tried producing a popular Broadway musical for southern Utah residents and discovered little interest. Challenged, he organized a production of *Romeo and Juliet*. Much to his delight, the play sold out its initial three-night run, and two more nights as well.

When Interstate 15 bypassed Cedar City's Main Street in 1962, city fathers became nervous that the town might die. The local Lions Club put up $1,000 for the first Shakespearean Festival in 1962. *The Taming of the Shrew, Hamlet,* and *The Merchant of Venice* were performed on an outdoor platform supporting a partial replica of an Elizabethan pavilion. The first festival drew 3,276 patrons, giving organizers enough of a profit to continue. The original company numbered 20 persons.

Nowadays, some 215 workers and actors—including 20 full-time employees—labor to produce the festival. Over 60,000 theater patrons enjoy a season lasting several months and featuring more than fifty evening performances. This mammoth undertaking produces $10 million for the local economy.

For a glimpse of Cedar City's pioneer past, spend some time browsing through **Iron Mission State Park** on Main Street. The town earned the name of "The Iron Mission" because iron was produced here, making the city exceedingly important to the survival of Mormon self-sufficiency in the territory's early days. The park illustrates pioneer life with a collection of horsedrawn vehicles started by Gronway

Parry in 1911, including a Wells Fargo Stagecoach, an original Studebaker White Top wagon, buggies, surreys, mail carts, horsedrawn farm machinery, an old milk wagon, and even a one-horse sleigh. The most popular item is probably the stagecoach that Butch Cassidy reputedly riddled with bullets during his gang's escapades in the Four Corners section of Utah.

The Robert Redford-Paul Newman movie *Butch Cassidy and the Sundance Kid* gave even more notoriety to these two already famous Western outlaws. According to folklorist Dave Stanley, who chronicles the history and folklore associated with southern Utah's national parks and monuments, southern Utah abounds with tales and evidence of the outlaw Robert LeRoy Parker, alias Butch Cassidy.

"He and the Sundance Kid and the

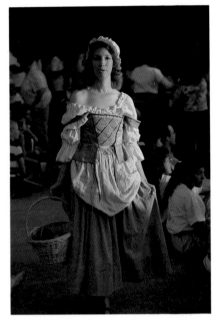

The Shakespearean Festival in Cedar City attracts more tourists than any other annual event in southern Utah.

rest of the Wild Bunch have been tracked through Bryce Canyon, Capitol Reef, and Canyonlands, especially in the Robbers' Roost country between Hanksville and Moab," writes Stanley. "Many of the Butch Cassidy stories treat him as a Robin Hood figure who robbed the rich and helped the poor. One tale concerns a local widow whose ranch was threatened by foreclosure. Butch and the boys robbed the local bank and delivered the cash to the woman, who paid off a surprised banker when he showed up at the ranch to evict her. On the way back to town, Butch held him up again and made off with the money."

Cedar City's festivals and proximity to major national parks, monuments, and forests have brought many amenities not found in cities of similar size. Restaurants, modern motels, and a community that welcomes out-of-towners make Cedar City a comfortable place to visit.

■ CEDAR BREAKS NATIONAL MONUMENT

Cedar Breaks National Monument sometimes does not open until mid-June, when the snow clears. With a drop of 2,500 feet (750 m) and a diameter of more than three miles (5 km), Cedar Breaks is shaped like a gigantic coliseum. Stone spires, columns, arches, and canyons in hues of tan, red, and orange change color and texture as the sun moves across the sky. Particularly enchanting is the short walk along the Alpine Pond Trail in early summer, when high meadows are ablaze with wildflowers.

Cedar Breaks was named, erroneously, by Mormon pioneers who settled Cedar City in 1851. The "cedars" growing near the base of the cliffs were actually juniper trees. The pioneers referred to the steep badland topography as "breaks"; their past works still dot the park.

Cedar Breaks is not simply a summer park, as we discovered during a January weekend vacation to the area. Winter might just be the best season for visiting this national monument. The operators of the nordic center at the nearby Brian Head Hotel have worked out a unique trail marking system. Utilizing plastic pipe tipped with flourescent orange paint, owner Bill Murphy and his fellow employees mark miles of cross-country ski trails. All are free, although there is a small charge for the trail maps. Brian Head nordic also offers tours and a variety of special programs, including ski tours under a full moon.

Visitors fortunate enough to glide quietly on cross-country skis around the rim of the amphitheater will find the view on a clear winter day breathtaking. Ancient bristlecone pines frame vistas of snow-covered red and tan rock below, and the icy silence magnifies the majesty of the entire place.

In the summer months, hikers can take a rugged 10-mile (16-km) backpacking trip into Rattlesnake Creek and the nearby U.S. Forest Service Ashdown Gorge Wilderness Area, located on the western boundary of the national monument. The trail descends an incredible 3,400 feet (1,030 m) into the gorge. Smart backpackers arrange to be picked up at the bottom of the hike rather than hiking back out.

Those who don't enjoy camping in the summer months may wish to rent a condominium or hotel room at off-season rates at the Brian Head ski area. Excellent mountain biking opportunities can be enjoyed as one of the ski resorts' lifts is available to carry mountain bikers to the top of the resort, making for an interesting trip down. Information, trail maps, guide services, and rentals are available at the shop inside the hotel. Brian Head offers a variety of other summer activities, including photography workshops, star-gazing parties, music festivals, and hikes.

Summer visitors to Cedar Breaks often take side trips to **Panguitch** and **Navajo lakes**. Both have rustic lodges and U.S. Forest Service campgrounds. Mountain bikers are discovering the challenging and scenic dirt roads and trails in this area.

■ ZION NATIONAL PARK

The Great White Throne, Angels Landing, Temple of Sinawava, the Guardian Angels, the Pulpit, Mount Moroni, the Tabernacle: the names of Zion's canyons, peaks, and rock formations reveal much about the nature of this land and the reverence for it held by the pioneers who settled this rugged country. Zion is Utah's oldest national park and one of its most beloved tourist destinations.

Nephi Johnson is believed to be the first non-Indian to enter Zion Canyon, in 1858. Isaac Behunin built the first cabin near the site of the present-day Zion Lodge in 1863. Zion first came under federal protection in 1909, when it was designated Mukuntuweap National Monument. Ten years later it became a national park.

Zion may be Utah's most "civilized" national park. Visitors can enjoy a stay in its recently refurbished lodge, or walk along paved hiking trails to the more popular attractions. Large developed campgrounds, a children's nature center, visitor facilities at both Zion Canyon and Kolob Canyon, ranger-guided hikes, naturalist programs, and evening campfire talks provide even more options for visitors. Just outside the park's southern boundary in the tiny town of **Springdale** are restaurants, motels, stores, and the O.C. Tanner Amphitheater, where Ballet West performs most summers, with Zion Canyon as a wonderful backdrop.

Yet, for all its civilized (and, in the summer, crowded) manner, Zion is essentially a wild place full of unexpected adventures for those willing to escape the confines of their cars and do some exploring. We'll never forget what appeared to be an easy spring stroll of just over a mile on the popular paved trail leading to the **Emerald Pools**. When a sudden thunderstorm hit the canyon, waterfalls began to pour over the trail. We had to cling to the sides of the cliffs as we crawled under the flowing water.

On a winter hike on the **East Rim Trail**, we explored a narrow passageway of twisted sandstone which almost formed a tunnel. We walked past ice frozen in bizarre shapes.

(previous pages) Winter adds a touch of white to Zion's familiar reds and greens.

Few who grip the chains on the **Angel's Landing Trail** to keep from falling into oblivion from the lip of a sheer sandstone cliff will forget the thrill.

Still, simply *driving* through the park is breathtaking. In Zion Canyon, the rock walls tower 2,000 to 3,000 feet (620-930 m) above your automobile. Negotiating the switchbacks up to the **Mt. Carmel Tunnel** and motoring past windows cut in the tunnel walls, you hardly dare to glance down at the chasm below. Emerging into daylight again, you find yourself on the edge of a great petrified sand dune carved into a checkerboard pattern, where large trees grow sideways out of bare rock. Appropriately, the feature is known as **Checkerboard Mesa**.

Zion is a four-season park. Fall rewards visitors with sights of blazing orange oaks and yellow cottonwoods shimmering at the bottom of gigantic crimson cliffs. Winter brings snowcapped sandstone peaks, ice formations, and cold solitude. The sound of the Virgin River swollen with runoff roaring through the canyon, and the smell of plants coming to life after a winter hibernation, greet springtime visitors. Summer brings blazing heat, which sends visitors scrambling to a cooling waterfall or the shade of a narrow canyon.

Parents visiting the park in the summer may want to consider signing their children up for the Junior Ranger Program at the **Zion Nature Center**, where rangers teach kids lessons in ecology, ethics, and biology.

More and more adventurers explore Zion by backpacking into canyons. In the remote **Kolob region** of the park, some 45 miles (72 km) east and north by road from Zion Canyon, backpackers can hike to Kolob Arch; with a span of 310 feet (96 m), it is the world's longest. Backcountry explorers may not always see wildlife like cougar, ringtail cat, bobcat, coyote, mule deer, and fox, but they can see signs of these critters in the dry sandy washes or on the banks of the tiny creeks which flow through this land of standing rocks.

■ UTAH'S DIXIE

As one motors south from Cedar City to Zion and then to **St. George**, it is easy to feel the change in the climate and see the difference in the landscape. The elevation at Cedar City is 5,800 feet (1,930 m). St. George, where locals claim the sun spends the winter, is 2,880 feet (960 m). Though the skyline of this bustling city is still dominated by the brilliant, white Mormon Temple, southern Utah's largest town enjoys newfound prosperity. The weather here is similar to Phoenix or Palm

The splendor of Zion National Park is apparent not only in the magnificent valley views but also in the park's hidden corners.

Springs, drawing thousands of Utahns south to swim, play golf and tennis, and bask in the winter sunlight. The city accommodates them with fine restaurants, modern hotels, pools and spas, and more than half a dozen golf courses.

In 1861, 300 Mormon families from Salt Lake City were led south by George A. Smith upon Brigham Young's request. (The town was named in honor of Smith, who was considered, after the Mormon tradition, a Latter-day Saint.) On orders from Brigham Young, who wanted Mormons to be independent from the outside world for their clothing, the settlers planted cotton—hence the name "Utah's Dixie."

Floods, drought, and disease hit the Mormons hard in Utah's Dixie. But the final blow to the cotton mission arrived with the completion of the transcontinental railroad in 1869, when cheaper cotton from the deep South became readily available.

For the hardy souls who stayed, and the lucky ones who came after, Utah's Dixie is now a gold mine. St. George is the fastest growing city in the state. The warm, dry climate and famous red rock lure thousands.

Travelers entering the valley from any direction still thrill to the sight of the spectacular white **Mormon Temple** framed by the red sandstone hills and dark green juniper and pinyon pine trees. Completed in 1877, it is the oldest temple still in use by the Latter-day Saints.

Take time to explore other pioneer sites, like the **Tabernacle**, the **Daughters of the Utah Pioneers Museum**, **Brigham Young's winter home**, the **Old Cotton Mill**, and the **Jacob Hamblin Home** in nearby Santa Clara, all of which provide glimpses of what early life was like here.

■ SIDE-TRIPS FROM ST. GEORGE

St. George is an ideal base for exploring Zion National Park, less than 40 miles (64 km) to the east. Zion, however, is only the most famous of the area's attractions.

North of St. George, the Pine Valley Mountains are a good place to escape the summer heat. **Pine Valley Recreation Area** and **Pine Valley Wilderness** are two promising hiking destinations, while water recreation is available at nearby **Gunlock Reservoir**, **Baker Dam Recreation Site**, and **Quail Creek Reservoir**.

West of the Pine Valley Mountains, just off Utah State Highway 18, is the **Mountain Meadows Massacre Historic Site**. A simple monument marks the place where 120 members of a California wagon train were attacked and executed by an alliance of Mormons and local Indians in 1857. Though the tightly knit Mormon community tried to cover up the incident, John D. Lee, who was in charge of Indian affairs in southern Utah at the time and was believed to be one of the leaders of the massacre, was brought to justice 20 years later, and executed in this same place. It is impossible to excuse their actions, but it must be understood that the Mormons felt besieged at the time of the massacre. The President had just sent Johnston's Army to Utah. The Mormons had heard what they considered threatening words from the gentile wagon train. They felt their isolation and security threatened by the outside world.

Naturalists and birdwatchers visiting the St. George area should not miss a fascinating oasis called **Beaver Dam Wash**, located south of the town of Shivwits in the extreme southwestern corner of the state. The southern region of the Great Basin, the western portion of the Colorado Plateau, and the northern part of the Mojave Desert all merge there at Utah's lowest elevation of 2,000 feet (667 m) above sea level. Brigham Young University, which worked with the Nature Conservancy to purchase the area, manages Beaver Dam Wash as a natural preserve. On a family hike one late December, we scared up a flock of mallards sitting on a pond. It may take some work to find the Beaver Dam Wash, but it's worth it.

If you only have time to visit one park (aside from Zion) in the St. George area, don't miss **Snow Canyon**, five miles (eight km) north of St. George off Utah State Highway 18. With hot showers and hookups for trailers, the scenic campground at Snow Canyon is among the best in this part of the state. If you hike to the small arch in the canyon, try to find the Indian pictographs on the canyon walls. Kids especially like to play in the sand dunes. The more adventurous can take flashlights into the lava caves. Many a photographer has stood at a Snow Canyon overlook and marveled at the contrasting colors of the red sandstone and black basalt formations of lava.

Near the town of Rockville, a few miles from the south entrance to Zion National Park, the ghost town of **Grafton** brings photographers by the dozens to snap pictures. Fans of Paul Newman will recognize the town, with its schoolhouse, store, and cabins, as the setting of the bicycle scene in *Butch Cassidy and the Sundance Kid.* A nearby graveyard (you may need to ask locals for directions to find it) preserves interesting hand-carved headstones.

Kanab is a pretty town located 41 miles (66 km) southeast of Zion on the Utah-Arizona border, close to both Lake Powell and Arizona's Grand Canyon. The town has been a center of the Western movie industry for many years. **Lopeman's Frontier Movie Town** has been built to show tourists a bit of the old West. Admission is free.

While in Kanab, be sure to visit the **Kanab Heritage House**, an 1895 Queen Anne-style Victorian built by one Henry Bowman. He lived in it only two years before being called away on a mission. A photo of the next owner, Thomas Chamberlain, along with his six wives and 55 children, is in the sitting room. The house is open for tours in the summer or by appointment with the city clerk.

Stark, ruddy-colored hills of sand are the main attraction at nearby **Coral Pink Sand Dunes State Park.** Its small campground provides an out-of-the-way experience that differs greatly from the larger, crowded campgrounds at Zion. We once watched the sunrise while eating breakfast at a lonely picnic table on the edge of the dunes. The shapes of the few juniper trees growing nearby took on a surrealistic appearance in the early-morning light.

One of the West's most vivid pictures of pioneer life is recreated in the living history program at **Pipe Spring National Monument** on Arizona State Highway

(above) The color of the dunes at Coral Pink Sand Dunes State Park near the Arizona border is enhanced by the setting sun. (opposite) Brigham Young's winter home in St. George.

389, southwest of Kanab. Stepping through the gates of the visitor center is like being whisked away in a time machine. The place is just as it was in pioneer times. In the summer, docents dressed in period garb act the parts of pioneers and profess to knowing nothing about the twentieth century. Each September, local citizens try to put together a covered wagon ride from Pipe Springs to St. George along the **Honeymoon Trail**. It takes about four days by wagon to cover what is a 90-minute automobile drive. The trail received its colorful name because Mormon couples from all over the Arizona Strip (that part of Arizona north of the Grand Canyon) used it to reach the temple in St. George, where they were married. Thus, they spent their honeymoon riding back on the trail.

■ BRYCE CANYON

Bryce is not really a canyon at all. It's a series of 14 huge amphitheaters which extend a thousand feet down through the pink and white limestones of the Paunsaugunt Plateau. Bryce Canyon has been described as the most colorful national park in the world. Depending on the time of season, the hour of the day, and the weather, the fantastic formations of limestone visible from Inspiration and Rainbow points turn vivid shades of white, orange, yellow, red, and purple. When you first approach Bryce Canyon, take time to sit on a bench at the edge of one of the amphitheaters and contemplate the extraordinary scene before you.

Indian legend claimed that Bryce was built as a city for the people of Coyote. Because they worked too long beautifying their city, Coyote became angry. He turned the people all to stone and overturned the paints they were using. They are still standing there, rows and rows of them, with the paint dried on their faces.

Who can resist striking out on the trails for such enchanting destinations as Queen's Garden, Navajo Loop, Peekaboo Loop, Under-the-Rim, and Fairyland? Trails give hikers intimate views of formations like the **Chinese Wall**, **Mormon Temple**, **Fairy Castle**, the **Cathedral**, the **Alligator**, the **Sinking Ship**, **Wall of Windows**, and **Boat Mesa**. Unfortunately for hikers who may not be in the best of shape, the walks down into the Bryce amphitheater are deceivingly easy. Climbing back out with elevation gains of anywhere from 300 to more than 800 feet (100-270 m) can be a real chore, especially during the hot summer months. The easiest hike is the 1.5-mile (2.5-km) **Queen's Garden Trail**, which begins at Sunrise Point and takes about two hours to complete. Once, visiting Bryce with friends, we took the advice of a ranger and left one of cars at the bottom of the canyon near the tiny town of Tropic. Driving back up to the amphitheater, we made the four-mile (6.5-km) hike, downhill all the way, and shuttled back to our campground.

Less crowded trails wander through the meadows of the **Paunsaugunt Plateau** on the west side of the park. In the spring, sego lilies, penstemons, asters, clematis, evening primrose, scarlet gilias, Indian paintbrush, and wild iris turn this part of Bryce into a garden full of wonderful color. Ancient bristlecone pines, alive during the time of Christ, still inhabit Bryce Canyon.

Though all of Utah's five national parks experience four distinct seasons, the extremes are greater at Bryce Canyon, mainly because of its high elevation, reaching 9,105 feet (2,937 m) at Rainbow Point. This means temperatures in winter dip well below freezing. Winter is one of the best times to see Bryce.

A few years ago, our family ventured into an all-but-deserted Bryce Canyon in the dead of winter wondering what we would do. The spires of crimson red limestone in the Bryce amphitheater were dusted with snow. Three to five feet (one-two m) of the white stuff could be seen on the Queen's Garden and Navajo Loop trails as we admired the wintery scene from overlooks. The ranger at the visitor center suggested we try some (free) snowshoes.

The six of us strapped the unwieldy things onto our boots and spent the next four hours alone in the magical paradise of Bryce. Large spires in strange shapes loomed above us on the trail. We lay down in the feathery, powdery snow and watched crystals float down from the canyon walls. In places the trail was so narrow that the towering rock formations all but hid the blue sky from our eyes. We were alone; no trains of horses, strings of hikers, or sounds of automobiles and buses could be heard. Instead, the winter silence gave our family a sense of what this place must have been like when it was initially inhabited by the Anasazi Indians, or when Ebenezer Bryce, a New England shipbuilder and stockman, came here in 1875.

A mistake made by many who visit Bryce Canyon is that they end their exploration of this part of Utah with the national park and fail to keep driving east on Utah State Highway 12, where some of the state's best-kept secrets can be unlocked. This road brings travelers to some of the most remote and isolated towns and backcountry; the stately alpine forests give this part of Utah an entirely different look from that of Zion or Capitol Reef.

■ KODACHROME BASIN

If our family were asked to pick its favorite place in Utah, we would probably select Kodachrome Basin State Reserve, a scenic little valley full of towering monolithic chimneys unlike anything else in the world. Yet, because Kodachrome Basin —which was named by the National Geographic Society—is located off the main highway on a (well-maintained) dirt road, most tourists miss it.

To our way of thinking, the 24-unit campground, located in the midst of the rock spires and pinyon/juniper forest, ranks among the best of its kind in the state, largely because each site is set so far from its neighbor. We've spent many an Easter weekend watching the children scramble up the sandstone walls, rolling Easter eggs in the soft, red soil, and soaking up the quiet solitude of this wonderful park.

Taking a hike to **Shakespeare Arch**, the small rock formation discovered by the superintendent of Kodachrome Basin while searching for a coyote den one afternoon, helps introduce visitors to the ecology of the desert. Hikers walk past typical plants like juniper, sagebrush, buffaloberry, Indian rice grass, false buckwheat, saltbrush, snakeweed, yucca, Mormon tea, and rabbitbrush. The plants, animal tracks in the tan sand, gnarled trees, and potholes seen along the way give clues to the forces which shaped this strange, almost surrealistic setting.

Kodachrome Basin always had fresh water available to campers, but until recently, primitive facilities kept some visitors away. Using largely volunteer labor, park superintendent Tom Shakespeare recently constructed a modern restroom facility, complete with showers, at the reserve campground. A concessionaire provides guided horseback, wagon, and stagecoach rides.

The rugged dirt road which leads south from Cannonville to Kodachrome Basin gets considerably rougher beyond the park (check with Kodachrome rangers before attempting to drive it). It goes to **Grosvenor Arch**, an unusual, yellowish-tan span named in honor of the founder of the National Geographic Society. Farther south, the unusual rock formations of **Cottonwood Canyon** greet surprised visitors. These rocks have been named the Cockscomb because they resemble the top of a rooster's head.

The Paria River runs through this area, leading into the **Paria Canyon-Vermillion Cliffs Wilderness Area** on the Utah-Arizona border. Backpackers, who sometimes must wade through waist-deep water, tell many stories of the narrow, twisting canyons of the Paria River.

Bryce Canyon is not an actual canyon at all, but a series of amphitheatres cut into the pink cliffs.

■ ESCALANTE CANYON COUNTRY

Returning to Cannonville and heading east on Utah State Highway 12, travelers pass through Henrieville en route to the red-rock country of the Escalante River, believed by most historians to be the last major river "discovered" by government surveyors in the continental United States. It's a wild land of arches, goblins, hoodoos, and assorted canyons. As it always has been, the river remains a major barrier to east-west transportation. Much of the area's colorful history involves pioneers trying to discover routes through the canyon and across the river. Hole-in-the-Rock Road, the Harris Wash-Silver Falls Canyon wagon route, the Boynton Road, the Boulder Mail (or Death Hollow) Trail, and the Old Boulder Road were all valiant attempts. The first bridge over the Escalante wasn't completed until 1935, making the town of Boulder one of the last places in the United States to be accessible to automobiles.

Before doing much exploring in this area, it is a good idea to stop at the BLM office in Escalante. Literature, safety information, maps, and historical data can all help visitors enjoy the canyons.

The Hole-in-the-Rock expedition is perhaps the most colorful story about the pioneers who were searching for a short cut into southeastern Utah. Pioneers discovered the Hole in the Rock, a narrow slit in the 2,000-foot (600-m) cliff overlooking the Colorado River. More than 200 people, 82 wagons with two or more teams of horses, about 200 additional horses, and more than 1,000 head of cattle made the 290-mile (470-km) journey, traversing 1.7 miles (2.7 km) per day.

Today, some of the **Hole-in-the-Rock Road** has been drowned by Lake Powell, but enough signs of the original trek remain that boaters on Lake Powell, or drivers willing to brave the rigors of a sometimes rugged 61-mile (98-km) county-maintained gravel road, can still view the places where pioneers struggled. The road passes **Dance Hall Rock**, a huge sandstone amphitheater where dances kept pioneer morale high, en route to the crevice above the Colorado, where the party used blasting powder and picks to open a passage to the river. If you thread your way down the steep, narrow sandstone slit, you will find yourself appreciating the immense hardships the pioneers endured.

Another interesting site is **Devil's Garden Outstanding Natural Area**, a fantastic collection of hoodoos reminiscent of Arches National Park and Goblin Valley.

Throughout southern Utah, narrow canyons, such as this one along the Virgin River, provide shelter from the blazing summer sun.

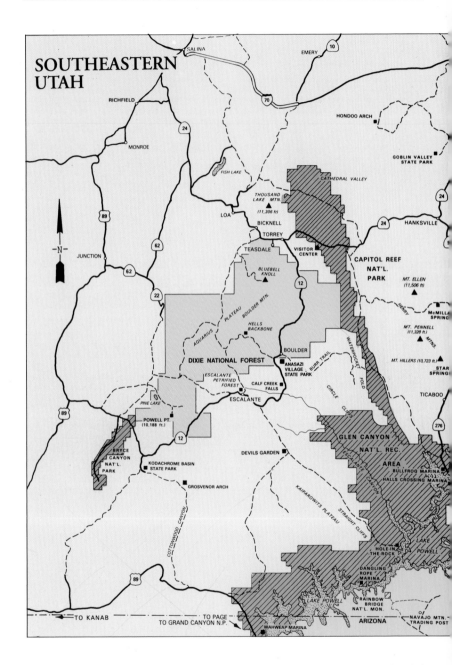

SOUTHEASTERN
UTAH

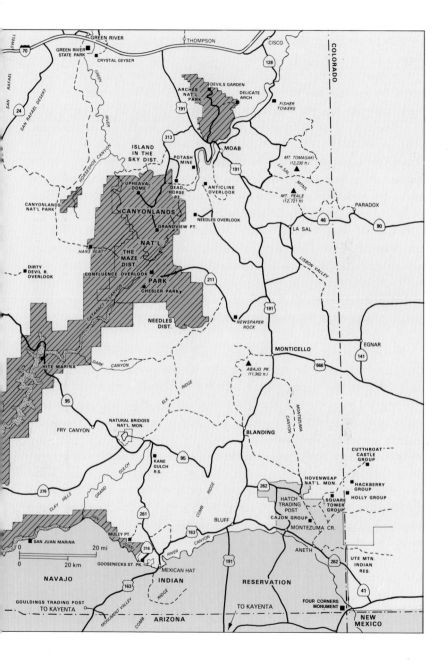

Devil's Garden also provides access to popular backpacking areas like **Harris Wash.** Our most memorable trip along Hole-in-the-Rock Road came on an Easter weekend a few years ago. Mel Davis, who published Rudi Lambrechtse's excellent book *Hiking the Escalante* (which should be required reading for anyone planning to explore this part of Utah), served as our guide into **Spooky Gulch** and **Peekaboo Canyon.** Both consisted of nothing more than narrow cracks cut by water through the sandstone. Spooky Gulch was so cramped in one spot that only the children and slimmest adults could pass. At one point in the Peekaboo Canyon hike, it was possible to scramble to the top of the canyon and look down at hikers 20 feet (six m) below while straddling the crack.

Perhaps the best-known Escalante destination is **Calf Creek Falls**, 15 miles (24 km) east of the town of Escalante. Small natural arches, thousand-year-old Indian rock art, an Anasazi ruin and, after a somewhat difficult hike, the falls itself, make this a special destination. Summer visitors can swim in the warm, shallow waters of Calf Creek to celebrate the finish of the trek. Camping and picnic sites, playground equipment, a volleyball court, and restrooms make this one of the nicest BLM facilities anywhere.

When the campground at Calf Creek is full, **Escalante Petrified Forest State Park** on the west end of Escalante makes a fine alternative. Backpackers regard this park with particular respect, largely because they like using its shower facilities after several days on the trail. The campground includes some shade, a grassy area, and access to Wide Hollow Reservoir, a good place to swim and fish. Hiking trails lead to the small petrified forest.

Anasazi Village State Park conserves the remains of an ancient village constructed on top of a mesa. With a year-round water supply, fertile fields, a broad view of the surrounding countryside, and abundant wild game, wood, and stone, the village was able to support 200 people for 75 years. The park museum explains how the Anasazi lived, while a reconstructed pueblo allows visitors to see for themselves. You can, for instance, try your hand at grinding corn the Indian way with a *mano* and *metate.* The University of Utah Natural History Museum sponsors annual digs here for amateur archaeologists who want to help excavate.

Passing through **Boulder**, Utah State Highway 12 climbs north to the 9,200-foot (3,067-m) summit of the Boulder Mountains, enjoying glimpses of Capitol Reef and the Waterpocket Fold to the east, the Aquarius Plateau to the west, and the Escalante canyons, Straight Cliffs, and Kaiparowits Plateau to the south. The temptation will be great to stay in one of three developed Dixie National Forest campgrounds along the road, from which you can hike into one of the many lakes on Boulder Mountain itself—lakes teeming with some of the largest brook trout found in the United States.

Our family likes to take the short drive south of Bicknell to the Division of Wildlife Resources **Perry Egan fish hatchery**, where trout eggs for all the other hatcheries in Utah are produced. Large cutthroat, albino, rainbow, and brown trout can be seen swimming in the concrete raceways. It's not rare to see fish hatchery workers stripping eggs from these huge trout. Workers are usually more than happy to take a minute or two to explain the process of obtaining eggs and raising fingerling trout to plant in lakes, reservoirs, and streams throughout the state.

■ CAPITOL REEF NATIONAL PARK

Capitol Reef gets its name from two geological curiosities of the **Waterpocket Fold**, a 100-mile (160-km) bulge in the earth's crust containing eroded pockets that catch water after each rainfall. Early settlers thought that the mountains, which dominate the landscape of the national park, resembled a coral reef. One of the white sandstone outcroppings, **Capitol Dome**, resembles that monument in our nation's capital. The area was designated a national monument in 1937 and transferred to national park status in 1971.

Influences of Mormon pioneer settlers remain in and around the little town of **Fruita**: a barn, a farmhouse, rock fences, an 1896 one-room schoolhouse, and acres of fruit orchards. These provide beautiful displays of blossoms in the spring, shade during the hot summer months, and fruit—apples, cherries, peaches, apricots, and pears—in the late summer and fall. The public is invited to pick them and pay a small per-pound or bushel price. The campground is located in the midst of one of these orchards. Deer and skunks—which often get too friendly with campers—frequent the area. The old weathered barn, situated against the red-rock cliffs guarding the campground, is one of the most frequently photographed structures in southern Utah.

The Fremont River runs through the middle of the park along Utah State Highway 24, a lifeline for the fruit orchards and cottonwoods. Archaeologists believe the Fremont Indians inhabited this area as long ago as A.D. 800. They left petroglyphs and storage bins, called *moki* huts, along the walls of the canyons.

Visitors can enjoy a nice drive through Capitol Reef on a fine paved road, but no trip can be complete without at least one short hike. Walking to **Hickman Bridge** or through **Capitol Gorge** and **Grand Wash** helps visitors appreciate the fascinating geology of the park. Kids especially love these strolls, where they can scramble up the easy-to-climb sandstone and through the little stone alcoves, playing hide-and-seek, for hours. Water pockets, or "tanks," can be viewed by hikers exploring the park. Longer, more difficult treks take walkers to **Cassidy Arch, Frying Pan Canyon** (where a shout turns into an echo

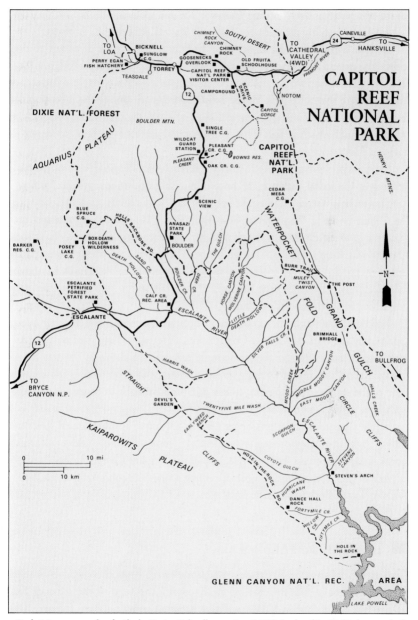

Early Mormon setttlers built the Fruita Schoolhouse circa 1896. It closed in 1941 due to a lack of students.

heard several times over), **Spring Canyon**, and the **Golden Throne**. An excellent hiking guide detailing the most popular trails is available at the visitor center.

Solitude seekers can take longer hikes from the **Burr Trail**, a dirt track cutting down the eastern boundary of the park, with one spur south to Lake Powell and another west to the town of Boulder. There are many washes to explore and arches to discover in this land. The **Muley Twist Canyons** are among the most popular backpacking destinations. As is the case in all of Utah's national parks, backpackers need a permit, which is free. This is dry country most of the year, so expect to carry in your own water.

Jeepers will enjoy exploring the rugged dirt road on the north end of the park leading to **Cathedral Valley**. Here, huge monolithic sandstone remnants form jutting buttes that resemble cathedrals in the desert. To the south, motorists may prefer a journey along the unpaved Burr Trail, which is passable by passenger cars (bring a good spare!). At first, farms and cattle ranches with lush green alfalfa contrasting with deep red soil dot the landscape. Then, after a harrowing drive up narrow switchbacks, the trail enters a sandstone canyon not unlike Zion's. Mountain bikers especially like traversing the Burr Trail in fall, spring, and even winter, taking advantage of the cooler weather.

The Burr Trail has been mired in an environmental controversy in recent years. Spurred by the Garfield County Commission, state leaders have tried to make improvements and even pave the scenic route to increase tourism in the area. Environmentalists, opposed to opening up adjacent potential wilderness areas on either side of the trail to development, fought the proposal both in court and in Congress, but parts of the road are now paved.

While no accommodations or restaurants are found inside Capitol Reef National Park, tiny Wayne County hamlets like Torrey, Bicknell, and Loa furnish some unexpected treats. For example, stop at the Sunglow Cafe in Bicknell and try a piece of pickle or pinto-bean pie. Or enjoy a fine Mexican dinner at La Buena Vida in Torrey. Both towns have small motels.

■ THE SAN RAFAEL SWELL

The stretch of Interstate 70 between Salina and Green River cuts through Fishlake National Forest (watch for deer on the highway), the heart of the red-rock San Rafael Swell and Sinbad Valley, without passing through a town for over 100

The muddy Colorado River winds through Cataract Canyon in Canyonlands National Park.

miles. Some devotees argue that this is one of the most scenic portions of interstate highway in the entire national system.

The Swell has been described as the jagged remains of a dinosaur backbone, an exposed sandstone coral reef, a saw blade, and a scene from the Arabian Nights. It's desolate but interesting country with a colorful history. Many believe it is worthy of national park status.

North of Interstate 70 at **Buckhorn Draw**, travelers can view the pictographs and petroglyphs left by ancient Indians who roamed this area thousands of years ago. Backpackers, horseback riders, and off-highway-vehicle enthusiasts can discover places like the Black Box, the Little Grand Canyon, Wedge Overlook, Black Dragon Canyon, the Muddy River, Crack Canyon, Iron Wash, Little Wildhorse Canyon, and the Copper Globe. Outlaws and cattle rustlers once hid in the narrow, winding canyons of the San Rafael Swell.

Maps and information for exploring the San Rafael Reef are available from the Price Chamber of Commerce and BLM offices in Salt Lake City, Price, and Hanksville. Michael Kelsey's guidebook, *Hiking Utah's San Rafael Swell*, also provides detailed information, photographs, and maps of trails inside the Swell.

■ GREEN RIVER

The 57-mile (92-km) drive on US Route 6/191 between Price and Green River gives glimpses of some of Utah's wildest, most desolate country. **Desolation Canyon**, a popular stretch of the Green River for rafting, is hidden from the road by the Tavaputs Plateau, Roan Cliffs, and Beckwith Plateau to the east. To the west, the northern portion of the San Rafael Swell looms on the horizon. On some stormy evenings, the sun plays tricks with the clouds. Thunderbolts slash across one part of the sky while a rainbow graces another. Save for the tiny coal-mining communities of East Carbon and Sunnyside to the east, there are no towns on this stretch of highway, leaving drivers free to relax while enjoying the grand vistas.

At first sight, **Green River** may seem desolate and bleak, but closer inspection reveals that this farm and tourist town has some interesting prospects. Built at an easy ford of the Green River, it's famous for its fine-tasting watermelons. Folks from all over Utah flock here in September to celebrate Melon Days, enjoy the early fall weather and, of course, buy melons from roadside stands.

For those who would like a taste of the rapids, canyons, and lore of the Colorado and Green rivers, the **John Wesley Powell River History Museum** offers telling glimpses of the famous explorer's journeys, as well as interpretive hands-on exhibits, art displays, a river runners' hall of fame, and a multimedia presentation.

Green River State Park south of town hosts campers in a lovely, shaded, grassy campground. It does fill at times during the summer, but there are nearby private campgrounds which almost always have space available. The park serves as a launching point for some Green and Colorado rivers rafting trips, and offers a fine stretch of flatwater for canoes. The Memorial Day weekend Friendship Cruise, on which powerboaters take a scenic two- or three-day journey down the Green River to its confluence with the Colorado River, and then up the Colorado to Moab, begins here.

A sandstone frieze at the John W. Powell River History Museum depicts Powell battling the rapids of the Green River.

■ THE ROADS TO LAKE POWELL

Southeast of the town of Green River, Utah State Highway 21 heads back toward Capitol Reef along the edge of the San Rafael Swell.

One of our family's favorite destinations is **Goblin Valley**, on the edge of the Swell, roughly midway between Interstate 70 and Hanksville. Goblin Valley is 17 miles (27 km) beyond a clearly marked turnoff.

Goblin Valley is filled with stone babies, goblins, ghosts, and toadstools that range in height from 10 to 200 feet (3-67 m). They stand like families of red goblins poured out, one by one, by a giant wizard and left frozen in time. The formations were made by uneven weathering of the sandstone; the softer material was removed by wind and water, leaving thousands of harder sections in unusual shapes. Water erosion and the smoothing action of windblown dust work together to shape the goblins.

There is something wonderful about wandering through the maze of goblins, toadstools, and hoodoos at night under a full moon. Children love to play hide-and-seek and turn this valley into a giant playground. It is easy to see the role rain plays in shaping Goblin Valley. We've witnessed an unexpected thunderstorm turn the hollows between the goblins into shallow streams resembling the chocolate river in *Willie Wonka and the Chocolate Factory*. Because there are few plants here, the mud flowed right off the formations. Minutes after the storm ended, the streams disappeared into the sand, and the goblins had taken new shapes.

Arthur Chaffin, who once owned and operated the Hite Ferry, stumbled upon Goblin Valley in the late 1920s while searching for an alternate route between Green River and Caineville. He called it Mushroom Valley. The area received protection as a scenic area in 1954, when it was under the control of the Bureau of Land Management, and officially became a state park on August 24, 1964.

Plan on spending at least several hours there, or better yet, stay a night at the campground. Showers, drinking water, and a trailer dump station are all available.

At **Hanksville**, travelers can either head west to Capitol Reef National Park, or south to Bullfrog and Hite marinas on Lake Powell in the Glen Canyon National Recreation Area.

Thunderstorms form over higher terrain, and the lower washes quickly turn into torrents, posing a serious risk to summer campers.

■ LAKE POWELL

Lake Powell, the second largest man-made reservoir in the world, is likewise Utah's second most popular tourist destination. Lake Powell receives some 3.2 million visitors a year—more than either Grand Canyon or Yellowstone national parks. The Glen Canyon Dam, located near Page, Arizona, has created a 186-mile (298-km) reservoir with a meandering, 1,960-mile (3,154-km) shoreline—longer than the entire western U.S. coastline. The recreation area itself consists of 1,869 square miles (4,840 sq km). Most of that is accessible only by boat, some of it can be reached by automobile, and other parts can be explored by hikers or rafters.

"There are few places on earth that cannot be adequately described," wrote Arizona author Bob Hirsch in his book *Houseboating on Lake Powell*. "Lake Powell is one of them. You'll know the first time you nudge the bow of your houseboat onto some sandy shore in a lonesome canyon far up the lake. It is quiet and peaceful and your eye delights in the patch of blue sky above, framed by soaring walls of buff and pink and light chocolate. The day is yours . . . from the time dawn tints a far-off butte from black to gray to the blush of rose, to the final hour storing up memories beside a driftwood fire, watching shadows dance on the ancient walls."

There is much to do at Lake Powell. At the very least, motorists should go to Bullfrog Marina and ride the small John Atlantic Burr Ferry to Halls Crossing. Inaugurated in 1985, the ferry provides a different route to southeastern Utah for vehicles and trailers of all sizes.

Bullfrog Basin, Hall's Crossing, and **Hite** are the preeminent marinas at the upper end of the reservoir, offering powerboat and houseboat rentals, beaches, and campgrounds. Tourists who don't want to steer their own boat can stay in modern lodges overlooking the lake at either Bullfrog or Wahweap and take a guided tour-boat ride.

Houseboating is an especially popular way to see Lake Powell. Some of the larger boats sleep up to 12 people. With gas available at the Dangling Rope Marina near Rainbow Bridge, boaters don't have to return to the main docking areas for days at a time. There are arches to discover, Indian ruins to find, and narrow canyons that lead into fine hiking areas. Taking a moonlight summer swim in the warm waters, or renting a water-ski boat adds much to a trip to Lake Powell.

As avid fishermen, we like to avoid the crowds of summer by renting a power-boat in either April or May or from mid-September to late October. Fishing for

Lake Powell's 1,960 miles of shoreline provide Utahns with a host of recreational opportunities.

large- and smallmouth bass, striped bass, crappie, northern pike, walleye, and channel catfish is best during those times of year. We like to pack all our tents, campstoves, and sleeping bags in the bow of the boat and head off to some secluded beach, where we can find some excellent fishing, swim, and enjoy a big driftwood fire in the evening.

Lake Powell boaters would do well to purchase one of Stan Jones's maps. Updated annually, these maps use a system of numbered buoys to help visitors find major landmarks, canyons, fishing areas, and other points of interest. Because this reservoir is so large, and because a boater can go miles before reaching the end of a flooded canyon, it is always possible to get lost or run out of gas.

Probably the most famous sight along Lake Powell is **Rainbow Bridge**. With a height of 290 feet (91 m) and a span of 270 feet (84 m), it is the world's largest natural bridge. This spot, sacred to the Navajo Indians, has been named one of the seven natural wonders of the world. If you visit this part of Glen Canyon National Recreation Area, search for the carving of author Zane Grey etched underneath a stone crevice behind the bridge. In Grey's day, only a few hearty souls made the long and difficult hike. Now, thousands of boaters visit the monument annually.

The **Henry Mountains** dominate the horizon to the northwest of the upper end of Lake Powell and furnish their own special kind of recreation. The dry, rugged character of the Henrys have kept them in a wild, natural state. Thousands of acres around the two highest peaks in the range, Mt. Ellen and Mt. Pennell, have been proposed for wilderness designation. John Wesley Powell named the range after Professor Joseph Henry of the Smithsonian Institute, one of his supporters. Prospectors have searched the Henrys for gold and other minerals since the turn of the century. Robbers' Roost, an important stopping point on the famed "Outlaw Trail" that stretched from Canada to Mexico, is found here. The remote canyons also made fine places for cattle rustlers to hide their bounty. The nearby **Dirty Devil River**, which now pours into Lake Powell, received its moniker because Powell and his men claimed "it stinks like a dirty devil."

The Utah Division of Wildlife Resources introduced 18 buffalo into the western foothills of the Henrys in 1941. Now hunters harvest surplus animals of what is one of the few wild, free-roaming buffalo herds in the country. In addition, the area is home to mountain lions, mule deer, snipe, chukar, blue grouse, and jackrabbits. Backpackers and four-wheel-drive enthusiasts seeking solitude enjoy dispersed recreation opportunities in this part of the state.

Rainbow Bridge is probably the largest natural arch in the world.

■ MOAB

Most visitors go to Moab by way of Interstate 70, turning south at US Route 191. A more scenic route awaits those who come by way of Cisco, however, where Utah State Highway 128 hooks south from the interstate. After crossing the Colorado River, it leads past Fisher Towers and through Castle Valley to Moab. **Fisher Towers** are isolated remnants of a 225-million-year-old floodplain. They gained some fame in 1964 and 1974 when helicopters placed cars on atop the pinnacles to make some automobile commercials. A 2.2-mile (3.5 km) hiking trail around the base of the towers takes about three hours to complete.

The town of **Moab**, with a population of just over 5,000, serves as the tourist hub of southeastern Utah. Though Monticello, Blanding, Mexican Hat, and Bluff to the south, all have a few tourist amenities, Moab offers much more than motels, concessionaires, restaurants, shops, and some unusual museums. Moab is, first and foremost, an incomparable base of operations for exploring the extraordinary canyonlands area of southeastern Utah, and in particular, Arches and Canyonlands national parks and the La Sal Mountains. It is also the preeminent base of operations for river trips, bicycle excursions, hikes, and four-wheel-drive expeditions through the red-rock country. On top of that, thousands of visitors from all over the United States come for the special yearly events, like the Moab Half-Marathon in March, the Easter Jeep Safari, the Friendship Cruise powerboat voyage on the Green and Colorado rivers, the Labor Day Jeep Jamboree, and the October Fat Tire Festival for mountain bikers. But most of all, Moab is the base for exploring some of the greatest canyon country in the world.

One word of advice to spring, summer, and fall travelers: arrive early in the day to get lodging, or better yet, make reservations. The campground at nearby Arches National Park is usually full from late March to late October. Though it does occasionally snow in the winter and temperatures can dip down below freezing, off-season travelers to this part of Utah generally enjoy relatively mild weather. We think the ideal months to visit the Moab area are April and October.

Founded in the 1870s by Mormon farmers and ranchers after an 1855 mission attempt failed, Moab was named for the biblical kingdom at the edge of Zion, the promised land. The town itself is located in a green valley on the edge of the Colorado River and is surrounded by high sandstone cliffs. With Utah's "Zion" of Salt Lake City located almost 300 miles (483 km) to the north, Mormon settlers must have felt that they, too, were living on the edge in this remote, often hot and dry place. Moab remained a quiet ranching community until the early 1950s, when a uranium boom tripled the town's population in three years and turned old prospectors like the near-legendary Charlie Steen into millionaires overnight. Steen earned and lost a fortune in just a few years. His home, named **Mi Vida** after the mine that made him rich, sits high above town and now serves as a scenic, historic restaurant. The town also became a center of potash mining, but as is the case in many mining ventures, the boom went bust and Moab turned to tourism for its survival.

Scenic country with a Western flavor helped turn Moab into a movie center. John Wayne films like *Rio Grande* and *The Comancheros*, the biblical movie *The Greatest Story Ever Told* with Max von Sydow, and more recently, *Indiana Jones and The Last Crusade* were filmed in the area. The recently opened **Hollywood Stuntman's Hall of Fame Museum**, at 100 East 100 West, provides further glimpses of the role Moab has played in movie making.

The Colorado River town of Moab is the gateway to Arches National Park.

First-time visitors to Moab should stop first at the **Chamber of Commerce** at the north end of town for free brochures and videos on such fascinating subjects as Moab area movie locations, walking tours of the city, car tours, restaurants, mountain bike trails, jeep trails, rental equipment, winter activities, hiking trails, and other kinds of recreation. (You can write to the Chamber of Commerce at 805 North Main Street, Moab, Utah 84532.)

Moab's reputation as the mountain-bike capital of the world grows each year. Some feel this town is to mountain biking what Aspen, Colorado, is to skiing. The first thing one will likely notice when driving toward this town is the number of mountain bikes being hauled on the top of automobiles and trucks. Though Rim Cyclery (94 West 100 North) was among the first to recognize Moab's mountain biking potential, many other shops in town rent bikes and offer information. The **Moab Slickrock Bicycle Trail**, originally constructed for use by trail machines and motorcycles, has been taken over by mountain bikers who enjoy the challenges of riding their all-terrain bicycles over the pale orange Navajo sandstone "petrified" dunes. The formation is almost entirely devoid of vegetation and provides excellent traction for trail bikes. A 2.3-mile (3.7-km) practice loop proved almost too much of a challenge for our family as we tried to negotiate the steep drops and rugged climbs with a guide from Rim Cyclery a few years ago. Overlooks at Updraft Arch, Negro Bill Canyon, Shrimp Rock, Abyss Viewpoint, and the aptly named Echo Point provide glimpses of the Colorado River, the La Sal Mountains, and Arches National Park.

Those with more mountain biking experience may want to take a day to explore the 10.3-mile (16 km) main loop ride. White arrows and caution zones painted on the rock keep bikers from straying into dangerous territory, but please make sure that your brakes are in good working condition. The four-wheel-drive roads and trails enjoyed by jeepers for years also provide excellent overnight or all-day mountain biking potential. Riding around the White Rim Trail in Canyonlands National Park, or exploring Monitor and Merrimac, Kane Creek Canyon Rim, Pritchett Canyon, Hurrah Pass, or the Gemini Bridges all provide challenging adventures. Still, the most exciting prospect for mountain bikers is the 128-mile (206-km) **Kokopelli's Mountain Biking Trail**, which will run, when completed, between Moab and Grand Junction, Colorado. Free brochures that rate the difficulty of trail sections can be picked up at most bike shops. Drinking water is not available along the route. The trail was named after Kokopelli, a humped-back flute-playing figure depicted in Indian art, who wandered from village to village with a bag of songs on his back. Legend holds that he was able to drive back winter with his flute playing.

Mountain biking is a relatively new activity in southeastern Utah, but Moab has long served as a base for river-running adventure. Day and night jet boat trips and one-day rafting trips make seeing the canyons relatively easy, but to really get to know the country, a longer expedition is in order. Most Colorado River trips into Cataract and Westwater canyons begin in Moab. When our family recently enjoyed a three-day Cataract Canyon trip, the thrill of shooting some of North America's most difficult rapids, coupled with the experience of swimming in the river, camping under the stars, exploring side canyons on foot, and enjoying the hospitality and knowledge of the guide, made for one heck of a vacation. We flew back to Moab in a small airplane, savoring spectacular views of the canyon country.

Thousands of miles of old mining roads, many unmaintained relics from the past, offer some excellent and rugged, four-wheel-drive experiences. If you like a challenge for your machine, this is the place. The old jeeper's creed of "never move a rock if you can drive around it—or over it" certainly applies on dozens of routes. Rental vehicles and guided trips are available in Moab. Also keep an eye out in town for Fran Barnes's jeep safari books and maps, which are among the best for the backcountry.

Hikers should investigate the uncrowded trails that cross the country around Moab *outside* the boundaries of Arches and Canyonlands national parks. **Portal Overlook**, **Corona** and **Bowtie arches**, **Mill Creek Canyon**, **Negro Bill Canyon**, **Hidden Valley**, and **Hunters Canyon** often reward explorers with contemplative solitude. Listen to the wind as it whistles through Corona Arch at sunset; it's an almost unearthly experience.

One of the more interesting stories involving the naming of these canyons surrounds Negro Bill Canyon. William Granstaff was a mulatto prospector who came to Moab Valley in 1877. Supposedly, he left in a hurry when other settlers charged him with selling whisky to Indians.

■ ARCHES NATIONAL PARK

If there is a more spectacular hike in the world than the trek to Delicate Arch, we have yet to discover it. The arch, once dubbed "The Schoolmarm's Bloomers" by local cowboys, graces the covers of many Utah books and is the star attraction of Arches National Park.

Just driving into the entrance of the park, four miles (six km) north of Moab, is a thrilling introduction to what lies ahead. The park contains over 90 natural arches, more than any other area in the world. Every year, more than half a million people come here for the spectacular scenery and the simple joys of hiking through soft sand and over slickrock.

Arches National Park is divided into six sections: **Courthouse Towers, The Windows, Delicate Arch, Fiery Furnace, Klondike Bluffs,** and **Devil's Garden.** Hiking guides and short, well-marked trails furnish glimpses of the natural arches, created by wind and rain in Entrada sandstone, which was laid down as coastal sand dunes some 150 million years ago.

Even lazy walkers can enjoy some of the trails of Arches, which for the most part are short, easy, and interesting. One of the best introductions to the park is taking the 2¹/2-hour, two-mile (3 km) ranger-led walk through the **Fiery Furnace.** Winding their way through a maze of narrow canyons, many hikers lose all sense of direction within moments and express relief that the ranger knows where he is going. Or does he? In places, visitors must squeeze through narrow spots on the trail, their bodies touching the walls on both sides.

Even toddlers enjoy short walks through **The Windows.** A quarter-mile (.4 km) hike leads to **Double Arch,** which appeared in *Indiana Jones and the Last Crusade.* Our children heard an echo here for the first time. Another favorite kids' hike is **Sand Dune Arch,** a .2-mile (.3 km) trek through a narrow canyon. Beneath the arch is a large sand dune. We've watched children spend an enchanted day playing in the fine, pink sand.

The longest series of maintained trails in Arches are found in the **Devil's Garden** area at the end of the paved road, just north of the campground. The five-mile (eight km) loop trail, with only a gentle 200-foot (62-m) gain in elevation, leads through narrow fins to **Double O Arch** and **Landscape Arch.** At 291 feet (90 m) long and 188 feet (58 m) high, Landscape is the longest span in the park and second longest in the world. No fewer than 60 arches, in fact, are found in this

(previous pages) Delicate Arch rises above a sandstone bowl, with the La Sal Mountains looming in the distance.

area. Take time to enjoy views of the fins, Salt Wash, and the La Sal Mountains along the way.

Still, the most famous sight in the park is **Delicate Arch**, an improbable natural wonder of salmon-colored sandstone, about 65 feet (20 m) high, and with an opening nearly 35 feet (11 m) wide. The 1.5-mile (2.4-km) trail to Delicate Arch begins at the historic **Wolfe Ranch**, built by Civil War veteran John Wesley Wolfe, who tried to make a living out of this desolate country in the late 1800s. The beauty of the hike is that the arch itself isn't visible until the last possible second. Viewing it for the first time can be compared to seeing the Statue of Liberty for the first time—a stunning sight that almost takes your breath away. Visitors tend to sit for hours contemplating the view in wonder and awe, especially at sunset, when the light and shadows play tricks with the arch and the natural amphitheater around it. Our most memorable trip to this place came on a cold, moonlit New Year's Eve. Frost on the willows near the swinging bridge sparkled like thousands of little fairies. The parking lot was empty, and snow covered parts of the trail. We reached sight of the arch just about midnight and brought in the new year in magnificent silence, standing in the moonlight, alone with the Delicate Arch.

UTAH'S NATURAL BRIDGES

In November 1909, under the guidance of Dr. John Williams of Moab, we visited a natural bridge on the edge of Grand County that deserves to be classed with those of San Juan County among the great natural wonders of our continent. This is a graceful arch with a total elevation of sixty-two feet, and a span of one hundred twenty-two feet long and forty-nine feet high. It stands beside the cliff on the western edge of Pritchett Valley; and has been fashioned under somewhat different conditions from those prevailing during the construction of the other Utah natural bridges. Here there has been no narrow zig-zag canyon through which the waters surged in former times, but quite a large valley, some three miles long and from one-fourth to one-half a mile wide. On the sides of this irregular basin rise rugged cliffs that jut into the valley here and there in sharp points and rounded domes. The upper surfaces of these cliffs stretch back in bare undulating fields of sandstone much eroded by wind and water. Caves have been hollowed out of these cliffs and various and numerous natural reservoirs are found scattered on the surface of these bare rocks where soft places have been found in the stone, or whirling eddies in former ages have ground out cisterns. Some of these are mere shallow tanks, while

others reach down twenty feet and more through the solid sandstone. Some are irregular and winding in their course, while others look as though they had been sunk by some Titanic drill when the gods were playing with the earth's crust. A few drain considerable areas of the cliff, and in time of storm many a rushing torrent loses itself in their depths. In a few instances such a reservoir has been formed directly behind a cave that was being hollowed out of the side of the cliff. As the walls of the cave gradually extended backward farther into the cliff, the reservoir was sunk deeper and enlarged little by little until its bottom broke through into the back of the cave. Then the waters formerly gathered into the reservoir and held surged through the cave and lost themselves in the valley below. Every downpour of rain and every driving wind carried the work a little farther until the former roof of the cave became an arch. When the reservoir held the waters until its depth about equalled that of the cave, then the gracefully curving arch of the cave became a real bridge as in the case of the fine arch already mentioned which we have christened Pikyabo (Pee-kya-bo), the Ute name for water tank.

—Byron Cummings,
The Great Natural Bridges of Utah, 1910

Storm clouds add to the intensity of a sunset glow over the Balanced Rock formation.

Landscape Arch covered in a mantle of snow. Arches National Park typically receives around 70 inches of snow every winter.

■ CANYONLANDS COUNTRY

The late Edward Abbey, iconoclast, cynic, and author of some of the best essays and fiction written about the deserts of southern Utah, described the Canyonlands country of southeastern Utah best when he called the place "the least inhabited, least developed, least improved, least civilized, most arid, most hostile, most lonesome, most grim bleak barren desolate and savage quarter of the state of Utah— the best part by far."

In terms of acres, Canyonlands is the largest of Utah's five national parks. First designated as a park in 1964, it was expanded to its present size in 1971. It is the least developed and most difficult to tour.

The park is divided into four principal districts. Island in the Sky is a broad, level mesa wedged between the Green and Colorado rivers. It serves as a kind of observation platform for the other three wards of this rugged park: the Needles District, the Maze, and the River District. A separate chunk of parkland, the Horseshoe Canyon Unit, lies northwest of the main body of the park.

The **River District**, which takes in Cataract Canyon and the confluence of the Green and Colorado rivers, can be visited only by river runners and experienced hikers. The other districts can by approached by road—though in some cases, *that* means only by four-wheel-drive vehicle or on foot.

Island in the Sky District is reached by Utah State Highway 313, which runs west from its junction with US Route 191, six miles (10 km) north of the turnoff to Arches National Park. The highway is a dead-end. One spur leads to Dead Horse Point State Park, and another into Canyonlands.

You can survey much of the park from **Grandview Point**. On a quiet, cold winter morning, the distant peaks of the La Sal, Henry, and Blue mountains stand like snow-covered sentinels in the midst of twisting, convoluted canyons. To the south, the Needles jut like monoliths erected by some ancient culture. Rock formations with descriptive names like Lizard Rock, the Doll House, Chocolate Drops, the Maze, and the Golden Stairs rise up in the southern background near the canyon of the Colorado River. Take some time to be alone in this outpost, to contemplate the vast tract of wilderness below you.

Long hiking trails and rugged dirt roads lead down to the **White Rim Trail**, remote arches, and interesting side canyons. Only the hardiest backpackers and experienced four-wheel-drive enthusiasts should attempt these routes. Everyone else can enjoy shorter hikes into places like Mesa Arch, Upheaval Dome, and Whale Rock. Standing on the brink of the cliff at Mesa Arch is like walking on the edge of infinity.

Do you enjoy a mystery? Then come up with your own theory of how Upheaval Dome was formed. The latest thinking is that the three-mile (five-km) long, 1,200-foot (372-m) deep crater may have been caused by a meteorite, but geologists really don't know for certain. Before coming up with your own theory, you may want to hike the eight-mile (13 km) trail that completely surrounds Upheaval Dome.

Dead Horse Point State Park also offers quite a view from the lip of a 2,000-foot (620-m) drop-off. Standing on the edge of this cliff gives a perspective of the depth, size, and majesty of the canyon country. Cowboys used to trap wild mustangs on the promontory by closing off the narrow neck of land. According to one legend, the gate was once left open so a band of corralled mustangs could return to the range. Instead, the mustangs remained on the point, dying of thirst within sight of the Colorado River, 2,000 feet below; hence the name of Dead Horse Point.

Traveling south from Moab, you can get a stunning glimpse of the Needles District by detouring to the **Canyon Rims Area** at the marked junction 32 miles (51 km) south of Moab. The view from **Needles Overlook** is simply staggering. The reserve, run by the BLM, also offers camping, hiking, and four-wheel-drive recreation. Ask directions to **Jail Rock**. Local legend has it that a sheriff's posse held a captured outlaw in the large pothole at the center of the rock. Another story says a rancher used to keep his wife there when he visited a local saloon.

Seven miles (11 km) south of the Needles Overlook road, Utah State Highway 211 heads west from US Route 191 toward Newspaper Rock and the Needles District of Canyonlands National Park.

Newspaper Rock State Park preserves a wall of sandstone covered with Indian petroglyphs that date as far back as 1,500 years ago. Several theories have been proposed to explain the meaning of the rock graphics. Contemporary Indians recognize some symbols; the Hopi, for instance, still use some in their religious ceremonies. Some graphics have been found to have direct connections to astrological occurrences. Archaeologists have used some as maps to lead them to water. Others see the strange man-like figures as records of extraterrestrial visits. Or was all this writing simply the doodling of passers-by, like the graffiti found in our time? The fun of visiting places like Newspaper Rock is in forming your own conclusions.

The **Needles District** is an amazing landscape of wind-carved sandstone fins. Plan on spending a day or two here camping in their midst and hiking to the **Roadside Ruin, Cave Spring,** or **Pothole Point.** Lovers of cowboy lore should visit the reconstructed line camp next to Cave Spring.

Few jeepers will ever forget an expedition over **Elephant Hill,** one of the wildest, roughest, most challenging stretches of "road" in the entire West. Narrow slots barely wide enough for a vehicle to get through, silver stairs of sheer rock, and

A sandstone pinnacle in Dead Horse Point State Park rises above Long Canyon.

(opposite) The pastel hues so often associated with desert light are a result of both the rocks' natural colors and a fine veil of dust in the air. Canyonlands National Park.

steep inclines force off-roaders to put their machines in the lowest possible gear. At one point in the 10-mile (16 km) loop, four-wheel-drives are forced to back to the edge of a steep cliff in order to make the turn! (We know of one woman who left the vehicle in tears at this point, and walked until she perceived the trail to be safe again. It was a long walk.) A few backcountry campsites can be found in **Chesler Park** along this road.

You can also hike to Chesler Park, as we did one Thanksgiving weekend. As we wound our way through narrow sandstone slits, ate lunch huddled under an alcove during a snowstorm, and then watched the gray sky turn blue, we witnessed the canyon country in all its glory.

The remote **Maze District**, located on the west side of the Colorado River, can be reached only by jouncing over some 60 miles (97 km) of dirt road from Utah State Highway 24 near the Goblin Valley turnoff. Only hikers and four-wheel-drive vehicles should attempt the last few miles. Or you can do as we did: at Hans Flat Ranger Station, we rode borrowed dirt bikes for the ride down the steep, rocky, perilous Flint Trail to the verge of the Maze.

Few hikes anywhere compare with a turn through the Maze. We made the steep descent to the bottom while clinging to chains and feeling for footholds cut into the sandstone. Thankful to have a veteran guide along to show us the way out, we kept thinking of two friends who did not. They descended into the maze of canyons from this same point for a day hike, only to run out of water and become hopelessly lost. After trying for hours to find their way out, the two noticed their parents standing at the top of the canyon and were able to locate the trail out. The moral is, if you hike into this pristine area, bring a good topographical map and know how to read it. This is difficult, seldom-traveled country—that's why it's so special, of course.

The road to the Maze passes through a section of Canyonlands National Park detached from the main body of the park: the **Horseshoe Canyon Unit**. Some of North America's most outstanding ancient Indian rock art can be found there in the **Great Gallery**. The gallery's huge, ghost-like pictographs are believed to have been made by a culture predating the Anasazi. Having seen the reproduction of these pictographs in Salt Lake City's Natural History Museum, we had long wanted to see the real thing in the sandy wash of Horseshoe Canyon.

Large graceful cottonwoods grow along the trail. In places the water surfaces to nourish cattails, horsetails, reeds, and willows. Seeping water in occasional alcoves

After even a small rain, a trickle can explode into a roaring torrent, in time carving creek beds into canyons.

nurse delicate flower gardens and lacy ferns. As we studied the land of the ancients, we tried to imagine how the residents of this canyon must have worked to make a living here. Would they have appealed to a higher force for help? Is that why the pictographs and petroglyphs are here?

The sand in the wash made walking hard. The dry wind blew sand into our eyes and plastered our hair. But we continued; we had seen other rock art before, but we knew this would be different. Perhaps it was partly exhaustion, partly the spirit in the canyon, but after rounding the bend and seeing the Great Gallery, we all stopped in our tracks and gasped. Life-sized apparitions seemed to float out of the wall above our heads. The armless, legless figures wore mask-like, ghost-like faces reminding us of souls from another world. We talked in whispers of what their creators were trying to tell us. Knowing the language of the canyon country, we somehow read the message. It was a feeling that could not be translated into words. We knew the haunting figures were meant to be felt, not explained. The canyons, mesas, and rivers of the Colorado Plateau have spirits of their own. If one spends enough time silently learning their secrets, it is the feeling of the place that seeps into the soul.

■ MOUNTAIN ESCAPES

Though desert, vast and dry, seems to dominate the landscape around Moab, just to the east rise the cool, verdant peaks of La Sal Mountains, proffering summer respite in their forests of aspen and pine. Cleared of snow from May through October, the **La Sal Mountain Loop** transports drivers into the mountains from Utah State Highway 128 north of Moab, and US Route 191 to the south. The 60-mile (97-km) loop takes about four hours to drive.

As you gain elevation, the pinyon and juniper trees give way to oak, then to larger pines and aspen, and finally to spruce and fir. Campers escape the desert heat by spending the night at the U.S. Forest Service campground at **Warner Lake**. The U.S. Forest Service office in Moab has produced an excellent guide to the 18 hiking trails on the La Sal Mountains. Many of these trails were made by miners who explored the country a century ago.

Pack Creek Ranch, Utah's premier dude ranch, sits at the base of the distinctive, pyramid-shaped crest of 12,483-foot (3,783-m) **Mount Tukuhnikivatz**. The mountain is named after a Ute word which means "the place where the sun shines longest." Increasing numbers of cross-country skiers discover the fine, untracked powder of the La Sals each year. Novices enjoy gentle tours through the Pack Creek campground, while experts can drive to higher slopes. Rim Cyclery in Moab offers rentals and information on avalanche conditions.

About 50 miles (80 km) below Moab, west of Monticello, the **Blue Mountains** provide another welcome furlough from the desert heat. Also called the **Abajos**, the Blues rise to elevations as high as 11,360 feet (3,462 m). The high alpine country here is remote and little visited. After a horsepacking trip in the remote **Dark Canyon Wilderness Area** on the western edge of the Blues a few years ago, we enjoyed views to the north of the Needles District. A bobcat scurried across the road in front of us. At an evening campout, local cowboys cooked steaks over a blazing fire in Horse Pasture Canyon and listened to the howls of coyotes, which seemed but a stone's throw away.

■ THE GRAND CIRCLE

The Grand Circle, the heart of Anasazi country, embraces the Four Corners area of Utah, Colorado, New Mexico, and Arizona. Within the 500-mile (805-km) circle, thousands of acres of public land have been set aside to preserve the ancient Anasazi villages and ruins. Visitors can become acquainted with the Anasazi and enjoy some spectacular scenery by following the **Trail of the Ancients** to the numerous Anasazi points of interest. Brochures describing the trail can be obtained at any of the sites along the trail, or by visiting or writing to Edge of the Cedars State Historical Park, south of Blanding.

The ruins at **Edge of the Cedars** are being stabilized, and we enjoyed talking to the archaeologist working on this project. The remains of an immense kiva have been found there. Such structures are common around Mesa Verde in Colorado and Chaco Canyon in New Mexico, but the Great Kiva at Edge of the Cedars is the northernmost one of its kind in Utah. It was probably roofed and its flat surface used by many clans for dances and ceremonies. The roof of a smaller kiva nearby has been restored. Most kivas we have seen have not been open, so the kiva at Edge of the Cedars was our only chance to actually climb down into the chamber and sit awhile and contemplate. The monument museum traces the settlement of San Juan County by Anasazi, Ute, Navajo, and Euro-American settlers, and also houses one of the largest Anasazi pottery collections in the Southwest. You can

buy Native American arts and crafts in the museum shop.

Butler Wash Rest Stop, about 15 miles (24 km) southwest of Blanding on Utah State Highway 95, looked like a convenient place to wait out a late summer rainstorm. The one-mile (1.6-km) roundtrip trail we took just after the storm led us on an adventure we'll never forget. Water from the storm flowed all over the smooth, salmon-colored slickrock. Streams and rivulets followed paths marked for them by previous cloudbursts. We tore off shoes and socks and scampered in the precious liquid. The source of life in this desert also brought us to life. We squealed with delight as newly formed waterfalls ran down our backs, drawn onward by the promise of more. Then suddenly, nestled far under the canyon's rim in a cozy alcove, we saw the Butler Wash ruins. Directly in front of the apartment-like complex, a waterfall cascaded like a curtain to the canyon floor. In the overhang to the right was a natural bridge where another waterfall plummeted over the edge. The ancient residents of this dwelling must have recognized the magic of this place.

Natural Bridges National Monument, 40 miles (64 km) west of Blanding on Utah State Highway 95, is famous for three impressive natural bridges. The trail down to White Canyon leads through a desert garden. It is easy to see why the Anasazi wanted to live here. A stream runs through the bottom of the canyon, and tracks of coyote, ringtail cat, deer, and other small game line its banks. About 200 Anasazi dwelling sites have been found there. Horse Collar Ruin is accessible from the trail between Sipapu and Kachina bridges.

The natural bridges were given Hopi names: **Kachina**, a

Ancient Anasazi remains near Junction Ruin in the Grand Gulch Primitive Area.

The La Sal Mountains are the backdrop to a formation known as the Fiery Furnace.

representation of Hopi gods; **Owachomo**, a flat-rock mound; and **Sipapu**, the gateway to this world from the other world below. Hopi clan symbols can be seen near several of the ruins. It is surmised that the White Canyon Anasazi may have migrated south to join the ancestors of the present-day Hopi.

The national monument was established in 1908 by President Theodore Roosevelt after *National Geographic* magazine publicized the three great bridges. Unfortunately, fame also brought vandalism, as it does all too often today. Consider the story told by Zeke Johnson, who was the custodian of the monument in 1926:

> *A* group of boys was going out to the bridges from Blanding, and I told them not to scratch their names on rocks inside the monument. One man who went along with the boys (I will just call him John Doe) told his boy that man Zeke Johnson had no police authority over those rocks, and he and his son wrote their names on top of Sipapu Bridge and dug it deep.
>
> Well, of course I explained the law and told him to get back out and rub it off, and he told me to go 'places.' The invitation to go some place was repeated several times, and I found it necessary to write to the director of national parks in Washington, D.C. The defendant got a letter telling him that unless he immediately complied with Custodian Johnson's instructions he would have a ride at his own expense from Blanding to Washington, D.C., to be arraigned before the U.S. Government. He soon hunted me up and asked what he should do. I said just do as I told you, track back out there and take off those initials. He offered me twenty bucks if I would do it, but I told him nobody could do it but him, and it was a five-day horseback trip in those days. Since then he has been a help to me. Several initial-cutters have been caught, and when they tried to lobby with me I just told them to step across the street and talk with Mr. John Doe. I can't give you chapter and verse, but the law is very plain, and I am obliged to enforce it.

Grand Gulch Primitive Area, south of the monument, preserves a winding, many-fingered canyon where numerous rock graphic panels can be found along the walls. Archaeologists have determined that the area was occupied as early as A.D. 200 by the Basketmaker Anasazi, but was abandoned and reoccupied two centuries later. Whoever wishes to explore Grand Gulch should check in with the BLM office in Monticello.

Bluff, 27 miles (43 km) south of Blanding, is another small Utah town on the Trail of the Ancients. Nearly every cliff or canyon slope within a 50-mile (80-km) radius of town harbors some sign of its ancient inhabitants. As in all explorations of Indian ruins, visitors should beware of hazards. Many ruins are located in inaccessible cliffs. People have been injured trying to climb into ruins by treacherous routes. Rattlesnakes and scorpions can be found in this part of the country. Go slow and be observant. Backcountry trails and roads can become treacherous in a flash flood. Guided tours of the backcountry by foot or four-wheel-drive are available at Recapture Lodge Tours in Bluff, and to the south at Goulding's Trading Post near Monument Valley Navajo Park.

Another stop on the Trail of the Ancients, 42 miles (68 km) east of Bluff, is **Hovenweep National Monument**. Hovenweep is a Ute word meaning "deserted valley." All access to the monument is on dirt roads generally passable by passenger cars, but tricky when it rains. Hovenweep is a curiosity in the Anasazi world because of its distinctive square towers. The Anasazi usually built round towers. Six separate ruined settlements are found here.

Hovenweep region was inhabited by Anasazi who migrated from Mesa Verde, nearly 100 miles (160 km) to the east, around A.D. 900. Perhaps they were migrants, maybe even outcasts. They lived in scattered villages and cultivated corn, beans, squash, and melons. From studying tree rings, it has been determined that by 1200, annual rainfall decreased substantially. The outlying farm villages were abandoned and new ones rebuilt near canyons with permanent springs. The style of the towers and the location of the dwellings in the cliffs suggest the inhabitants of Hovenweep may also have been preparing for attack by other Anasazi clans or Shoshone raiders looking for food and water. Each tower contained only one small doorway protected by a parapet. Most towers also have peepholes pointing outwards—away from the canyon.

Archaeologists have offered another theory concerning the use of the towers. At least three sites at the monument, including the major ruin, **Square Tower**, may have been used as observatory sites. Certain windows in the towers are situated in such a way that sunlight enters only during the summer and winter solstices and the autumn and vernal equinoxes, striking particular points marked on the interior walls.

When the last springs dried up, the Hovenweep Anasazi were forced to leave, archaeologists surmise, and join the Zuni Pueblo in western New Mexico. By 1300, the Hovenweep region was deserted.

The **Navajo Indian Reservation**, which covers large areas of Arizona and New Mexico, also reaches into Utah's rugged southeastern corner. Traditional Navajo hogans dot the landscape. Famous the world over, the majestic buttes of **Monument Valley** have served as the backdrops for many famous Western movies. **Goulding Trading Post** and the **Navajo Tribal Park** nearby provide meals and accommodations for visitors. The Navajos manage the entrance to a small monument at the **Four Corners Monument**, the only place in the United States where a visitor can stand in one spot and be in four states—Utah, New Mexico, Colorado, and Arizona.

Boulder House in Hovenweep National Monument was occupied by the Anasazi around A.D. 900.

(opposite) The Anasazi used natural landscape features, such as this cave, to quarry the stone for their structures.

PURPLE SAGE

It was the moment when the last ruddy rays of the sunset brightened momentarily before yielding to twilight. And for Venters the outlook before him was in some sense similar to a feeling of his future, and with searching eyes he studied the beautiful purple, barren waste of sage. Here was the unknown and the perilous. The whole scene impressed Venters as a wild, austere, and mighty manifestation of nature. And as it somehow reminded him of his prospect in life, so it suddenly resembled the woman near him, only in her there were greater beauty and peril, a mystery more unsolvable, and something nameless that numbed his heart and dimmed his eye. . . .

❖ ❖ ❖

Venters looked out upon the beautiful valley—beautiful now as never before—mystic in its transparent, luminous gloom, weird in the quivering, golden haze of lightning. The dark spruces were tipped with glimmering lights; the aspens bent low in the winds, as waves in a tempest at sea; the forest of oaks tossed wildly and shone with gleams of fire. Across the valley the huge cavern of the cliff-dwellers yawned in the glare, every little black window as clear as at noonday; but the night and the storm added to their tragedy. Flung arching to the black clouds, the great stone bridge seemed to bear the brunt of the storm. It caught the full fury of the rushing wind. It lifted its noble crown to meet the lightning. Venters thought of the eagles and their lofty nest in a niche near the arch. A driving pall of rain, black as the clouds, came sweeping on to obscure the bridge and the gleaming walls and the shining valley. The lightning played incessantly, streaking down through opaque darkness of rain. The roar of the wind, with its strange knell and the recrashing echoes, mingled with the roar of the flooding rain, and all seemingly were deadened and drowned in a world of sound.

—Zane Grey, *Riders of the Purple Sage,* 1912

THE GREATEST SNOW ON EARTH

THE SNOWSTORM RAGED THROUGH MUCH OF THE NIGHT, dumping prodigious amounts of fluffy powder on ski slopes throughout Utah. Cars full of skiers anxiously waited for the canyon roads to be cleared and for the avalanche rangers to declare the resorts safe.

As the road opened, the skies began to clear. A few fluffy white clouds rolled off to the eastern horizon just as the sun peaked over the mountain, bathing the ski slopes in light. Skiers quickly buckled their boots, snapped into their bindings, and hopped aboard the chairlifts. The untouched powder was knee deep. This was the kind of day Utah skiers love.

❄   ❄   ❄

When compared with their gigantic counterparts in California, Colorado, Europe, or the eastern United States, many of Utah's ski resorts seem quaint and small. But there is a certain magic that surrounds Utah ski resorts that has its source in what many have called the best quality skiing snow in the world.

There is a reason Utah's snow conditions are often better than those in surrounding states.

"Most of the winter storms that affect Utah have their origin in the northern Pacific Ocean," said William Alder, chief meteorologist for the National Weather Service in Salt Lake City. "These storms move southeastward across the Sierra Nevada and Cascade Mountains, where they lose some of their moisture. When they hit the high Wasatch and Utah's south-central mountains, the orographic (air forced against mountains) lifting occurs and squeezes out much of the moisture. This is what produces the colder, drier powder snows for which Utah is noted.

"The secret of Utah's unique and wonderful powder is the structure of the individual snow crystals. Under cold, relatively dry conditions, light crystal-type snowflakes called dendrites are produced. These snowflakes are thin and symmetrical in shape, and they float down through the cold atmosphere, accumulating like fluffy down or powder on Utah's mountains. Many times cold northwest winds will follow a storm and prolong this powder snowfall over the higher mountains. When deep enough, the powder snow gives skiers the feeling they are floating on air as they ski down, and that's what makes the Greatest Snow on Earth."

UTAH SKI AREAS

Courtesy, Utah Ski Association.

Utah Alpine Ski Area Statistics

	ALTA 742-3333	BEAVER MTN. 753-0921	BRIAN HEAD 677-2035	BRIGHTON 943-8309	DEER VALLEY 649-1000	ELK MEADOWS 439-5433	NORDIC VALLEY 745-3511	PARK CITY 649-8111	PARK WEST 649-5000	POWDER MTN. 745-3772	SNOWBASIN 399-1135	SNOWBIRD 742-2222	SOLITUDE 534-1400	SUNDANCE 225-4107
Average Annual Snowfall	500"	450"	400"	430"	300"	400"	300"	350"	300"	500"	400"	500"	410"	320"
Vertical Drop Serviced By Lift	2,000'	1,600'	1,250'	1,745'	2,200'	1,200'	960'	3,100'	2,200'	1,300'	2,400'	3,100'	2,030'	2,150'
Top Elevation	10,550	8,840	10850	10,500	9,400	10,400	6,400	10,000	9,000	8,900	8,800	11,000	10,030	8,250
Lifts (D=Double Chair / T=Triple Chair/Q=Quad Chair)	6D / 2T	3D / 5T	2D / 5T	2Q-3D / 1T-1tow	1D / 9T-1Q	2D-1TBar2D / 1T-1Poma	—	5D-2Q / 5T-1G	7D / —	2D 1T / 3 tow	1D / 4T	7D / —	4D / 2T	2D / 2T
Gondola/Tram/ DQ=Detachable Quad	—	—	—	—	—	—	—	1DQ 1Gond	—	—	—	1Tram	1Q	—
% Beginner Terrain	25%	35%	38%	24%	15%	14%	30%	17%	22%	10%	20%	20%	20%	20%
% Intermediate	40%	40%	43%	38%	50%	62%	50%	49%	30%	60%	50%	30%	55%	40%
% Advanced	35%	25%	19%	38%	35%	24%	20%	34%	48%	30%	30%	50%	25%	30%
# Runs	39	16	55	61	58	30	12	83	50	33	39	45	60	41
Adult All-Day Lift Pass	$23	$18	$28	N/A	$43	$25	N/A	$40	N/A	$20	N/A	$30* $37**	N/A	$22
Child All-Day Lift Pass	$18	$14	$18	10 & under $28 free		$15	N/A	$18	N/A	$13	N/A	$17* $22**	N/A	$15
Night Skiing	No	XP	No	N/A	No	No	N/A	$8	No	Yes	No	No	No	No
Skiable Acres	2,200	364	825	850	1000	345	85	2,200	850	1,600	1,800	2,000	1,100	450
Snowboards Allowed	No	Yes	Yes	Yes	No	Yes	No	Yes	Yes	Yes	Yes	Yes	No	No
Nursery/Child Care	Yes	No	Yes	No	Yes	Yes	No	Yes	Yes	No	No	Yes	No	Yes
Distance From Salt Lake City	26 mi.	111 mi.	260 mi.	29 mi.	34 mi.	228 mi.	49 mi.	32 mi.	28 mi.	54 mi.	52 mi.	24 mi.	27 mi.	51 mi.

* = Chairs Only ** = All Area Including Tram XP = By Prior Arrangement N/A = Not Available At Press Time

There are 16 ski resorts in Utah. Visitors to the Wasatch Front have a choice of 11 ski resorts, all within an hour's drive of the airport. In addition, hundreds of roads in the national forests are ideal for cross-country skiing. To help you decide where to ski, call Ski Utah at (801) SKI-UTAH or write for their *Utah Winter Vacation Planner,* which contains information on specific resorts as well as on lodging, ski pass rates, seasons, hours, and other important details. (Address: 150 West 500 South, Salt Lake City, Utah, 84101.) For information about winter snow conditions call (801) 521-8102.

■ HISTORY OF SKIING IN UTAH

Skiing started in Utah during the early 1900s when a few miners and trappers adopted skis for getting around the mountains during winter. Robert F. Marvin was one of the few miners to leave a first-hand account of early ski equipment and "technique."

"Let me tell you about Alta, before it became effete and a play-place for kids, before it was converted from a mining camp to a ski resort," wrote Marvin in an unpublished manuscript. "Let me tell you of the men who lived and labored there, of men who plied their trades as miners, as haulers of ore and freight, as hewers of wood. Let me describe the lives they lived and the works they wrought with strong backs and calloused hands and precious little help from things mechanical. I'll tell you about these things as they were in the early years of this century, as I first saw them in the closing days of 1916.

"To begin then, Alta was not in those days a ski resort. There were no hotels, no accommodations—and almost no skis. In 1916 the onset of winter found exactly two pairs of skis in the camp, not counting the stubby, broad and double-edged skis the Finlander miners brought in from the old country. I had to send far away for my first pair, all the way to St. Paul, where someone had begun to manufacture them. When the skis came, they were hickory, thick and heavy and exactly 11 feet long. The thinking was that the longer the skis were the better they would ride atop the snow and not sink in. I was about the only person in camp long-legged enough to make a kick turn with them, and it was an effort like a high-kickin' chorus girl's. Ski poles we had none; they were to us an unknown. Instead, we had a single long pole, usually cut from creek-side brush, preferably water birch because the bark was so smooth. This pole we used like an oar or gee-pole, always on the uphill side, right or left. Also, there was no ski harness, only a leather toe-strap (sometimes tied to the ankle with a short length of cord to prevent the skis going home by themselves in case of a tumble). With this primitive gear, we 'rowed' ourselves uphill and down to all the places your tows and lifts take you now, and beyond; to the top of Baldy on occasion."

The Utah ski industry grew from these humble beginnings. Alta, second only to Sun Valley, Idaho, as the oldest resort in the United States, constructed its first lift in 1938. It was followed by Snowbasin in Ogden Canyon and Brighton in Big Cottonwood Canyon. Construction of the huge Park City complex—one of the few Utah resort areas which can compare in size and scope to Aspen, Vail, and Mammoth Mountain—started in 1963. Park West and the exclusive Deer Valley followed, as did other Wasatch Front resorts, like Robert Redford's Sundance east of Provo, Powder Mountain and Nordic Valley in Ogden Valley, Solitude in Big Cottonwood Canyon, and Beaver Mountain in Logan Canyon. Snowbird, a huge, modern complex located below Alta in Little Cottonwood Canyon, appeared on the scene in the early 1970s, bringing with it an often acrimonious debate over how much development should take place in the canyons east of Salt Lake City. With Utah bidding to host the Winter Olympics in 1998, the controversy over how much development should be allowed in the precious Wasatch Front canyons continues to rage.

For an account of these controversies, as well as the most detailed information on the colorful history of Utah skiing, pick up a copy of Alexis Kelner's *Skiing in Utah: A History.*

Each Utah resort occupies its own niche. The giant resorts, like Park City and Snowbird, rank with the top ski areas in the world in terms of facilities, number of runs, and nightlife. Smaller resorts, like Beaver Mountain, Brighton, and Alta, bring to mind simpler times in the ski business when only the quality of the snow and the ski runs seemed important.

■ LITTLE COTTONWOOD CANYON

Alta and Snowbird, two resorts located just a few miles from one another at the top of Little Cottonwood Canyon east of Salt Lake City, could not be more different.

Alta, with its world-famous powder and comparatively low lift rates, is a re-minder of what skiing in the United States used to be like. Its eight lifts service a mountain which compares favorably to any on earth as a place to ski. Its lodges are small, quaint, and few in number. Even on holiday weekends, when a skier may have to wait in line for 40 min-utes before boarding an Alta lift, the wait seems worth the effort. Resort managers work hard not to put too many people on the mountain at one time, and avoided a national trend toward building high-speed quad lifts or triple chairs, invoking a philosophy that too many people on a hill at the same time can ruin a skier's expe-rience.

Alta has a well-deserved reputation for giving skiers some of the best powder in the world and is also an excellent place for beginners to learn the sport. Its slopes are well-groomed and the Albion Lift services one of the longest and best begin-ners' slopes found in Utah. Moguls, tree skiing, and deep powder off the Wildcat Lift challenge even the most expert of skiers.

On-site lodging is available at Alta, ranging from the elegant Alta, Rustler, and Peruvian lodges to the more rustic and considerably less expensive Goldminer's Daughter Lodge. But the Utah Transit Authority bus service which brings skiers from downtown to Alta for a $2 roundtrip fare makes staying in town and then skiing at Alta a relatively easy proposition.

If Alta is an example of a quaint, laid-back resort with a charm dating back to its beginnings, then **Snowbird** is an unabashed giant working hard to create an image of technological wonder.

From the monolithic cement condominiums at the resort base to the gleaming red and blue trams which whisk skiers to the top of 11,000-foot (3,333-m) Hid-den Peak, Snowbird presents itself as a gleaming, well-planned, modern ski area. The shopping centers, restaurants, tennis courts, swimming pools, convention center, spa, and bars reflect the vision of founders Dick Bass and Ted Johnson. Skiers straight off the slopes can head to a spa where they can enjoy a massage, nail care, herbal wraps, and hair care, or visit the shops, restaurants, bank, post office, laundry, medical clinic, and pharmacy.

Snowbird is a slightly more difficult resort to ski than Alta. Some runs range up to 3 1/2 miles (5.6 km) in length. Only 20 percent of the runs are rated for begin-ners with 30 percent for intermediate and a whopping 50 percent for experts. Fine skiers like the challenge of taking the tram and the Peruvian and Little Cloud lifts

Utah is a candidate for the 1998 Winter Olympics, which would be based in Park City.
(Photo by Tim Kelly)

to ski the expert runs. Snowbird skiers can choose from seven double chairlifts. The vertical drop of 3,100 feet (939 m) is the sharpest at any Utah resort.

In many ways, the proximity of the two Little Cottonwood resorts to one another is a boon to skiers. Alta and Snowbird have distinct personalities. Try both and choose your favorite.

■ BIG COTTONWOOD CANYON

Brighton, named after William S. Brighton who constructed a small hotel near the site of the present Big Cottonwood Canyon resort east of Salt Lake City in 1874, bills itself as "the place Utah learns to ski."

Dave Farmer, a lift supervisor at the resort, put things another way.

"People learn to ski at Brighton and then go on to enjoy all types of expert powder skiing at the other resorts, only to return here when they get older and their knees start going bad."

Alexis Kelner, in his book on the history of Utah skiing, says simplicity and sincerity were the hallmarks of the original 1870s' Brighton venture. Brighton has recently been purchased by a large corporation, Boyne U.S.A. which has raised lift ticket prices and is busy constructing new lifts. If its masterplan is completed, this resort will become Utah's second largest.

Brighton boasts some the state's best powder. About 30 percent of its runs are rated for experts. Powder hounds love blasting through the deep stuff on the Scree run near the Millicent Lift or skiing between the pines under the Snake Creek triple chair after a heavy snowfall. Most of the runs serviced by the Majestic and Mary's lifts are lit for night skiing.

Several trails connect Brighton to Solitude, its downhill skiing neighbor in Big Cottonwood Canyon. A day pass can be purchased to allow those who demand variety in their skiing to ride the lifts at both resorts in a single day.

Solitude might be described as a "poor-man's Snowbird." The resort recently underwent major expansion and now offers a high-speed quad detachable chairlift, a lift capable of moving skiers up the mountains twice as fast as a normal chair but which slows up to allow skiers to load and unload.

Though Solitude managers list 20 percent of its runs for beginners, 55 percent for intermediates, and 25 percent for experts, the skiing terrain, like Snowbird's, possesses many mogul hills and places to enjoy great powder after a heavy storm.

Big Cottonwood Canyon in a winter storm.

Opened in 1957 by a colorful miner named Bob Barrett, Solitude had its share of troubles in its early days. Barrett, an independent sort, believed in doing things his own way. He ran into trouble with both Salt Lake City officials trying to protect the Big Cottonwood Canyon watershed, as well as U.S. Forest Service bureaucrats charged with issuing special-use permits for the part of the resort which rested on its property. Barrett was a do-it-yourself buff and his lifts, unique to Solitude, became legendary for both their construction and numerous breakdowns. The new phase of Solitude began in 1975 when Richard Houlihan took over the resort and, two years later, constructed three state-of-the-art chairlifts.

Now under new ownership, Solitude boasts the largest hourly lift capacity of the four Cottonwood Canyon resorts. Skiers can use the high-speed quad, two triple chairs, and four double chairs to ski on 60 different runs.

■ PARK CITY SKI AREAS

Not long ago, Park City's Main Street was on the verge of turning into a ghost town. Old mining equipment, an abandoned railroad station, and wooden shacks hanging precariously on the hills seemed to litter the landscape. Mining activity in the old community, which had produced some of Utah's richest and most eccentric community leaders, had all but ceased. A few curious tourists made the 32-mile (51-km) drive from Salt Lake City during the summer to shop for antiques or have a soda at the old fountain. Park City still served as the home of Utah's oldest weekly newspaper, *The Park Record.* Some colorful characters would tell visitors of the fires, different cultures, 30 Main Street saloons, and the wealthy mining magnates that were all part of the history of this place. Fewer than 2,000 residents lived in what was once a booming town.

What a contrast to the bustling 1990s' atmosphere brought on by the development of Park City, ParkWest and Deer Valley—three of Utah's largest ski areas. Though Main Street is still listed on the National Register of Historic Places, the town has become a huge ski resort. Park City is headquarters for the Mrs. Fields Chocolate Chip Cookie empire and houses some 45 restaurants, 20 clubs and bars, 50 shops, and a dozen art galleries in its restored buildings. In addition to skiing, visitors now can ride a hot-air balloon, go ice skating, take a moonlight sleigh ride, ski cross-country on groomed trails, take a snowmobile journey, and play tennis and racquetball. Live theater performances and the Sundance Film Festival add to the allure of the town. In the summer, visitors can entertain themselves with golf and miniature golf, bicycling, hiking, and an alpine slide that careens riders down a mountainside on a wheeled car. The Park City Arts Festival in August is one of the biggest events of its kind in the state.

The landscape of this once quaint mining town is now dotted with hundreds of condominiums, built in many different styles and catering to numerous incomes and tastes. Park City is as close as Utah gets to imitating the atmosphere and nightlife of huge ski areas like Vail, Aspen, or Sun Valley.

With the possible exception of Park West, the way Park City caters to out-of-state skiers is reflected in the price. Skiing at Park City is more costly than anywhere else in the state, and the exclusive Deer Valley has the highest lift ticket prices in the United States.

With a four-passenger gondola, a high-speed detachable quad lift, two quad lifts, five triple chairlifts, and five double chairlifts, **Park City Resort** is easily Utah's largest. It can handle 20,900 skiers an hour on its 93 designated runs, 650 acres of wide-open bowl skiing and more than 2,200 acres of skiable terrain. Nobody has to ski the same run or use the same lift twice in a single day. The kids can enjoy the First Time or Three Kings beginner chairlifts, while the more experienced can explore miles of intermediate terrain. Expert skiers head to the Jupiter Bowl at the top of the resort to discover some of the best powder skiing Utah has to offer. In terms of services offered and variety of terrain, nightlife, and facilities, Park City is hard to beat. The town serves as headquarters for the United States ski team and as the site of numerous professional and World Cup skiing races. Should Utah receive a future Olympics bid, Park City would be the host for most alpine skiing events.

Deer Valley, located just east of Park City, spoils skiers. *Skiing* magazine calls it ". . . the crème de la crème of ski destinations, devoid of most hassles that vacationing mortals are heir to, with uncrowded runs groomed to silky perfection . . . advanced terrain as good as anywhere . . . a cornucopia of slope-side extras, which in the aggregate spell the difference between routine and luxury."

Even the moguls seem like they are groomed at Deer Valley. Expect help unloading the skis from your vehicle and look for attendants clad in elegant green ski suits to help load you on the lifts. Deer Valley is a place to beat the holiday crowds because the number of skiers allowed on the mountain at any given time is limited.

Reservations to ski on the hill during busy times of the year can be made. Lighted signs advise Deer Valley skiers about lines in the restaurants. There are even places to recline in the snow on lounge chairs during skiing breaks. Don't expect the traditional paper plates and plastic silverware in even the least expensive cafeterias at the resort—everything is served on china. The Stein Erikson Lodge at the resort upholds a reputation as one of Utah's most elegant dining spots.

Those who use Deer Valley's quad, triple chairs, and double notice a feeling of quiet elegance. Each run seems perfectly groomed. Details like keeping the lifts free of snow, the walkways shoveled, and tissue boxes at the bottom of the lifts are not ignored.

Skiing takes place on two mountains—9,400-foot (2,848-m) Bald Mountain and 8,400-foot (2,545-m) Bald Eagle—with 15 percent of the runs rated as easy, 50 percent as more difficult, and 35 percent as most difficult. Not many locals can afford the stiff lift-ticket prices at Deer Valley, but the few who splurge enjoy being treated like royalty.

ParkWest is located just north of Park City near the community of Snyderville. The atmosphere there, though not exactly like Brighton or Alta, differs from the huge resort atmosphere of Park City or the high prices of Deer Valley. Many Utahns learned to ski here as high school students.

ParkWest is often somewhat of a surprise for first-timers. Only a small part of the resort can be seen from the entrance road off Interstate 80, giving the impression that it is a small, unchallenging resort for beginners.

Actually, seven double chairlifts serve 50 designated ski trails on three different mountains. The beginner's area at the base is gentle, smooth, and a good place to try downhill skiing for the first time. The trails at the top challenge even the best of skiers (48 percent of the resort is rated as expert). Prices are often $11 to $15 less than the other two Park City area resorts and comparable to Brighton, Solitude, and Alta. There are four restaurants and a number of condominiums on site. Nearby Park City offers much more in the way of nightlife.

ParkWest has turned into a popular summer resort, too. Its annual summer concert series draws thousands of music fans from all over the Wasatch Front, who come to hear the music of Bob Dylan, the Beach Boys, Crosby, Stills, Nash and Young, and the Grateful Dead, under the stars.

In 1923, *The Park Record* published an article predicting that Park City would turn into a "mecca" for winter sports. It may have taken almost three-quarters of a century but that prediction has become a reality.

■ SUNDANCE

A skier can explore the many nuances of Utah County's only ski resort for years and never catch a glimpse of its famous owner, Robert Redford. Yet Redford's spirit seems to live in every part of Sundance. The actor purchased a tiny ski area in the Uinta Forest called Timp Haven in 1969, renamed it after the character he played opposite Paul Newman in the movie *Butch Cassidy and the Sundance Kid,* and slowly turned it into an arts center, ski resort, and home. Redford also filmed a movie about a mountain man, *Jeremiah Johnson,* near here. Views of 11,788-foot (3,572-m) Mt. Timpanogos dominate both the movie setting and the ski resort. This is not a flashy resort—one has to search to find the few condominiums located on the site. The base facilities are small, quiet, and tasteful.

Sundance is located on a fine ski hill. Though relatively small even by Wasatch Front standards, the resort's two double and two triple chairs lead to 30 trails on 400 acres. Beginners can find places to fit their abilities at Sundance, but the terrain challenges good skiers, especially after a heavy snowfall. As a rule, the higher the elevation of the lift at Sundance, the more difficult the runs.

■ OGDEN VALLEY RESORTS

Some might question why a skier would want to travel the longer distances from Salt Lake City to ski Ogden Valley's three small resorts—Snowbasin, Powder Mountain, and Nordic Valley.

Variety is one reason, the quality of snow is the other. Some of the highest quality powder in Utah can be found at tiny Powder Mountain, a resort consisting of three mountains and three lifts.

"The greatest snow. . . .What are we really talking about," wrote Williams in his Utah Geographic Series *Utah Ski Country.* "The amount? The moisture content? Yes, but for a ski resort there is more. Is it easy to get to, and does it last? And, my big question—Are powder skiers happy? At Powder Mountain, the answer is 'yes' all around."

The view from **Powder Mountain**, northeast of the tiny community of Eden, is alone worth the price of a lift ticket. One can see the sun setting over the Great Salt Lake, peer into Cache Valley to the north, or see the distant ski runs cut out of the mountainside of Park City to the south.

Those who have never skied Powder Mountain may be deceived into thinking that a resort with only three lifts is small. The resort's one triple and two double chairs are smartly constructed to cover the largest possible skiing area. In some cases, shuttles are used to transport skiers from one lift to the next. Another oddity is that the resort facilities are located near the top of the ski area instead of at the base. One actually needs to ski down from the main resort complex to reach a lift. There are 33 runs here, including an excellent night skiing hill serviced by the aptly named "Sundown Lift."

Nordic Valley, located just across the valley to the west of Powder Mountain, is the smallest ski resort on the Wasatch Front. It consists of two double chairlifts capable of serving 1,800 skiers. There are only 12 runs at this resort, but all are lit at night. Nordic Valley provides some of the best night skiing along the Wasatch Front. With its excellent teaching programs, it is a good place to introduce the kids to the sport of skiing.

In terms of lift capacity, the largest of the three Ogden Valley ski areas is **Snowbasin**, located below the back of Mt. Ogden. Since the completion of the Trappers Loop Highway, which makes the drive from Salt Lake International Airport to the resort about the same distance as Park City, Snowbasin looks as if it could turn into Utah's next super resort. The fact that it is now owned and managed by the same company that operates the huge and famous Sun Valley, Idaho, resort gives further indication that it will likely get much larger in the future. There may be no on-site lodging now, but that promises to change, as well.

To an intermediate skier, Snowbasin is ideal. The runs are steep enough to be challenging but well-groomed enough not to contain many surprises. Its vertical drop of 2,400 feet (727 m)—ranking third in Utah for steepness—gives skiers a chance to enjoy long, scenic runs. Snowbasin a good place to avoid lift lines on crowded weekends because it is still relatively unknown and is serviced by four triple chairs and one double.

The thing we like best about Snowbasin is the scenery. Mt. Ogden is magnificent. On the drive up to the base of the resort, keep an eye out for wintering moose foraging in the willows at the side of the road. Don't forget to take along your cross-country skis! Have a picnic and enjoy the view.

■ BEAVER MOUNTAIN

The best way to describe Beaver Mountain is to call it a "college-town resort." At the top of Logan Canyon near the Utah-Idaho border you'll find this small, family-operated resort, which serves the outdoor-oriented students of nearby Utah State University.

In many ways, the area resembles a small-scale Brighton. Its three double chairlifts service 16 major runs and provide access to beginner and intermediate hills and to a few expert runs, as well.

We enjoy skiing cross country over the groomed U.S. Forest Service trail near the side road that leads to the resort. We then spend the evening soaking in the outdoor pools and hot tubs at Crystal Hot Springs, located in nearby Honeyville. Some fine condominiums are found at neighboring Bear Lake, which are seldom, if ever, crowded during the winter months.

■ SOUTHERN UTAH RESORTS

One might not expect to find places for nordic and alpine skiing in the midst of what many picture as red-rock desert. But the Brian Head and Elk Meadows ski areas feature high elevations, good powder, uncrowded conditions, and modern facilities.

Brian Head, located 12 miles (19 km) east of the town of Parowan, possesses a bit of the alpine atmosphere of Utah's northern ski areas but looks more like southern Utah. Skiers taking the resort's Giant Steps Lift, one of seven at the resort, find themselves standing under 11,307-foot (3,426-m) Brian Head Peak—an impressive red sandstone mountain some say may have been named (but misspelled) after the famed bald-headed politician William Jennings Bryan. On a clear, cold winter day, skiers peer down on a scene of fire and ice, looking out toward Zion National Park and the red-rock deserts.

The town of Brian Head comes alive in winter. The resort is large enough to provide for thousands of skiers, while retaining a quaintness that makes it a quiet alternative to the huge California and Colorado resorts. Smaller lodges near Duck Creek and Panguitch Lake offer rustic, out-of-the-way settings to visitors looking for "big city" escapes. Less expensive lodging can be found in Cedar City and Parowan.

Elk Meadows, east of Beaver and one of Utah's newest resorts, is a fine place for families and has one of the best "learn-to-ski" packages in the state. Nestled in an alpine canyon at an elevation of 9,200 feet (2,788 m), with runs reaching as high as 10,400 feet (3,437 m), this quiet ski area receives 350 inches (9 m) of snowfall annually. Its two newest lifts serve primarily intermediate runs. Skiers can choose from two double chairs, one triple chair, one poma lift, and one T-bar at a resort that is rarely crowded. Lodging is available at the ski area itself or in nearby Beaver.

Utah's smallest resort is **Blue Mountain,** located near the town of Monticello in southeastern Utah. Although the area is served by one small poma-style lift, it gives area residents a place to learn to ski in a canyonlands setting.

■ CROSS-COUNTRY SKIING

In many ways, much of Utah could be called a "ski resort." Most of the state receives plentiful snow, and where the white stuff falls, cross-country skiers often find open areas to enjoy their sport. It is not unusual to see the tracks of "skinny skis" on golf courses or parks in the middle of the city.

Most nordic skiers, however, take to the backcountry. Experts can be seen telemarking down steep powder runs in alpine canyons. Beginners, on the other hand, might take advantage of a road closed to auto traffic in the winter months to see pine trees dusted with snow, quiet canyons in frosty settings, or brooks flowing around magnificently shaped frozen shorelines. On certain days, it is even possible to ski across the slickrock after a snowstorm has covered the red rock with a white coating.

Destination resorts also cater to nordic skiers. These cross-country resorts provide a variety of services, including trail grooming, rental services, night skiing, backcountry huts, day and overnight tours, and lessons. In addition, helicopter ski services drop experts at the top of mountains, where they can ski through the world's best powder on runs untouched by others.

Nordic areas close to Salt Lake City include **Mountain Dell** in Parleys Canyon and the **Solitude Nordic Center** in Big Cottonwood Canyon. Most of the skiing in these areas takes place on beautiful, groomed trails. The Mountain Dell area is a relatively open golf course free of trees, and it will be here that Olympic events are held should Utah get a Winter Games bid. The Solitude Nordic Center connects the Brighton and Solitude downhill ski areas. Nordic enthusiasts glide through

Snowfall in southern Utah tends to be wetter and less persistent than in the north.

alpine splendor, occasionally finding a hill to match their skills. Because the two alpine resorts are located nearby, the nordic center is a good place for families who enjoy both alpine and nordic skiing.

For those who enjoy more of a resort atmosphere, **The Homestead** in the town of Midway—a 48-mile (77-km) drive from Salt Lake City—holds a special appeal. This country inn, built near some hot springs before the turn of the century, is one of Utah's oldest. New owners have recently restored the old hotel to its original elegance and have constructed newer lodging facilities and a golf course. Skiers can use both the resort's golf course and another larger adjacent links at Wasatch Mountain State Park. Leave time at the end of the day to soak in the hot-springs pools. For special occasions, spend the night and take a romantic moonlit ride on a horse-drawn sleigh. Top it off with a catered dinner for two near the fireplace at the resort's restaurant.

Ruby's Inn at the edge of Bryce Canyon National Park may be the best of southern Utah's nordic ski areas. Skiers staying at the motel can glide across groomed trails into the nearby national park, where they can ski along the edge of the Bryce Amphitheater. If you have the good fortune to arrive in clear weather after a heavy snowfall, the sight of powder snow, blue skies, and bright red rock will reward your skiing efforts. Unlike summer, when crowds of people gather on the edge of Bryce, there are days when you can have the entire park to yourself. Ruby's also grooms trails into nearby national forests.

Ski tours are also available from the **Pack Creek Ranch**, 14 miles (22 km) south of Moab. We spent a memorable holiday weekend a few years ago skiing on the La Sal Mountains and enjoying views of the red-rock country below us. The trip was capped by a midnight hike on New Year's Eve to Delicate Arch at nearby Arches National Park. The beauty of a trip to Pack Creek Ranch is that you can ski one day, mountain bike the next, and hike the third.

The venerable **White Pine Ski Touring Center**, located on the Park City Golf Course, is Utah's oldest. This is a good place for beginners to get a feel for nordic skiing before attempting a more difficult canyon run.

The **Sherwood Hills Resort**, 15 miles (24 km) south of Logan, serves a primarily northern Utah clientele. Though groomed trails are available on the golf course at the resort, don't be afraid to drive to Logan Canyon to try skiing on U.S. Forest Service trails. Crystal Hot Springs Resort, located in nearby Honeyville, is open year-round and is a great place to soak after a day of skiing.

Several state parks also groom trails specifically for cross-country skiers. **Pioneer Trail State Park** on the east bench of Salt Lake City and **Rockport State Park** near Park City both groom marked trails. We like Rockport because the sagebrush-juniper scenery differs from many of the forest areas and because it is possible to view many different types of wildlife in the winter from the trail.

Don't hesitate to ask about other nordic ski possibilities—especially at U.S. Forest Service district ranger offices. We've discovered a variety of small, little-known trails in the Wasatch, Uinta, and Manti-La Sal national forests. Particular favorites include **Mill Creek Canyon** east of Salt Lake City, the **Huntington Canyon** area in Emery County, and the **Tibble Fork Reservoir** area in the north Fork of American Fork Canyon.

■ SNOWMOBILING

Vast expanses of Utah's most scenic forest and red-rock country lie almost untouched in the winter. Thousands of people drive the Mirror Lake Highway between Kamas and Evanston, Wyoming, during summer, but only a few ever view the snowcapped High Uinta Mountains from the road in the winter. Those few ride snowmobiles on the Mirror Lake Highway, one of several major complexes of trail systems established and groomed by the Utah Division of Parks and Recreation.

Snowmobiles require registration in Utah. Registration fees go toward the grooming and marking of trails by rangers from the Division of Parks and Recreation. Close to 500 miles (800 km) of backcountry roads and trails encompassing all sorts of different terrain and scenery are groomed.

The **Wasatch Mountain State Park-Mirror Lake Complex**, located close to the Wasatch Front, includes 150 miles (240 km) of groomed trails traversing both the Wasatch and Uinta ranges. In addition to the groomed areas are numerous wide-open spaces where snowmobilers can play in powder snow. The 50-mile (80-km) Mirror Lake Highway is covered with snow most years from November until May. Though snowmobiles are not allowed in the adjacent wilderness areas, the views of both the High Uintas and the Wasatch Range are a sight to behold on a crisp, clear winter day. Snowmobiles can be rented at Wasatch Mountain State Park, the state's finest and most complete snowmobiling facility.

Trailheads at **Midway, Park City,** and **American Fork Canyon** offer plowed parking areas, restrooms, designated play areas, warming stations, and 60 miles (96 km) of groomed trails.

Snowmobilers searching for a chance to view red-rock canyons coated with snow usually head for the **Cedar Mountain Complex,** just east of Cedar City on a high plateau. Trails lead into Cedar Breaks National Monument, which is closed to automobile traffic in the winter. Much of the trail leads through the pines and aspens of the Dixie National Forest, but views of the red-rock country are common. Access to the complex is available from the Brian Head, Duck Creek, Strawberry, Navajo, and Midway trailheads, with some package tours offered out of Brian Head.

One of our favorite complexes is the **Logan Canyon-Monte Cristo-Hardware Ranch** area in northern Utah. The 150 miles (240 km) of groomed trails here connect with hundreds more trail miles in neighboring Idaho. Be sure to stop by the Hardware Ranch to see the winter feeding grounds of the wild elk. Though snowmobiles are not allowed near the huge animals, visitors can take a horse-drawn sleigh ride near the elk herds. The visitor center provides heated restrooms, a warm fire, vending machines, and information about the elk. The wide-open spaces on **Ant Flat** between Hardware Ranch and Monte Cristo and in the Sinks area of Logan Canyon give snowmobilers plenty of area to enjoy untouched powder.

In central Utah, you might enjoy a snowmobile ride across a portion of **Skyline Drive** where elevations reach nearly 12,000 feet (3,636 m). About 75 miles (120 km) of trails are groomed in this scenic complex, with trailheads found on both sides of the Manti Range. We like the ride from Huntington Canyon into Joe's Valley Reservoir.

On occasion, the Division of Parks and Recreation also grooms snowmobile trails near Strawberry Reservoir and in the Vernal area. This depends on the availability of groomers. If you are in the mood for a bit of adventure and have confidence in your snowmobiling abilities, these are two good areas to try.

Maps and information on snowmobiling in Utah are available from any Division of Parks and Recreation office or any state park. See "PRACTICAL INFORMATION" for addresses.

PRACTICAL INFORMATION

Listings

FOLLOWING IS A SELECT LIST OF INFORMATION WE HOPE will be useful to the Utah traveler. Further information may be obtained through the Utah Chamber of Commerce, (801) 364-3631 (large towns also have their own chambers of commerce); the Convention and Visitors Bureau, (801) 521-2822; and the Utah Travel Council, (801) 538-1030.

■ AREA CODE

The area code for all Utah is 801.

■ CLIMATE

Utah's climate is as varied as its scenery. With at least one notable exception—St. George, in extreme southwestern Utah—most parts of Utah experience four distinct seasons. (St. George is mild enough in winter for golf!) Almost everywhere else in Utah, including Salt Lake City, winter can be cold.

Summer temperatures throughout most Utah valleys hover around 85-100 degrees F (26-38° C), while the nearby mountains might enjoy a cool 60 degrees F (16° C). At night, temperatures in the mountains may cool off to 40-50 degrees F (5-10° C).

Spring and fall are the most comfortable seasons to visit southern Utah because daytime temperatures are in the 60-70 degree F (16-19° C) range. There are many times in northern Utah where, during April and May, visitors can spend the morning skiing in the mountains and the afternoon golfing in the valleys.

■ HOW TO GET THERE

Most major air routes to the state lead through Salt Lake City. Salt Lake International Airport, six miles (10 km) west of downtown, services more than 460 flights daily, with a capacity of 55,000 seats. Commercial service is available from Salt Lake City to Cedar City and St. George, while charter service can be arranged to smaller towns around the state.

Amtrak serves the Salt Lake area with four scheduled trains arriving and departing daily from the historic Rio Grande Depot. In addition, Amtrak makes stops at Provo, Ogden, Milford, Helper, and Thompson.

Salt Lake City's Greyhound bus station is located just west of Temple Square.

■ FINDING YOUR WAY AROUND UTAH CITIES

Nearly every Utah city was planned in advance by the Mormon pioneers. Streets are in checkerboard fashion, with wide, square blocks and streets running true north-south and east-west; finding an address is a relatively easy proposition. Cities have meridian markers from which most main streets are numbered; street addresses increase by increments of 100 every block from that point. Salt Lake City's marker is at the southeast corner of Temple Square. Thus, if you want to find an address at 500 South 700 East, you would simply drive five blocks south and then seven blocks east from Temple Square. Similar numbering systems are used throughout the state.

■ ACCOMMODATIONS

Utah's urban areas offer modern, full-service hotels operated by major national chains like Red Lion, Marriott, Hilton, Holiday Inn, Howard Johnsons, and Doubletree. The newer hotels feature indoor pools and recreation complexes. In addition, expect to find most national chains, like Motel 6, Days Inn, Comfort Inn,

TraveLodge, Super 8, La Quinta, and Quality Inn, represented. Most are listed in the Utah Travel Council's Travel Guide, published annually and available free of charge (Utah Travel Council, 538-1030).

As is the case in most of the United States, more and more bed-and-breakfast establishments are opening in Utah. Many are found in historic mansions restored to their former glory. In Salt Lake City, most are located in residential areas. The Utah Travel Council has compiled a list of bed-and-breakfast houses.

Some interesting accommodations are found near ski resorts. Elegant Cliff Lodge at Snowbird and the Stein Eriksen Lodge near Deer Valley draw an elite clientele. More rustic experiences can be enjoyed at smaller resorts like Alta or Brighton.

A number of rustic dude ranches or cabins next to fishing areas offer visitors a taste of the Wild West lifestyle. See the *Utah Tour Guide*, published annually by the Utah Travel Council, for a list.

Prices, based on double occupancy per night, are indicated as follows:
B = Budget under $40   M = Medium $40-$75   L = Luxury over $75

ANTIMONY
Rockin' R Ranch, family-style dining, Highway 22, 624-3250; M

BEAR LAKE
Sweetwater Condominiums, located next to lake, 946-8745; M

BEAVER
Elk Meadows Ski Resort Condominiums, fireplaces in some rooms, Beaver Canyon, 438-5444 or (800) 248-SNOW; M
Paradise Inn Best Western, great indoor pool, spa, I-15 Exit 112, 438-5464; M
Paice Motel Best Western, quiet, 461 South Main, 438-2438; M
Sleepy Lagoon Motel, 882 South Main, 438-5681; M

BICKNELL
Sunglow, close to Boulder Mountains, Utah 24, 425-3821; B

BLANDING
Best Western Gateway Motel, nice Indian jewelry sold there, 88 East Center, 678-2278; M
Cliff Palace Motel, southwestern architecture, 132 South Main, 678-2264; B

B L U F F
Recapture Lodge, near Monument Valley, 672-2281; B

B R I A N   H E A D
Brian Head Hotel, outside hot tubs, (800) 468-4898; L
Brian Head Condominium Reservations, alpine setting, inexpensive in summer.
677-2045, (800) 722-4742; L

B R Y C E   C A N Y O N
Bryce Canyon National Park Lodge, recently remodeled cabins and motel units,
586-7686; M

C E D A R   C I T Y
El Rey Inn Best Western, closest to Southern Utah University, 80 South Main,
586-6518 or (800) 528-1234; M
Holiday Inn, nice exercise room, 1575 West 200 North, 586-8888 or (800) HOLI-
DAY; M
Quality Inn, downtown, 18 South Main, 586-2433 or (800) 228-5151; M
Town and Country Best Western, next to Old Train Station, 200 North Main,
586-9911 or (800) 528-1234; M

D E L T A
Plaza Motel Best Western, near golf course, Junction US 50 and 6, 864-3882; B
Motor Inn, 527 East Topaz Blvd. 864-3882 or (800)-528-1234, FAX 864-4834; B

D U C K   L A K E
Meadeau View Lodge, in red rock country, Duck Creek Village, 682-2495; M-L

E P H R A I M
Iron Horse Motel, near Snow College, 670 North Main, 283-4223; B

E S C A L A N T E
Moqui Motel, near Escalante Canyons, 480 West Main, 826-4210; B

F I L L M O R E
Paradise Inn Best Western, indoor pool and spa, 800 North Main near I-15 exit,
743-6895 or 800-528-1234; M

F I S H   L A K E
Bowery Haven Resort, modern units, fishing boat rentals, 836-2788; B

Fish Lake Lodge, historic log cabins, 836-2700; B-M

FLAMING GORGE
Flaming Gorge Lodge, best in area, Dutch John, 889-3773; M

GREEN RIVER
River Terrace Best Western Motel, next to river, 880 East Main, 564-3401; M
West Winds, popular with truckers, 525 East Main, 564-3421; B

HANKSVILLE
Poor Boy Motel, on the way to Lake Powell, Utah 24, 542-3471; B

HEBER CITY
Hylander, in middle of town, 425 South Main, 654-2150; M
Swiss Alps Inn, 167 South Main, 654-0722; B

HURRICANE
Weston's Lamplighter Inn Best Western, quiet alternative to bustling St. George,
    280 West State, 635-4647; M

KANAB
Coral Sands, 60 South 100 East, 644-2616 or (800) 654-0805; M
Four Seasons Motel, one of largest in area, 36 West 100 North, 644-2635; M
Parry Lodge, collection of old movie memorabilia, 89 East Center, 644-2601; M
Red Hills Motel Best Western, pool, 124 West Center, 644-2675; M
Shilo Inn, pool, spa, free continental breakfast, and mini suites, 296 West 100
    North, 644-2526 or (800) 222-2244; L
Stagecoach Inn Ranch, 644-2452; M

LAKE POWELL
Bullfrog Resort, next to lake on red rock ledge, (800) 528-6154; M-L

LOGAN
Baugh Motel, nicely landscaped, 153 South Main, 752-5220; M
Center Street Bed and Breakfast, in older home, 169 East Center, 752-7443; M
Westin Inn Best Western, indoor pool, 250 North Main, 752-5700 or (800) 528-
    1232; M

MANTI
Manti Motel, near Mormon Temple, 445 North Main, 835-8533; B

MIDWAY

The Homestead, historic property near hot spring, completely renovated with golf course, 700 North Homestead Dr., 654-1102 Midway, 649-2060 Park City, (800) 327-7220 out of state; L

MOAB

Apache Motel, quiet location, 166 South 400 East, 259-5727; M
New Canyonlands Motel, nicest property in town, 16 South Main, 259-5167; E
Park Creek Ranch, Utah's best dude ranch, 259-5505; L
Ramada Inn, river runners headquarters, 182 South Main, 259-7141; M
The Virginian Motel, full kitchens, 70 East 200 South, 259-5951; B

MONTICELLO

Canyonlands Motor Inn, nice indoor pool, spa, 197 North Main, 587-2266; M
Wayside Inn Best Western, close to city park, 195 East US 666, 587-2261; M

MONUMENT VALLEY

Gouldings, modern motel with large gift shop—old trading post is now a small museum, two miles west of US 163, Monument Valley turnoff, 727-3231, (800) 874-0902; FAX 727-3334; M

MT. CARMEL JUNCTION

Thunderbird Best Western, nice par 3 golf course, US 89, 648-2203; M

NEPHI

Whitmore Mansion Bed and Breakfast, historic old home, 110 South Main, 623-2047; M

OGDEN

Flying J Motel Inn, outdoor pool, 1206 West 21st St., 393-8644 or (800) 343-8644; M
Radisson Suite Hotel, downtown with large rooms, 2510 Washington Blvd., 627-1900 or (800) 228-9822; M

PANGUITCH

New Western Motel Best Western, close to Bryce and Zion National Parks, 180 East Center, 676-8876; M
Sand's Motel, 390 North Main, 676-8874; M

PANGUITCH LAKE

Lake View Resort, cabins, RV parks, store, boat ramps, 676-2650 summer, 628-2719 winter; B

PARK CITY

Blue Church Lodge and Townhouses, renovated old church, 424 Park Ave., 649-8009; L

Deer Valley Lodging, one of Utah's most luxurious accommodations, 1375 Deer Valley Dr. South, 649-4040 or (800) 453-3833; L

Old Miners Bed and Breakfast Inn, old-time Park City atmosphere, 615 Woodside Ave., 645-8068; L

Park City Reservations, for all condos in area, 1790 Bonanza Dr., 649-9598; L

Park Plaza Resort, 2060 Sidewinder Dr., 649-0870; L

Radisson Inn, heated outdoor pool, 4346 Park Ave., 649-5000, (800) 228-9822; L

Stein Ericksen Lodge, Deer Valley Resort, 649-3700 or (800) 453-1302; L

The Yarrow Resort, central location, 1800 Park Ave., 649-7000, (800) 327-2332; L

PAROWAN

Swiss Village Inn Best Western, inexpensive winter alternative to Brian Head, 580 North Main, 477-3391 or (800) 538-1234; M

PRICE

Crest Motel, budget family units, 625 East Main, 637-1532; B

Day's Inn, indoor pool, 838 Westwood Blvd., 637-8880 or (800) 325-2525, FAX 637-7707; M

PROVO

Cotton Tree Inn (Best Western), pool, close to BYU campus, 2230 North University Parkway between Provo and Orem, 373-7044 or (800) 528-1234; M

Excelsior, nicest in area, 101 West 100 North, 377-4700 or (800) 824-4193, FAX 377-4708; M

Hotel Roberts, southwestern architecture, 192 South University Ave., 373-3400; M

University Comfort Inn, 1555 North Canyon Rd., 374-6020 or (800) 221-2222, FAX 374-0015; M

RICHFIELD

Best Western Apple Tree Inn, business district, 145 South Main, 896-5481; M

Day's Inn, 333 North Main, 896-6476 or (800) 325-2525, FAX 325-3535; M

ROCKVILLE

Blue House Bed and Breakfast, modern home off highway with beautiful rooms, 125 East Main, 772-3912; M

ROOSEVELT
Frontier Motel, business district location, 75 South 200 East, 722-2201, (800) 248-1014; B

ST. GEORGE
Coral Hills Best Western, pool, spa, 125 East St. George Blvd., 673-4844 or (800) 542-7733; M

Day's Inn Four Seasons, some rooms have a jacuzzi, 747 East St. George Blvd., 673-6111, (800) 635-4441; M

Green Valley Resort, pools, golf course, and tennis courts, 1515 West Canyon View Dr., 628-4663; L

St. George Hilton Inn, close to golf course, 1450 South Hilton Inn Dr., 628-0463 or (800) 662-2525, FAX 628-1501; L

St. George Holiday Inn, nice indoor sports complex and pool area, 850 South Bluff St., 628-4235 or (800) 457-9800, FAX 628-8157; M

SALINA
Cedar Creek Inn, business district, 60 North State, 529-7469; M

Shaheen's Best Western Motel, near entrance to Salina Canyon, 1225 South State, 529-7455, (800) 538-1234; M

SALT LAKE CITY
Airport Hilton, 5151 Wiley Post Way, 539-1515 or (800) 999-3736, FAX 539-1113; M

Alta Rustler Lodge, near famous ski area, beautiful alpine setting, Little Cottonwood Canyon, 742-2200, (800) 451-5223; L

Doubletree, closest to Delta Centers, 215 West South Temple, 531-7500 or (800) 528-0444 FAX 328-1289; L

Embassy Suites, large, beautiful atrium, 110 West 600 South, 259-7800 or (800)-362-2779; L

Little America Hotel, fine dining, 500 South Main, 363-6781, (800) 453-9450; L

Marriott Hotel, across from Salt Palace, 75 South West Temple, 531-0800 or (800) 228-9290; L

Red Lion Hotel, elegant dining ambience, 255 South West Temple, 328-2000 or (800) 325-3535, FAX 359-2938; L

Residence Inn by Marriott, full kitchen units, 765 East 400 South, 532-5511; L

Salt Lake Hilton, great suites, heart-shaped tubs, 150 West 500 South, 532-3344 or (800) 255-3050, FAX 532-3344; M

Saltair Bed and Breakfast, older home, 6151 South 900 East, 268-8762; M
Spruces Bed and Breakfast, near historic Wheeler Farm, 6151 South 900 East, 268-8762; M

S P R I N G D A L E
Cliff Rose and Garden, some kitchen units, nicely landscaped yard, 281 Zion Park Blvd., 772-3234, (800) 243-8824, FAX 772-3900; M
Driftwood Lodge Best Western, cool, shady units, 1515 Zion Park Blvd., 772-3262; M
Flanigan's Inn, nice patio units and budget units, 428 Zion Park Blvd., 772-3244; M-L
Terrace Brook Lodge, some units off highway, 990 Zion Park Blvd., 772-3932; B
Under the Eaves Guest House, historic home, 980 Zion Park Blvd., 772-3457, (800) 243-8824; M

T O R R E Y
Capitol Reef Inn, modern, 360 West Main, 425-3271; M
Rim Rock Ranch, close to Capitol Rock, 3 miles east of Torrey, 425-3843; M

V E R N A L
Antlers Best Western, 423 West Main, 789-1202; M
Dinosaur Inn Best Western, 251 East Main, 789-2660 or (800) 528-1234, FAX 789-2467; M
Weston Lamplighter Inn, 120 East Main, 789-0312; M

Z I O N
Zion Lodge, cabins with fireplaces and motel, 586-7686, FAX 586-3157; M

■ LIQUOR LAWS

Outsiders view Utah's liquor laws as strange. And they are. Still, most visitors will find it relatively easy to purchase an alcoholic beverage. Because the state controls the price of alcohol, travelers may also discover they usually get more for their money. The state owns liquor stores in convenient locations throughout the state. In fact, package liquor agencies are a part of many hotels, resort centers, and lodges. The stores are open every day of the week except Sundays and holidays, with varying hours. Beer (which is 3.2 percent alcohol) and wine coolers are available in most grocery stores. Stronger beer is carried by liquor stores.

Most fine restaurants in Utah have liquor licenses. Patrons may purchase mixed drinks,wine and beer at restaurants with these licenses. You can also bring your own wine into a restaurant for a corkage fee.

Visitors to Utah may wish to purchase a two-week membership to a private club for $5. Private clubs of this type sell liquor by the drink. Some hotels offer the membership as a courtesy. Lounges and taverns sell only 3.2 beer and do not offer wine service or mixed-drink set-ups. Liquor or wine may not be brought into these establishments.

■ DINING OUT

Utahns love to dine out. The great number and variety of restaurants found throughout the state, especially along the Wasatch Front, give testimony to the fact.

In Salt Lake City, for example, it's possible to find a sampling of many different ethnic specialties as well as traditional American meat-and-potato fare. A large restaurant center, with many fine establishments located in restored old buildings, is growing up around the Salt Palace Convention Center. Visitors can find a number of excellent restaurants in Trolley Square. And for fast food, the Richards Street Courtyard in the basement of the Crossroads Mall, with a number of fast-food establishments situated right next to one another, is available. It is possible to find Mongolian, several types of Chinese, Mexican, German, Japanese, Thai, Italian, French, Lebanese, Navajo Indian, Vietnamese, and Korean cuisine of fine quality.

One can also find a surprising number of good restaurants in places like Ogden, Provo, Cedar City, Moab, St. George, and Brigham City. Eating in smaller Utah towns can be an adventure. Often, restaurants are operated by interesting, colorful characters who not only serve a fine meal but can tell you about local history and attractions. When in doubt, order the chicken-fried steak when visiting a cafe or diner in rural Utah. It is usually excellent. Small town drive-ins (not franchises) often mix up a fine milk shake or malt. This is especially true if you happen to be visiting a rural area at a time when local fruit is ripening. For example, drive-ins around Bear Lake serve great raspberry malts and sundaes in late summer. Try eating a fresh peach pie in the Willard area when the peaches become ripe. In Navajo country in southeastern Utah, order a Navajo taco instead of a hamburger.

If Utah has one bit of outstanding cuisine, it is its ice cream. Salt Lake City possesses a surprising number of local ice cream companies. The atmosphere in a

Snelgroves, Fendalls, or Fernwood parlor takes visitors back to soda fountains of the 1940s and 1950s. Order a malt made the old-fashioned way, and it will be served in a glass accompanied by the metal cannister it was mixed in. Confections like banana splits, hot fudge sundaes, phosphates, cherry cokes, chocolate sodas, and root-beer floats are a delight.

In major tourist areas like St. George, Cedar City, Salt Lake City, Ogden, Logan, Park City, and Moab, local visitor centers can provide lists of available places to eat. Following are some of our favorites.

■ RESTAURANTS

Prices for one, excluding drinks and tip, are indicated as follows: B=Budget, up to $6; M=Moderate, $6-$12; E=Expensive, over $12.

BEAVER
The Black Steer Steak House, American, Beaver Canyon, 438-2242; M
Ponderosa, American, 330 South Main, 438-2856; M

BICKNELL
Sunglow Cafe, American, unusual pies, 425-3701; B

BLANDING
Elk Ridge Restaurant, American, 123 East Center, 678-3390 B;
Patio Drive-Inn, Navajo tacos-fast food, North Highway 191, 678-2177; B

BLUFF
Sunbonnet Cafe, Navajo food, Bluff Historic Loop; M
Turquoise Restaurant, American-Indian-chuck wagon, Main Highway; M

BOULDER
Burr Trail Cafe, nicely cooked American food, friendly ambience, center of village on Highway 12; B

BOUNTIFUL
The Mandarin, Chinese, 348 East 900 North, 298-2406; E

BRIAN HEAD
The Edge, steak and seafood, 677-3343; E

BRYCE CANYON
Bryce Canyon National Park Lodge, elegant, varied menu, in park, 586-7686; E
Ruby's Inn, American, good salad bar, entrance to park, 834-5341; M

CEDAR CITY
Sullivan's Cafe, American, potato bar (not to be confused with a piano bar), inexpensive prime rib, 86 South Main, 586-6761; M
Milt's Stage Stop, steaks, excellent prime rib, scenic canyon setting, Utah 14, Cedar Canyon, 586-9344; E
Pizza Factory, pizza, 124 South Main, 586-3900; B
The Black Swan, Shakespearean theme, 164 South 100 West, 586-7673; E

DELTA
The Pizza House, extensive Italian menu, 69 South 300 East, 864-2207; B

DUCHESNE
El Cid's Steakhouse, American, 339 West Main, 738-5540; M

ECHO
Echo Cafe, American, great truck stop food, Echo Canyon, 336-5642; B

FISH LAKE
Bowery Haven, rustic atmosphere, north end of lake; M

FLAMING GORGE
Flaming Gorge Lodge, don't miss the record trout! Dutch John, 889-3773; M

GREEN RIVER
Ray's Tavern, huge burgers, funky atmosphere, pool, 564-3511; B
Tamarack, American, near river on highway, 564-8109; M

HANKSVILLE
Red Rock Restaurant, American, 226 East 100 North, 542-3235; M

HEBER CITY AREA
Blazing Saddles, Mexican, 605 West 100 South; B
The Homestead, continental, elegant setting, Midway, 654-1102; E

KAMAS
Kamas Cafe, American, Main Street, 783-4389; B

KANAB
Chef's Palace, American, great double cheeseburger, 151 Center, 644-5052; B
Parry's Lodge, American, movie star memorabilia, 89 East Center, 644-2601; M
Territorial Inn, American, 85 South 200 West, 644-5744; M

LOGAN
Bluebird, American, great chocolate factory, 19 North Main, 752-3155; E

Gia's Restaurant, Italian, 119 South Main, 752-8384; M

Zanavoo Lodge Restaurant, American, a beautiful building in Logan Canyon, 753-5675; M

MILFORD

Hong Kong Cafe, Chinese, 433 South Main, 387-2251; B

MOAB

Dos Amigos Cocina Mexicana, Mexican, 56 East 300 South, 259-7903; B

Golden Stake, American, good prime rib, 550 South Main, 259-7000; M

Grande Old Ranch House, American, historic farm house on north edge of town, 259-5753; E

La Hacienda, Mexican, 574 North Main, 259-6319; B

Mi Vida, overlooks Moab, north edge of town, 259-7146; E

Milt's Stop and Go Drive In, great chili, Millcreek Drive, 259-7424; B

Sundowner, international menu—German food's the best, north edge of town, 259-5201; M

Westerner Grill, diner, 331 North Main, 259-9918; B

MONTICELLO

La Cocita, Mexican, 280 East US 66, 587-2959; B

Juniper Tree, American, 133 East US 66, 587-2870; B

MORGAN - WANSHIP

Spring Chicken Inn, great fried chicken, in Morgan call 829-6082; in Wanship call 336-5334; B

OGDEN

El Matador, Mexican, 2654 Ogden Ave., 393-3151; B

Graycliff Lodge, American, five miles up Ogden Canyon, 392-6775; E

Lee's Mongolian Barbecue, Mongolian and Chinese, 2866 Washington Blvd., 621-9120; M

Paisano's, Italian, 3050 Grant Ave., 392-9701; M

Prairie Schooner, American, seating in covered wagons, 445 Park Blvd., 392-2712; E

PANGUITCH

Flying M, American, good homemade bread, 614 North Main, 676-8008; M

PARK CITY

Cafe Mariposa, continental, elegant atmosphere, Deer Valley Resort, 649-1005; E

The Claimjumper, steaks, 573 Main Street, 649-8051; E
The Eating Establishment, American, 317 Main Street, 649-8284; M
Grub Steak, American with great salad bar, 2000 Sidewinder Dr., 649-8060; E
Mileti's, Italian, 412 Main Street, 649-8211; M
Red Banjo Pizza Parlour, pizza, 322 Main Street, 649-9901; B
The Glitretind, continental in elegant surroundings, Stein Ericksen Lodge, Deer
    Valley, 649-3700; E
Utah Coal and Lumber, Mexican, 201 Heber Ave., 649-9390; M

P R I C E
China City Cafe, Chinese and American 350 East Main, 637-8211; B
Greek Streak, Greek, 30 West 100 South, 637-9217; B

P R O V O
El Azteca, Mexican near BYU campus, 746 East 820 North, 373-9312; M
Los Hermanos, Mexican, 16 West Center, 375-5732; M
Maglebys, European, Village Green, 374-6249; E
The Brick Oven, pizza and Italian, 150 East 800 North, 374-8800; B

R I C H F I E L D
Topsfield Lodge, continental, good prime rib, 1200 South Main, 896-5437; E

R O O S E V E L T
Frontier Grill, American, 665 South 200 East, 722-3669; M
Cow Palace, steaks, east downtown, 722-2717; M

S T .   G E O R G E
Andelin's Gable House, continental, 290 East St. George Blvd., 673-6797; E
Dick's Cafe, American, 114 East St. George Blvd., 673-3841; B
Rickshaw, Chinese, 212 North 900 East, 628-1511; M
Los Hermanos, Mexican, 46 West St. George Blvd., Ancestor Square, 628-5989; M
Paula's Cazuela, Mexican, 745 West Ridgeview Dr., 673-6568; M
Pizza Factory, 100 West St. George Blvd., 628-1234; B

S A L T   L A K E   C I T Y   A R E A
Alta Rustler Lodge, American, Little Cottonwood Canyon, 742-3500; E
Baci Trattoria, gourmet Italian, 134 Pierpont Ave., 328-1500; E
Blind Miner, continental, Brighton Store, Big Cottonwood Canyon, 649-9156; E
Cafe Pierpont, Mexican, 122 W. Pierpont Ave., 364-1222; M
Cedars of Lebanon, Lebanese, 154 East 200 East, 364-4096; M

Cordova's El Rancho, Mexican, 543 West 400 North, 355-1913; E
Della Fontana, nine-course Italian dinners, 336 South 400 East, 328-4243; E
Finn's, continental, 2675 Parley's Way, 466-4682; E
Five Alls, continental, 1458 S. Foothill Drive, 582-1400; E
Hibachi, Japanese, 238 E. South Temple, 364-5456; E
Hunan, Mandarin and Szechuan cuisine, Arrow Press Square, 165 West Temple, 531-6677; M
Kyoto, Japanese, some private rooms, 1080 East 1300 South, 487-3525; E
La Caille at Quail Run, continental, fanciest in valley, 9565 S. Wasatch Blvd., 942-1751; E
La Frontera, Mexican with live music, several locations throughout the valley; B
Lamb's, American, oldest in state, 163 South Main, 364-7166; M
Le Parisien, French, 412 South 300 East, 364-5223; M
Log Haven, famous Sunday brunch, Millcreek Canyon, 272-8255; E
Marianne's Delicatessen, German deli, 149 West 200 South, 364-0513; B
Market Street Broiler, seafood, 258 South 1300 East, 583-8808; E
Mikado, Japanese, 67 West 100 South, 328-0929; E
Mulboon's, huge shrimp bowls, locations at Trolley Corners and the Olympus Hotel in Salt Lake City; also in Midvale, Layton, and Ogden.
Oceans, seafood, 4760 South 900 East, 261-0115; E
Panda, Mongolian barbecue, 1701 South State, 485-3226; B
Perry Pub and Cafe, unusual continental cuisine, Perry Hotel, 110 West 300 South, 521-8919; E
Rio Grande Cafe, Mexican, located at Rio Grande train station, 450 West 300 South, 364-3302; M
Santa Fe, continental, Emigration Canyon, 582-5888; E
Siegfriend's Delicatessen, German, 69 West 300 South, 355-3891; B
The Orient, Vietnamese, 4768 Redwood Road, 966-3659; M
The Park Cafe, across from Liberty Park, 600 East 1300 South, 487-1670; E
The Pie Pizzeria, student hangout near U of U, 1320 East 200 South, 582-0193; B

S P R I N G D A L E
Bumbleberry Inn, American, great berry pie, 897 Zion Park Blvd., 772-3224; B
Driftwood Lodge, American, 1515 Zion Park Blvd., 772-3263; M
Flanigan's Inn, American, 428 Zion Park Blvd., 772-3244; E
Bit and Spur, Mexican, famous for Zuni stew, 772-3498; E

T O O E L E
Glowing Embers, variety of American favorites, 494 South Main, 882-0888; M

T O R R E Y
La Buena Vida, Mexican, great atmosphere, 425-3759; M

V E R N A L
Casa Rios, Mexican, 2015 West Highway 40, 789-0103; M

W E L L I N G T O N
Pugs Drive-Inn, burgers in a drive-in setting; B

W I L L A R D - P E R R Y
Maddox Ranch House, great turkey steak, US 89, 723-5683; M

■ MAJOR FESTIVALS

J A N U A R Y
Utah Winter Games, first two weeks in January, northern Utah
United States Film Festival, late January, Park City

M A R C H - A P R I L
Easter Jeep Safari, Easter week, Moab

M A Y
Golden Spike Anniversary Reenactment of Driving of Golden Spike in 1869,
    May 10, Golden Spike National Historic Site
Green River Friendship Cruise, Memorial Day weekend, Green River and Moab

J U N E
Utah Summer Games, late June, Cedar City
Ute Indian Pow Wow, late June, Fort Duchesne
Salt Lake Arts Festival, third week of June, Salt Lake City

J U L Y
America's Freedom Festival, around July 4th, Provo
Oakley Rodeo, near July 4, Oakley
Ute Stampede, early July, Nephi
Greek Festival Days, mid-July, Price
Mormon Miracle Pageant, mid-July, Manti
Days of '47, near July 24th, Salt Lake and Ogden with statewide celebrations

Festival of the American West, late July, Logan
Shakespearean Festival, July to early September, Cedar City

AUGUST
Park City Arts Festival, first weekend in August, Park City
Railroaders Festival, mid-August, Golden Spike National Historic Site
Bonneville Nationals Speed Week, third week of August, Bonneville Salt Flats

SEPTEMBER
Park City Miners Day Celebration, Labor Day, Park City
Swiss Days, Labor Day weekend, Midway
Peach Days, early September, Brigham City
Southern Utah Folklife Festival, second weekend in September, Zion National
    Park and Springdale
Autumn Aloft Balloon Festival, mid-September, Park City
Melon Days, mid-September, Green River
Salt Lake Greek Festival, mid-September, Salt Lake City
Utah State Fair, mid-September

OCTOBER
Fat Tire Festival, October, Moab
World Senior Games, mid-October, St. George

NOVEMBER
Festival of Trees, late November, Salt Lake City
Temple Square Christmas Lighting, last weekend in November, Salt Lake City

■ UTAH'S PUBLIC LANDS

Utah almost literally belongs to the nation. Nearly 80 percent of its land is controlled by government agencies for public uses such as recreation, timber, and wildlife management, mineral leasing, and livestock grazing. Utah's six national forests give outdoor enthusiasts over nine million acres to explore. The forests range from alpine peaks covered with aspen, pine, and fir, to red-rock mountains rich with juniper, pinyon, and ponderosa pine. Hikers, boaters, campers, skiers, and people simply taking a Sunday drive can all enjoy Utah's national forest lands. You can obtain maps and travel planners designating roads and areas open to off-highway motorized travel at ranger districts and forest supervisor offices throughout the state.

Utah's five national parks, six national monuments, two national recreation areas, and one national historic site are all open year-round. The road into Cedar Breaks National Monument does close in the winter months, but the monument can still be seen by skiers and snowmobilers. Some of the most popular parks are crowded in the summer, but there is always lodging and camping available in private facilities nearby. If you want to camp in Arches, Bryce, Capitol Reef, or Zion national parks in summer, plan on arriving early in the day to assure yourself a camping space.

The Utah Division of Parks and Recreation administers 45 developed state parks encompassing over 94,000 acres of land and over a million surface acres of water. Its state parks contain individual or group campsites and facilities for boating, hiking, off-highway vehicle use, and other outdoor sports. In addition, several parks contain cultural and natural history museums.

The Bureau of Land Management (BLM) administers 43 percent of the land in Utah. Off-road vehicle use, hiking, and camping are popular in most of these areas. The BLM administers river rafting in both Desolation and Westwater canyons on the Green and Colorado rivers, as well as in a number of primitive areas. Several million acres of BLM land are under consideration for national wilderness area designation. When driving through Utah, BLM offices located throughout the state often provide a good source for topographical maps and advice on hiking and camping conditions. Popular developed BLM recreation sites, like the Little Sahara Sand Dunes near Delta, the Dixie Red Cliffs near St. George, and the Calf Creek area near Escalante, give campers a chance to get away from the more crowded conditions often found in nearby national and state parks.

Before venturing into Utah's thousands of miles of backcountry roads and trails, check with the administering agency about fire restrictions and other regulations. Permits are required in some BLM primitive areas. Travel maps listing places open to off-highway vehicle use are available from local U.S. Forest Service and Bureau of Land Management offices. Backpackers going into National Park Service-administered lands are required to pick up a free permit from a ranger station or visitor center.

■ CAMPING

Camping in most national forests, national parks, recreation areas, and BLM lands is allowed on a first-come, first-served basis. Large group sites, however, can be reserved in advance.

The view through a window at Monument Valley.

Campground reservations for some national forests may be made by calling the MISTIX Reservation center's toll-free number: (800)284-CAMP (2267). If payment is made by credit card, instant confirmation of the campsite reservation is given. Mail-in applications can be obtained at all state parks and some national forests, or a request for a mail-in application can be sent to MISTIX Reservation Center, P.O. Box 680039, Park City, Utah 84068-0039. To reserve state park campgrounds in advance, call 322-3770 inside Utah or (800) 322-3770 outside the state.

Expect to pay fees for overnight camping and/or day use at most public campgrounds, depending on the facilities at the individual campground. A Golden Eagle Passport is available for $25 for persons over 62, and provides free or discounted entrance to national parks and monuments where an entry fee is normally charged. The Golden Access Passport is available to the blind and permanently disabled. These passports can be obtained at the parks or agency offices and provide a 50 percent discount on single-family campsites and other features where a use fee is charged. They also provide free or discounted entry to the national parks.

The Utah Campground Owners Association manages private campgrounds throughout the state, most of which offer more amenities (swimming pools, hookups, showers) than those found in public facilities. Write to the association for a free brochure listing private facilities. **Utah Campground Owners Association VIP Campground**, 1370 West North Temple, Salt Lake City, Utah 84116. Call 521-2682 for information on private campgrounds within Utah.

■ FISHING AND HUNTING

Utah's fishing season—with a few exceptions—is year-round. The sport is regulated by the Utah Division of Wildlife Resources. Licenses can be purchased at their offices in Salt Lake City, Ogden, Springville, Vernal, Price, and Cedar City, as well as at most sporting goods stores. Pick up a free fishing update for details on special regulations, limits, and license fees. Anglers can catch trout, bass, walleye, bluegill, whitefish, Bonneville Cisco, yellow perch, crappie, and catfish. Hunting seasons are set for deer, elk, antelope, pheasant, duck, geese, sage grouse, forest grouse, chukar partridge, mourning dove, wild turkey, cottontail rabbit, and snowshoe hare. Special permits may be purchased to hunt bear, mountain lion, and bobcat. Once-in-a-lifetime permits for buffalo, desert bighorn sheep, moose, and Rocky Mountain goat are also available via special lottery drawings. Antelope and some deer and elk hunts are on a lottery basis only. Specific hunting regulations are issued annually by the Utah Division of Wildlife Resources. To hunt or fish in Utah, purchase a license at any Utah Division of Wildlife Resources office or in most sporting goods stores. **Utah Division of Wildlife Resources**, 15 West North Temple, Salt Lake City, Utah 84116, 533-9333. Call the following for recorded information on: birds 530-1299; fishing 530-1298; hunting 530-1297.

■ BOATING AND RIVER RAFTING
Although Utah is a dry state, it ranks sixth in the nation in surface acres of boatable waters. Power boats and sail craft must meet both Utah and Coast Guard regulations on reservoirs, lakes, and rivers. Some areas restrict the use of motors. For information, contact the Division of Parks and Recreation, the agency charged with managing boating in Utah.

Utah is world-famous for its rafting opportunities. More than 25 outfitters are eager to show visitors the state's whitewater rapids and calm scenic waters. There are more than 400 miles (640 km) of raftable rivers in the state. For more detailed information, write to the Utah Travel Council and request the *Utah Tour Guide:* **Utah Travel Council**, Council Hall/Capitol Hill, Salt Lake City, Utah 84114, 538-1030, FAX 538-1399.

■ PUBLIC LANDS INFORMATION

■ NATIONAL PARKS AND MONUMENTS
Arches National Park, Box 846, Moab, Utah 84532, 259-8161
> DEVILS GARDEN CAMPGROUND is located 2 miles south of park headquarters and has 54 total units.

Bryce Canyon National Park, Bryce Canyon, Utah 85717, 834-5322
> NORTH CAMPGROUND, located just east of park headquarters, has 11 units.
> SUNSET CAMPGROUND is located two miles south of park headquarters and has 115 units.
> Bryce Canyon Lodge, a lovely old-time lodge, 586-7686, FAX 586-3157

Canyonlands National Park, Moab, Utah 84532, 259-7164
> SQUAW FLAT CAMPGROUND is located 35 miles west off US 191 on Highway 211 and has 26 units.
> WILLOW FLAT CAMPGROUND is located 41 miles west off US 191 on Highway 313 and has 12 units.

Capitol Reef National Park, Torrey, Utah 84775, 425-3791

CAPITOL REEF CAMPGROUND, located 1.3 miles off Highway 24, has 53 units.

CEDAR MESA CAMPGROUND, located 20 miles off Highway 24, has five units.

Cedar Breaks National Monument, Box 749, Cedar City, Utah 84720, 586-9451

POINT SUPREME CAMPGROUND is located two miles north of the south entrance and has 30 units.

Dinosaur National Monument, Box 210, Dinosaur, Colorado 81610, (303) 374-2216

QUARRY VISITOR CENTER, 789-2115

GREEN RIVER CAMPGROUND is located five miles east of the Dinosaur Quarry and has 100 units.

RAINBOW PARK is located 25 miles from Dinosaur Quarry and has four units.

SPLIT MOUNTAIN, located four miles east of the Dinosaur Quarry, has 35 units.

Flaming Gorge National Recreation Area, P.O. Box 278, Manila, Utah 84046, 885-3315

ANTELOPE FLAT CAMPGROUND, 10.9 miles northwest off Highway 260, has 122 units.

ARCH DAM GROUP CAMPGROUND, located 2.8 miles southwest off Highway 260, has 200 units.

CANYON RIM CAMPGROUND, located 15 miles southwest off Highway 44, has 19 units.

CEDAR SPRINGS CAMPGROUND is located 6.2 miles southwest off Highway 260, has 23 units.

DEER RUIN CAMPGROUND, located 5.8 miles southwest off Highway 260, has 19 units.

DRIPPING SPRINGS CAMPGROUND, located three miles southeast off Highway 260, has 5 units.

FIREFIGHTERS MEMORIAL CAMPGROUND is located 6.5 miles southwest off Highway 260, has 7 units.

GREEN LAKE CAMPGROUND, located 14 miles southwest off Highway 44, has 19 units.

MUSTANG RIDGE, located 4 miles southwest off Highway 260, has 73 units.

RED CANYON, located 15.8 miles north off Highway 44, has 8 units.

SKULL CREEK, located 12.5 miles southwest off Highway 44, has 17 units.

Claret cup cactus in Arches National Park.

Glen Canyon National Recreation Area, Box 1507 Page, Arizona 86040, (602) 645-2471

BULLFROG CAMPGROUND, located 70 miles south of Hanksville on Highway 276, has 86 units.

HALLS CROSSING CAMPGROUND, located 95 miles southwest of Blanding on Highway 263, has 65 units.

HITE CAMPGROUND, located 45 miles south of Hanksville on Highway 95, has 6 units.

WAHWEAP CAMPGROUND, near Page, Arizona, has 100 units.

Golden Spike National Monument, P.O. Box W, Brigham City, Utah 84302, 471-2209; no campground

Hovenweep National Monument, McElmo Route, Cortez, Colorado 81321, (303) 529-4465

SQUARE RUIN CAMPGROUND is located 15 miles north of Aneth off Highway 262 and has 31 units.

Natural Bridges National Monument, c/o Canyonlands National Park, Moab, Utah 84532, 259-7164

CAMPGROUND located 4 miles northwest off Highway 95 and has 13 units.

Pipe Spring National Monument, Moccasin, Arizona 86022; no campground

Timpanogos Cave National Monument, Route 3, Box 200, American Fork, Utah 84003, 756-0351; no campground

Zion National Park, Springdale, Utah 84767, 772-3256

LAVA POINT CAMPGROUND, located 26 miles north off Virgin, off Highway 9, has 4 units.

SOUTH CAMPGROUND is located near the south entrance to the park and has 144 units.

WATCHMAN CAMPGROUND is located near the south entrance to the park and has 229 units.

■ U.S. FOREST SERVICE OFFICES

Ranger District offices within each forest may be reached by calling the forest headquarters listed below.

Intermountain Region Headquarters, 324 25th Street, Ogden, Utah 84401, 625-5182

Ashley National Forest Headquarters, Ashton Energy Center, 1680 West Highway 40, Suite 1150, Vernal, Utah 84078, 789-1181

Dixie National Forest Headquarters, 82 North 100 East, P.O. Box 580, Cedar City, Utah 84720, 586-2421

Fishlake National Forest Headquarters, 115 East 900 North Richfield, Utah 84701, 896-4491

Manti-La Sal National Forest Headquarters, 599 West Price River Drive, Price, Utah 84501, 637-2817

Uinta National Forest Headquarters, 88 West 100 North, P.O. Box 1428, Provo, Utah 84603, 377-5780

Wasatch-Cache National Forest Headquarters, 8226 Federal Building, 125 South Street, Salt Lake City, Utah 84138, 524-5030

■ B U R E A U   O F   L A N D   M A N A G E M E N T   O F F I C E S

Cedar City District Office, 176 East D.L. Sargent Drive, P.O. Box 724, Cedar City, Utah 84720, 586-2401

Moab District Office, 82 East Dogwood, P.O. Box 970, Moab, Utah 84532, 259-6111

Richfield District Office, 150 East 900 North, Richfield, Utah 84701, 896-8221

Salt Lake District Office, Bear River Resource Area, Pony Express Resource Area, 2370 South 2300 West, Salt Lake City, Utah 84119, 524-5348

Utah State Office, 324 South State Street, Salt Lake City, Utah 84111, 524-5330

Vernal District Office, Diamond Mountain Resource Area, Book Cliffs Resource Area, 170 South 500 East, Vernal, Utah 84078, 789-1362

■ S T A T E   P A R K S   I N F O R M A T I O N

Utah Division of Parks and Recreation, 1636 West North Temple, Salt Lake City, Utah 84116, 538-7221 for state parks and Utah boating information; for camping reservations, call (800)-322-3770.

■ ART AND CULTURE

In Salt Lake City, the Salt Lake Art Center adjacent to the Salt Palace and the Utah Museum of Fine Arts on the University of Utah campus host excellent permanent

(following pages) Goblin Valley in winter.

displays as well as traveling visual-arts exhibits. A number of private galleries can be found in the Salt Lake area as well. Listings of current art shows appear in the Arts Section of both Salt Lake City daily newspapers each Sunday. Ballet West, the Salt Lake Acting Company, Pioneer Theatre Company, Ririe-Woodbury Dance Company, the Utah Symphony, the Repertory Dance Company, and the Utah Opera Company all are based in Salt Lake City. Seasons schedules and specific dates for shows can be obtained by contacting the Salt Lake County Convention and Visitors Bureau at West Temple and 200 South adjacent to the Salt Palace, or by calling the individual arts group. The Hansen Planetarium is located in the old Salt Lake City Library. It offers star shows, laser shows, and small science exhibits.

In Utah County, the Springville Museum of Art displays works of many well-known painters and sculptors and features a month-long National Art Exhibit each April. Sundance Summer Theatre at Sundance Resort offers musical productions on alternating nights from June to Labor Day. The Pageant of the Arts in American Fork, where live actors and actresses portray famous paintings, is held in June and July. Theater and dance departments at Brigham Young University perform throughout the year. The Payson Community Theater also presents two productions annually.

In northern Utah, the Nora Eccles Harrison Museum of Art in the Daryl Chase Fine Arts Center at Utah State University regularly features national and local exhibits. The university also hosts many dance programs and concerts, including the classical music workshops of the Irving Wasserman Festival each year. A "Music in the Parks" series is performed in Logan annually. "The West: America's Odyssey" is a highlight of Utah State University's Festival of the American West. Logan hosts a Summerfest Art Faire. Ogden art galleries include the Myra Powell at Union Station, the Collett Art Gallery at Weber State University, and the Eccles Community Art Center on Jefferson Avenue. Weber State University regularly schedules live theater, music, and dance.

In southern Utah, several galleries exhibit the work of local artists from the surrounding red rock country in Moab, which is fast becoming a small artists' colony. In Blanding, Edge of the Cedars State Park has year-round art and photo exhibits. The Braithwaite Fine Arts Gallery is located on the campus of Southern Utah State University in Cedar City. The premier attraction hereabouts is the Utah Shakespearean Festival, which runs from July through the first week of September.

A summer concert series, ranging from symphonic music to ethnic dancing, is held at the O.C. Tanner Amphitheater in Springdale, just outside the entrance to Zion National Park. The Southwest Symphony, based in St. George, presents a season of concerts from October through May each year.

■ PROFESSIONAL SPORTS

The Utah Jazz of the National Basketball Association is one of the state's two major league franchises. Getting a ticket to see this team perform in the Delta Center can be difficult. The team is so popular that nearly every game sells out. The Delta Center also serves as the home of the Salt Lake Golden Eagles professional hockey team of the International Hockey League. In the spring, the Salt Lake Sting professional soccer team, the other major-league team, plays at venerable Derks Field. The old but well-kept Derks Field is also home of the Salt Lake Trappers, a rookie-league baseball team which gained national attention by winning a professional baseball record of 29 straight games during July of 1987. Since then, this successful Pioneer League team has continued to attract record crowds.

■ INFORMATION RESOURCES

A R T S

Utah Arts Council, 617 East South Temple, Salt Lake City, Utah 84102, 533-5895. General information and publications pertaining to Utah arts organizations. Utah Arts Resources Directory. Glendenning Gallery and Chase Home Exhibition, featuring the State Fine Arts Collection.

C A M P G R O U N D S / P R I V A T E

Utah Campground Owners Association VIP Campground, 1370 West North Temple, Salt Lake City, Utah 84116, 521-2682. Information on private campgrounds within Utah. (For public campgrounds, see listings under "Public Lands Information.")

G E N E R A L   I N F O R M A T I O N

Utah Travel Council, Council Hall/Capitol Hill, Salt Lake City, Utah 84114, 538-1030, FAX 538-1399. For recorded summer calendar of events and winter snow conditions, call 521-8102. Provides multipurpose maps, travel publications, posters. Yearly Utah travel guide. Bed and Breakfast information. *Utah Tour Guide* includes listings of airlines, taxis, ground tours, guides and outfitters, aerial tours, bicycle tours, backcountry tours, four-wheel-drive tours, hunting and fishing guides, instructional schools, dude ranches, marinas, cabins, river-running, boat tours, Salt Lake City tours, tour operator index.

Utah Chamber of Commerce, 400 South Second East, Salt Lake City 84111, 364-3631. Cities and large towns also have their own chambers of commerce.

Utah Convention and Visitors Bureau, 180 South West Temple, Salt Lake City 84101, 521-2822.

GEOLOGY/MINERALS

Utah Geological and Mineral Survey, 2363 S. Foothill Dr., Salt Lake City, Utah 84109, 469-7970. Numerous publications on all aspects of Utah geology. Resource library.

GUIDES

Utah Guides and Outfitters, 3131 South 500 East, Salt Lake City, Utah 84106, 466-1912. Directory of professional river-runners, outfitters.

HIGHWAYS/ROAD CONDITIONS

Utah Department of Transportation, 4501 South 2700 West, Salt Lake City, Utah 84119. Road report, 964-6000 (Salt Lake Area) or (800) 752-7600 (toll free anywhere within Utah). Utah Highway Map. Road conditions, construction sites.

HISTORY

Utah State Historical Society, 300 Rio Grande, Salt Lake City, Utah 84101, 533-5755. Library: Utah, Mormons, the West. Photograph collection: Utah, Mormons. Historical publications. Historical preservation.

HISTORY TOURS

Utah Heritage Foundation, 355 Quince Street, Salt Lake City, Utah 84103, 533-0858. Nonprofit organization. Historic Salt Lake City tours. Publications.

HOTELS

Utah Hotel Association, 9 Exchange Place, Suite 715, Salt Lake City, Utah 84111, 359-0104. Information on accommodations.

MAPS

U.S. Geological Survey, 125 South State, Salt Lake City, Utah 84138, 524-5652. Topographical and geological maps, publications.

SKIING

Utah Ski Association, 150 West 500 South, Salt Lake City, Utah 84101, 534-1779.

WILDLIFE

Utah Division of Wildlife Resources, 15 West North Temple, Salt Lake City, Utah 84116, 533-9333. Recorded information: birds 530-1299; fishing 530-1298; hunting 530-1297.

Stream channel in the Great West Canyon of Zion National Park.

RECOMMENDED READING

■ DESCRIPTION AND TRAVEL

Aitchison, Stewart. *Utah Wildlands.* Utah Geographic Series, Inc. 3 (1987): 112. Photographs and text explore Utah's proposed and designated wilderness areas.

Carr, Stephen L. *The Historical Guide to Utah Ghost Towns.* Salt Lake City: Western Epics, 1986. Maps, historical photos, and many details.

Hirsch, Bob. *Houseboating on Lake Powell.* Phoenix: Primer Press, 1988. A good guide about a great way to see Lake Powell.

Hirsch, Bob and Stan Jones. *Fishin' Lake Powell.* Sun Country Publications. Helpful advice on where and how to catch the lake's gamefish.

Hoefer, Hans, et al. *American Southwest.* Englewood Cliffs: APA Insight Guides, 1984. A full-color guide to southern Utah and adjacent states.

Jones, Stan. *Boating and Exploring Map: Lake Powell and Its 96 Canyons.* Sun Country Publications, 1985. This map points out natural features, marinas, Indian sites, hiking trails and four-wheel-drive tracks, points of interest, navigation, history, fishing, and wildlife.

Porter, Elliot. *The Place No One Knew: Glen Canyon on the Colorado.* San Francisco: Sierra Club Books, 1963. Beautiful color photos and thoughtful quotations from many individuals.

Roylance, Ward J. *The Enchanted Wilderness: A Red Rock Odyssey.* Four Corners West, 1986. A personal account of Roylance's experiences on the Colorado Plateau.

Stegner, Wallace, ed. *This is Dinosaur: Echo Park Country and its Magic Rivers.* Boulder: Roberts Rinehart, Inc., 1985. Essays on this rugged land—its geology, dinosaurs, wildlife, Indians, explorers, river-running, and visiting Dinosaur National Park.

Stokes, William Lee. *Dinosaur Tour Book of the Western United States, Southcentral Canada, and Baja.* Starstone Publishing Company, 1980. An illustrated guide for those who wish to see all the dinosaur bones they can. Also by Stokes is

Scenes of the Plateau Lands and How They Came To Be (Starstone Publishing Company, 1969), a must for any visitor to southern Utah. Finally, Stokes's *The Great Salt Lake* (Starstone Publishing Company, 1984) is full of scientific facts as well as interesting trivia about Utah's famous landmark.

Thompson, George A. *Some Dreams Die: Utah's Ghost Towns and Lost Treasures.* Salt Lake City: Dream Garden Press, 1982. With his fascinating tales, Thompson encourages readers to seek the lost treasures of the ghost towns.

Till, Tom. *Utah: Magnificent Wilderness.* Newport Beach: Westcliffe Publishers, Inc., 1989. A photographic essay by Tom Till. The foreword was written by Pulitzer Prize winner Wallace Stegner.

Trimble, Stephen. *Blessed By The Light.* Layton: Gibbs M. Smith, Inc., 1986. An anthology of great writing and photography about the Colorado Plateau.

Utah Division of Wildlife Resources. *Lakes of High Uintas.* A series of 10 booklets, 1981-1985, available from Utah Division of Wildlife Resources (1596 West North Temple, Salt Lake City, UT 84116). $1 plus postage. A good practical guide for hikers, fishermen, campers, and packhorse enthusiasts.

Utah Writers' Program of the Work Projects Administration. *Utah: A Guide to the State.* New York: Hastings House, 1941. Libraries usually have a copy of this detailed book, which was used extensively by the authors of this one.

Wharton, Tom. *Utah! A Family Travel Guide.* Salt Lake City: Wasatch Publishers, Inc., 1987. How to enjoy Utah's outdoors in a way families and older travelers find relaxing.

Wilson, Ted. *Utah's Wasatch Front.* Utah Geographic Series, Inc., 4 (1987): 118. Full-color photos illustrate the text written by Salt Lake City's former mayor.

■ HIKING, BICYCLING, SKIING, AND CLIMBING

Barnes, F. A. *Canyon Country Hiking and Natural History.* Salt Lake City: Wasatch Publishers, Inc., 1977. Hiking the canyons and mountains of southeastern Utah.

Bjornstad, Eric. *Desert Rock: A Climber's Guide to the Canyon Country of the Southwest American Desert.* Denver: Chockstone Press, Inc., 1988. Climbing routes on the towers, spires, buttes, and cliffs of the Four Corners region.

Coello, Dennis. *Bicycle Touring in Utah.* Salt Lake City: Dream Garden Press, 1984. Tour descriptions and how to get started.

Davis, Mel. *High Uinta Trails.* Salt Lake City: Wasatch Publishers, Inc., 1974. Guide to hiking, backpacking, camping, and fishing in the High Uintas Wilderness of northeastern Utah.

Hall, David. *The Hiker's Guide to Utah.* Helena: Falcon Press Publishing Co., Inc., 1982. Day and overnight hikes all over Utah, ranging in difficulty.

Kelner, Alexis. *Skiing in Utah: A History.* Self-published, 1980. Full of anecdotes as well as facts.

Kelner, Alexis and David Hanscom. *Wasatch Tours.* Salt Lake City: Wasatch Publishers, Inc., 1976. A guide to about 100 cross-country ski tours near Salt Lake City.

Kelsey, Michael R. *Canyon Country Hiking Guide to the Colorado Plateau.* Provo: Kelsey Publishing, 1986. A good guide with maps to hikes in the Utah, Colorado, and New Mexico areas of the Colorado Plateau. Also by Kelsey, *Hiking and Exploring Utah's Henry Mountains and Robbers Roost* (Provo: Kelsey Publishing, 1987) contains trail descriptions and maps as well as historical information. Kelsey's *Hiking Utah's San Rafael Swell* (Provo: Kelsey Publishing, 1986) provides historical information and maps of the Swell's hidden canyons.

Lambrechtse, Rudi. *Hiking the Escalante.* Salt Lake City: Wasatch Publishers Inc., 1985. Descriptions and maps for 42 hikes of varying difficulty.

Ringholz, Raye Carleson. *Park City Trails.* Salt Lake City: Wasatch Publishers, Inc., 1984. Tour descriptions of hikes and cross-country treks in the mountains and canyons surrounding this historical mining town.

Schimpf, Ann and Scot Datwyler. *Cache Tours.* Salt Lake City: Wasatch Publishers, Inc., 1977. Descriptions of thirty cross-country ski tours near Logan in northern Utah.

Williams, Brooke. *Utah Ski Country.* Utah Geographic Series, Inc. 2 (1986): 126. Color photos accompany this guide to the state's ski resorts and backcountry ski areas.

Veranth, John. *Hiking the Wasatch.* Salt Lake City: Wasatch Publishers, Inc., 1988. Hiking trails of varying difficulty through the Wasatch Mountains east of Salt Lake City.

Wood, John. *Cache Trails.* Salt Lake City: Wasatch Publishers, Inc., 1987. Hiking trails in the mountains of northern Utah near Logan.

■ RIVER-RUNNING

Abbey, Edward. *Down the River.* New York: E.P. Dutton, 1982. Abbey's descriptions of travels along rivers through deserts of the West. River-runners like to quote from this book.

Huser, Vern. *Canyon Country Paddles.* Salt Lake City: Wasatch Publishers, Inc., 1978. An introduction to river-running by kayak, canoe, and raft in southeastern Utah.

Zwinger, Ann. *Run, River, Run: A Naturalist's Journey Down One of the Great Rivers of the American West.* New York: Harper and Row, 1975. The author's experiences along the Green and Colorado rivers mixed with her knowledge of geology, Indian ruins, plants, and wildlife.

■ HISTORY

Dunn, Marion. *Bingham Canyon.* Salt Lake City: Publishers Press, 1973. Mr. Dunn is a sportswriter who grew up in Bingham Canyon. His book is full of personal accounts from the people who lived there.

Fradkin, Philip L. *A River No More.* New York: Alfred A. Knopf, 1981. Historical account of water usage in Utah.

Morgan, Dale L. *The Great Salt Lake.* Albuquerque: University of New Mexico Press, 1947. A history of the lake minus the developments of the late twentieth century.

Powell, John Wesley. *The Exploration of the Colorado River and Its Canyons.* New York: Dover Publications, 1961. First published in 1895, Powell's descriptions are a must for all river lovers.

Smart, William. *Old Utah Trails.* Utah Geographic Series, Inc. 5 (1988): 135. William Smart guides the reader along all the old Utah trails by foot or car while he tells tales of the original trailblazers.

Wallace, Irving. *The Twenty-seventh Wife*. New York: E.P. Dutton, 1962. An account of the private life of Brigham Young, particularly in relation to his twenty-seventh wife. Includes comments from Young's comtemporaries and from other historians and students of Mormonism.

■ ARCHAEOLOGY

Jones, Dewett and Linda S. Cordell. *Anasazi World*. Portland: Graphic Arts Center Publishing Company, 1985. Written with an archaeologist, this book outlines the development of the Anasazi, their demise, and the coming of the Europeans. Using what is known about the modern pueblo Indians, the authors speculate about life in the Anasazi world.

Stokes, William Michael and William Lee Stokes. *Messages on Stone*. Starstone Publishing Co., 1980. Possible explanations for petroglyphs and pictographs.

■ NATURAL SCIENCES

Barnes, F.A. *Canyon Country Geology for the Layman and Rockhound*. Salt Lake City: Wasatch Publishers, Inc., 1978. Geologic history and rockhounding guide.

Craighead, John J. *A Field Guide to Rocky Mountain Wildflowers*. Boston: Houghton Mifflin Co., 1963. Illustrated with line drawings and photos.

Fiero, Bill. *Geology of the Great Basin*. Reno: University of

Harry Longbaugh a.k.a. the Sundance Kid and Etta Place (Utah State Historical Society).

Nevada Press, 1986. Comprehensive and fairly easy for the non-geologist to understand.

Haywood, C. Lynn, et al. *Birds of Utah*. Salt Lake City: Brigham Young University Press, 1976. Descriptions of the Great Basin, focusing on where and when to sight birds.

Haywood, C. Lynn. *The High Uintas: Utah's Land of Lake and Forest*. Salt Lake City: Monte L. Bean Science Museum, 1983. A guide to the geology, plantlife, birds, and animals of the Uintas.

Sigler, William F. and Robert Rush Miller. *Fishes of Utah*. Salt Lake City: Utah Division of Wildlife Resources, 1963. Descriptions, illustrations, and life histories of Utah's fish.

Welsh, Stanley L. and Bill Ratcliffe. *Flowers of the Canyon Country*. Moab: Canyonlands Natural History Association, 1986.

■ REFERENCE

Geer, Deon C. *Atlas of Utah*. Salt Lake City: Weber State College and Brigham Young University Press, 1981. A comprehensive atlas of the state, including Utah's geography, climate, geology, flora and fauna, history, social institutions, government, economy, and recreation.

■ MISCELLANEOUS

Grey, Zane. *Riders of the Purple Sage*. New York: Pocket Books, Inc., 1974. Also by Grey is *The Rainbow Trail* (Santa Barbara: Santa Barbara Press, 1985).

Kelly, Tim, et al. *Utah: Gateway to Nevada!* Salt Lake City: Dream Garden Press, 1984. A humorous look at Utah's history, places, and institutions.

Twain, Mark. *Innocents Abroad* and *Roughing It*. New York: Library of America, 1984.

I N D E X

COMPASS AMERICAN GUIDES

WRITTEN FOR THE "LITERATE TRAVELER," this series of guides conjures up the images, explores the myths and legends, and reveals the spirit of America, its cities and states, and Canada.

Compass American Guides are available in general and travel bookstores, or may be ordered directly by calling 1-800-733-3000; or by sending a check or money order, including the cost of shipping and handling, payable to: Random House, Inc. 400 Hahn Road, Westminster Maryland 21157. Books are shipped by USPS Book Rate (allow 30 days for delivery): $2.00 for the 1st book, $0.50 for each additional book. Applicable sales tax will be charged. All prices are subject to change. Or ask your bookseller to order for you.

"Books can make thoughtful (and sometimes even thought-provoking) gifts for incentive travel winners or convention attendees. A new series of guidebooks published by Compass American Guides is right on the mark."—SUCCESSFUL MEETINGS *magazine*

Consider Compass American Guides as gifts or incentives for VIP's, employees, clients, customers, convention and meeting attendees, friends and others. Quantity discounts and customized editions are available.

Chicago   Veteran newsman and inveterate Chicagoan, Jack Schnedler, who writes regularly for the *Chicago Sun-Times*, captures the essence of this brawny, exuberant city, covering its history from swamp to skyscrapers, its architecture and urban essences.
Author: Jack Schnedler—Photographer: Zbigniew Bzdak
ISBN 1-878867-28-8; 320 pp; Price $16.95 (paper). ISBN 1-878867-29-6; Price: $24.95

Las Vegas   Deke Castleman's rollicking introduction to the capital of glitz, with a tale of fifty hotels, a celebration of tacky museums, a guide to quick weddings and sign language, and, of course, a system for playing slots, craps, blackjack, poker, and other games of chance.
Author: Deke Castleman—Photographer: Michael Yamashita
ISBN 1-878867-18-0; 304 pp; Price $14.95. Second edition.

Los Angeles   A hip and fast-moving tour of Los Angeles with special attention to those places where movies were filmed, movie stars lived and loved, and legends were born.
Author: Gil Reavill—Photographer: Mark S. Wexler
ISBN 1-878867-17-2; 324 pp; Price $14.95.

San Francisco and the Bay Area   San Francisco has something for everyone, whether your taste runs to cappuccino or dim sum, to downtown honky tonk or Davies Symphony Hall. Special emphasis on the surrounding Bay Area, from the Napa Valley to the markets of the East Bay.
Author: Barry Parr—Photographer: Michael Yamashita
ISBN 1-878867-16-4; 400 pp; Price $14.95. Second edition.

Arizona   From hidden canyons to museums of archaeology, from the civilized pleasures of Phoenix to jagged wildlands, author Larry Cheek reveals Arizona's scenic, cultural, and historical attractions and colorful eccentricities.
Author: Larry Cheek—Photographer: Michael Freeman
ISBN 1-878867-32-6; 288 pp; Price $16.95. Second edition.

Colorado Champagne powder and cattle ranches, deserts and mountains, clean civilized cities, and classic American small towns—author Klusmire describes them all with wit, folksy humor, and a native's insight.
Author: Jon Klusmire—Photographer: Paul Chesley
ISBN 1-878867-07-5; 318 pp; Price $14.95 (paper). ISBN 1-878867-20-2; Price $22.95 (cloth)

Hawai'i Some credit Hawai'i's magic to climate and scenery, others to its handsome people and spirit of *aloha*—but all are stirred by its royal history and its connection to the cultures of Polynesia. This guide helps you discover Hawai'i's magic for yourself.
Author: Moana Tregaskis—Photographers: Wayne Levin and Paul Chesley
ISBN 1-878867-23-7; 364 pp; Price $15.95 (paper). ISBN 1-878867-24-5; Price $22.95 (cloth)

Montana Love of land and sky runs deep in Montana. Mountain ranges with names like the Crazies and the Sapphires. Legendary rivers—the Madison, Big Hole, and Yellowstone. Curiouser creeks—Froze-to-Death, Stinking Water, and Hellroaring. High plains, once home to buffalo, still offer wide vistas to the eye and soul. This land of the Big Sky may well be the last best place.
Author: Norma Tirrell—Photographer: John Reddy
ISBN 1-878867-10-5; 320 pp; Price $14.95 (paper). ISBN 1-878867-13-X; Price $22.95 (cloth)

New Mexico Space, light, purity—New Mexico has cast a magical spell of mystery over its inhabitants for centuries. Rich in history, New Mexico has seen the sophisticated Anasazi culture, Spanish conquistadors searching for gold, 16th century colonists, and Pancho Villa. This truly is a Land of Enchantment.
Author: Nancy Harbert—Photographer: Michael Freeman
ISBN 1-878867-06-7; 336 pp; Price $15.95 (paper). ISBN 1-878867-22-9; Price $22.95 (cloth)

Utah Unspoiled as the day Brigham Young proclaimed "this is the right place," this land of red-rock canyons and snow-capped mountains offers glorious scenery and a glimpse of the magnificent cliff-dwellings of the ancient Anasazi Indians. Special emphasis on outdoor recreation.
Author: Tom & Gayen Wharton—Photographer: Tom Till
ISBN 1-878867-31-8; 352 pp; Price $16.95. Second edition.

Wyoming High, wide, and handsome, a land where tales of Indians, pioneers, gun slingers, cattle barons, cowboys and other characters of the Old West still cling to life. Nat Burt, son of pioneering dude ranchers, roams the state where the myth of the cowboy was born.
Author: Nathaniel Burt—Photographer: Don Pitcher
ISBN 1-878867-04-0; 392 pp; Price $14.95 (paper). ISBN 1-878867-03-2; Price $22.95 (cloth)

Canada Veteran journalist Garry Marchant approaches the second largest country in the world as not one, but six different nations. Special sections on the Inuits, Canadian sports, rail hotels, 'Newfies,' Quebecois culture and the Calgary Stampede.
Author: Garry Marchant—Photographer: Ken Straiton
ISBN 1-878867-12-1; 308 pp; Price $14.95

■ ABOUT THE AUTHORS

Tom and Gayen Wharton are natives of Utah who have spent much of their lives exploring and enjoying the many cultural and recreational opportunities found in their state.

The Whartons both graduated with honors from the University of Utah, where Gayen earned her degree in education and Tom studied journalism.

Tom has been a sports writer and outdoor editor for the *Salt Lake Tribune* since 1970. His first book, *Utah! A Family Travel Guide,* appeared in 1987. His work has been published in many magazines, including *Field and Stream* and *Outdoor Life.* A member of the Outdoor Writers Association of America, he has captured numerous national and local awards for his journalism. He is listed in *Who's Who in the West.*

Gayen has taught elementary school for eight years, and has been active in a number of community service projects. She served as vice-chairman of her local community council, a member of the Board of Directors of the Salt Lake City YWCA, and as a member of the Utah League of Women Voters.

Tom and Gayen, with their four children, love to spend as much time as possible in Utah's great outdoors, camping, hiking, backpacking, fishing, and skiing.

■ ABOUT THE PHOTOGRAPHER

Tom Till is one of the premier American Landscape photographers in the United States. His work has appeared in a number of books on the American West and Southwest, including *Colorado, Images from Above,* an aerial portrait of the state, which he also authored. His photography frequently appears in magazines such as *Audubon, Wilderness, Sierra* and *Omni,* as well as in calendars for both the National Geographic Society and the Audubon Society.

When not on the road capturing images for his photo stock library, Tom makes his home in Moab, Utah, where he enjoys the beauty of Utah's magnificence with his wife Marcy and their two children.